DUTCH
PHRASEBOOK

Compiled by
LEXUS

ROUGH
GUIDES

www.roughguides.com

Credits

Dutch Phrasebook

Compiled by: Lexus with
Susan Ridder
Lexus series editor: Sally Davies
Layout: Pradeep Thapliyal
Pictures: Nicole Newman

Rough Guides Reference

Director: Andrew Lockett
Editors: Kate Berens, Tom Cabot,
Tracy Hopkins, Matthew Milton,
Joe Staines

Publishing information

First edition published in 1999.
This updated edition published September 2011 by
Rough Guides Ltd, 80 Strand, London, WC2R 0RL
Email: mail@roughguides.com

Distributed by the Penguin Group:
Penguin Books Ltd, 80 Strand, London, WC2R 0RL
Penguin Group (USA), 375 Hudson Street, NY 10014, USA
Penguin Group (Australia), 250 Camberwell Road, Camberwell,
Victoria 3124, Australia
Penguin Group (New Zealand), Cnr Rosedale and Airborne Roads,
Albany, Auckland, New Zealand

Rough Guides is represented in Canada by Tourmaline Editions Inc.,
662 King Street West, Suite 304, Toronto, Ontario, M5V 1M7

Printed in Singapore by Toppan Security Printing Pte. Ltd.

248 pages

A catalogue record for this book is available from the British Library.

978-1-84836-736-4

3 5 7 9 8 6 4 2 1

CONTENTS

How to use this book

The Rough Guide Dutch Phrasebook is a highly practical introduction to the contemporary language. It gets straight to the point in every situation you might encounter: in bars and shops, on trains and buses, in hotels and banks, on holiday or on business. Laid out in clear A–Z style with easy-to-find, colour-coded sections, it uses key words to take you directly to the phrase you need – so if you want some help booking a room, just look up "room" in the dictionary section.

The phrasebook starts off with Basics, where we list some essential phrases, including words for numbers, dates and telling the time, and give guidance on pronunciation, along with a short section on the different regional accents you might come across. Then, to get you started in two-way communication, the Scenarios section offers dialogues in key situations such as renting a car, asking directions or booking a taxi, and includes words and phrases for when something goes wrong, from getting a flat tyre or asking to move apartments to more serious emergencies. You can listen to these and download them for free from www.roughguides.com/phrasebooks for use on your computer, MP3 player or smartphone.

Forming the main part of the guide is a double dictionary, first English–Dutch, which gives you the essential words you'll need plus easy-to-use phonetic transliterations wherever pronunciation might be a problem. Then, in the Dutch–English dictionary, we've given not just the phrases you'll be likely to hear (starting with a selection of slang and colloquialisms) but also many of the signs, labels and

instructions you'll come across in print or in public places. Scattered throughout the sections are travel tips direct from the authors of the Rough Guides guidebook series.

Finally, there's an extensive **Menu reader**. Consisting of separate food and drink sections, each starting with a list of essential terms, it's indispensable whether you're eating out, stopping for a quick drink or looking around a local food market.

Goeie reis!
Have a good trip!

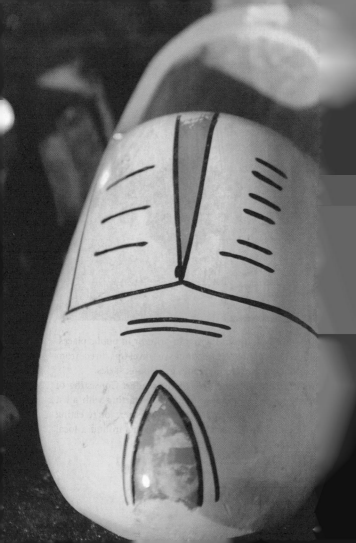

Pronunciation

In this phrasebook, the Dutch has been written in a system of imitated pronunciation so that it can be read as though it were English, bearing in mind the notes on pronunciation given below:

a	as in Petra
ah	a long 'a' as in cart
ay	as in may
e	as in get
g	always hard as in goat
ī	as the 'i' sound in might
J	like the 's' in pleasure
KH	like the 'ch' in the Scottish pronunciation of loch
o	as in pop
oo	as in soon
∞	like the 'ew' in few but without any 'y' sound, as in the French pronunciation of tu
OW	as in now, but pronounced much further forward in the mouth, with lips pursed as if to say 'oo'
uh	like the 'e' butter
y	as in yes

Letters given in bold type indicate the part of the word to be stressed.

Abbreviations

adj adjective	*fam* familiar	*pl* plural
pol polite	*sing* singular	

Note

In Dutch, there are two words for **'the'**: de duh and het het. For example, **'the city'** de stad; **'the restaurant'** het restaurant. The plural form is always de. The correct Dutch word for 'the' has been given throughout the dictionary sections, so you don't need to worry about which one to use.

BASICS

Basic phrases

yes ja ya

no nee nay

OK oké

hello hallo

good morning goedemorgen
KHooyuh-**mor**KHuh

good evening goedenavond
KHooyuh-**ah**vont

good night goedenacht
KHooyuh-na**KH**t

goodbye tot ziens zeens

please alstublieft a**lst**oobleeft

yes, please ja, graag ya KHrahKH

thank you (*pol*) dank u wel oo vel
(*fam*) dankjewel d**a**nk-yevel

thanks bedankt

no, thanks nee, bedankt nay

thank you very much (*pol*)
dank u vriendelijk oo **vree**ndelik
(*fam*) dank je vriendelijk yuh

don't mention it graag gedaan
KHrahKH KHed**ah**n

how do you do? aangenaam
kennis te maken **ah**nkHenahm
kennis tuh m**ah**kuh

how are you? hoe gaat het
met u? hoo KHaht uht met oo

fine, thanks uitstekend, dank u
owtst**ay**kent

pleased to meet you
aangenaam (kennis te maken)
ahnkHenahm (kennis tuh m**ah**kuh)

excuse me
(to get past, to get attention) pard**o**n
(to say sorry) neemt u mij niet
kwalijk naymt oo mi neet kva**h**lik

(I'm) sorry sorry

sorry? (didn't understand)
pard**o**n, wat zei u? vat zi oo

I see/I understand
ik begrijp het beKH**ri**p

I don't understand
ik begrijp het niet neet

do you speak English?
spreekt u **E**ngels? spraykt oo

I don't speak Dutch
ik spreek geen Nederlands
sprayk KHayn **nay**derlants

**could you speak more
slowly?** kunt u wat langzamer
spreken? koont oo vat l**a**nkzahmer
spr**ay**kuh

could you repeat that?
zou u dat kunnen herhalen?
zow oo dat k**oo**nnuh herh**ah**luh

could you write it down?
kunt u het opschrijven?
koont oo uht **o**psKHr**i**vuh

I'd like... ik wil graag...
vil KHrahKH

can I have a...? mag ik een... (hebben)? maKH ik uhn... (hebbuh)

do you have...? heeft u...? hayft oo

how much is it? wat kost het? vat

cheers! (toast) proost! prohst (thanks) bedankt!

it is... het is...

where is...? waar is...? vahr

is it far from here? is het ver hier vandaan? vair heer vandahn

Dates

Dates are expressed using ordinal numbers (see p.12):

the first of July één juli ayn yooli

on the first of July op één juli

the twentieth of March twintig maart tvintikH mahrt

on the twentieth of March op twintig maart

Days

Monday maandag mahndaKH

Tuesday dinsdag dinsdaKH

Wednesday woensdag voonsdaKH

Thursday donderdag donderdaKH

Friday vrijdag vrīdaKH

Saturday zaterdag zahterdaKH

Sunday zondag zondaKH

Months

January januari yanooahri

February februari faybrooahri

March maart mahrt

April april ahpril

May mei mī

June juni yooni

July juli yooli

August augustus OWKHOOstOOs

September september

October oktober

November november

December december

Time

what time is it? hoe laat is het? hoo laht is uht

it's one o'clock het is één uur ayn oor

it's ten o'clock het is tien uur teen

five past one vijf over één vif ohver ayn

ten past two tien over twee teen ohver tvay

twenty past one** twintig over één tvintikH ohver ayn

quarter past one kwart over één kvahrt ohver ayn

quarter past two kwart over twee tvay

half past one* half twee hal-f

half past two* half drie dree

ten to two tien voor twee
teen foor tvay

twenty to ten twintig voor tien
tvintiкн

quarter to two kwart voor twee
kvahrt

quarter to ten kwart voor tien
teen

at one o'clock om één uur
ayn ∞r

at ten o'clock om tien uur teen

at half past ten* om half elf hal-f

14.00 twee uur tvay ∞r

17.30 half zes hal-f

noon twaalf uur's middags
tvahlf ∞r smiddaкнs

midnight middernacht
midderna кнt

am 's morgens smorкнens

pm 's middags smiddaкнs

an hour een uur ∞r

a minute een minuut min∞t

a second een seconde sekonduh

a quarter of an hour
een kwartier kvarteer

half an hour een half uur
hal-f ∞r

three quarters of an hour
drie kwartier dree kvarteer

* The half hour always refers to
the following hour rather than
the previous one: **'half past**

one' is half twee (literally 'half
two' meaning 'half before two').

** People also refer to the time
in relation to the half hour: **1.20**
can be either twintig over een
'twenty past one' or tien voor
half twee **'ten to half past one'**.

Note: to indicate that the word
een means **'one'**, rather than **'a/
an'**, it may be given accents: één.

Numbers

0 nul n∞l

1 een, één ayn

2 twee tvay

3 drie dree

4 vier feer

5 vijf vif

6 zes

7 zeven zayvuh

8 acht aкнt

9 negen nayкнuh

10 tien teen

11 elf

12 twaalf tvahlf

13 dertien dairteen

14 veertien vayrteen

15 vijftien vifteen

16 zestien zesteen

17 zeventien zayventeen

18 achttien aкнteen

19 negentien na**y**KHenteen

20 twintig tv**i**ntiKH

21 eenentwintig **ay**nentvintiKH

22 tweeëntwintig tv**ay**entvintiKH

30 dertig d**ai**rtiKH

31 eenendertig **ay**nendairtiKH

32 tweeëndertig tv**ay**endairtiKH

40 veertig v**ay**rtiKH

50 vijftig v**i**ftiKH

60 zestig z**e**stiKH

70 zeventig z**ay**ventiKH

80 tachtig ta**KH**tiKH

90 negentig na**y**KHentiKH

100 honderd h**o**ndert

101 honderd een ayn

110 honderd tien teen

200 twee honderd tvay

1,000 duizend d**ow**zend

1,000,000 een miljoen ayn milyoon

Ordinals

1st eerste **ay**rstuh

2nd tweede tv**ay**duh

3rd derde d**ai**rduh

4th vierde v**ee**rduh

5th vijfde v**i**fduh

6th zesde z**e**sduh

7th zevende z**ay**venduh

8th achste a**KH**tstuh

9th negende na**y**KHenduh

10th tiende t**ee**nduh

Regional accents

The pronunciation given in this book is typical of the Standard Dutch you will hear in the north of the Netherlands. But there are a great variety of different accents.

There are also local dialects which vary in vocabulary and grammar, as well as pronunciation. In the eastern provinces of Groningen, Drenthe, Gelderland and Overijssel, the dialects are related to those in northern and western Germany. In the southern

provinces of Brabant, Limburg and Zeeland, the dialects are similar to those in neighbouring Belgium. The main difference between the northern and southern Dutch dialects is the pronunciation of g, which is harsh in the north, but soft in the south. There are vowel differences too. The word huis (**house**) is pronounced hoos in the north, hoos in the east, and hows in the west and south; ijs (**ice**) is pronounced ees in the north, east and southwest, and is in the west and south.

	Dutch word	Standard Dutch as in the north	Amsterdam	
z becomes s	zoon	zohn	sohn	
v becomes f	even	**ay**vuh	effuh	
ay becomes ay-uh	veel	vayl	fayl	
oh becomes ow or o	telefoon	telefohn	telefohn	
KH softens to h	groot	KHroht	KHroht	
v becomes w	waar	vahr	vahr	
t in -ti- becomes s	nationaal	natshohnahl	natshohnahl	
final t before a consonant is dropped	Utrecht	ootrecht	ootrecht	
loanwords pronounced as though they were Dutch	plafond	plahfon	plahfon	
ī becomes a	plein	plīn	plīn	
ow becomes uh	buiten	bowtuh	bowtuh	
ow becomes a	blauw	blow	blow	
ah to o	gaan	KHahn	KHahn	

Speakers of different Dutch dialects don't always understand each other, but they all speak Standard Dutch too, and they will certainly have no difficulty understanding your pronunciation.

Flemish, spoken in northern Belgium, is similar to Dutch but has some minor vocabulary differences, sometimes borrowing words from French (for example, **fork** is vork in Standard Dutch but fourchette in Flemish).

The table below gives examples of the key differences you may hear in the various Dutch accents.

Rotterdam	The Hague	Utrecht	southern Netherlands	Flemish
zohn	zohn	zohn	zohn	zohn
effuh	effuh	effuh	effuh	**ay**vuh
fay-uhl	**fay**-uhl	fayl	vayl	vayl
telefo**wn**	telefo**wn**	telefo**n**	telefo**hn**	telefo**hn**
кнroht	кнroht	кнroht	hroht	hroht
vahr	vahr	vahr	wahr	wahr
natshohn**ahl**	natshohn**ahl**	natshohn**ahl**	nahshon**ahl**	nahshon**ahl**
∞trecht	∞trecht	∞trech	∞trecht	∞trecht
plahfo**n**	plahfo**n**	plahfo**n**	plahfo**n**	plahfo**nt**
plīn	plan	plīn	plīn	plīn
bowtuh	**buh**tuh	**bow**tuh	**bow**tuh	**bow**tuh
blow	blow	blah	blow	blow
кнahn	кнahn	кнon	кнahn	кнahn

SCENARIOS

Download these scenarios as MP3s from
www.roughguides.com/phrasebooks

1. Accommodation

▶ Is there an inexpensive hotel you can recommend?
Kunt u mij een goedkoop hotel aanbevelen?
kOOnt OO mī uhn KHootkohp hotel ahnbevayhluh

▶▶ I'm sorry, they all seem to be fully booked.
Sorry, ze zitten allemaal vol.
sorry zuh zittuh alluhmahl vol

▶ Can you give me the name of a good middle-range hotel?
Kunt u mij de naam van een goed hotel in de middenklasse geven?
kOOnt OO mī duh nahm van uhn KHoot hotel in duh midduh-klassuh KHayvuh

▶▶ Let me have a look, do you want to be in the centre?
Eens even kijken, wilt u een hotel in het centrum?
ayns ayvuh kīkuh vilt OO uhn hotel in uht sentrOOm

▶ If possible.
Als het kan.
als uht kan

▶▶ Do you mind being a little way out of town?
Vindt u het erg om iets buiten de stad te zitten?
vint OO uht airKH om eets bOWtuh duh stat tuh zittuh

▶ Not too far out.
Niet te ver weg.
neet tuh vair veKH

▶ Where is it on the map?
Waar is het op de kaart?
vahr is uht op duh kahrt

▶ Can you write the name and address down?
Wilt u de naam en het adres opschrijven?
vilt OO duh nahm en uht ahdres opsKHrīvuh

▶ I'm looking for a room in a private house.
Ik ben op zoek naar een kamer in een particulier huis.
ik ben op zook nahr uhn kahmer in uhn partikOOleer hOWs

2. Banks

bank account	bankrekening	bank-raykuhning
to change money	geld wisselen	KHelt visseluh
cheque	cheque	shek
to deposit	storten	stortuh
euro	euro	urroh
pin number	pincode	pinkohduh
pound	pond	pont
to withdraw	opnemen	opnaymuh

▶ Can you change this into euros?
Kunt u dit in euros wisselen?
k00nt 00 dit in urrohs visseluh

> ▶▶ How would you like the money?
> Hoe wilt u het geld?
> hoo vilt 00 uht KHelt

▶ Small notes.   Big notes.
Kleine biljetten.   Grote biljetten.
klīnuh bilyettuh   grohtuh bilyettuh

▶ Do you have information in English about opening an account?
Heeft u informatie in het Engels over het openen van een
bankrekening?
hayft 00 informahtsee in het engels over het openuh van uhn bank-raykuhning

> ▶▶ Yes, what sort of account do you want?
> Ja, wat voor rekening wilt u?
> yah vat vohr raykuhning vilt 00

▶ I'd like a current account.
Ik wil graag een betaalrekening.
ik vil KHrahKH uhn betahl-raykuhning

> ▶▶ Your passport, please.
> Uw paspoort, alstublieft.
> 00 paspohrt alst00bleeft

▶ Can I use this card to draw some cash?
Kan ik met deze kaart geld opnemen?
kan ik met dayzuh kahrt KHelt opnaymuh

> ▶▶ You have to go to the cashier's desk.
> Dat kunt u bij het loket doen.
> dat k00nt 00 bī uht loket doon

▶ I want to transfer this to my account at…
Ik wil dit naar mijn rekening bij de… overschrijven.
ik vil dit nahr mīn **ray**kuhning bī duh… **o**versкнrīvuh

▶▶ OK, but we'll have to charge you for the phonecall.
Goed, maar we moeten u wel de kosten voor het
telefoongesprek in rekening brengen.
кноot mahr vuh **moo**tuh ∞ vel duh **ko**stuh vohr uht tayluh**foh**n-кнesprek
in **ray**kuhning **bre**nguh

3. Booking a room

shower	douche	doosh
telephone in	telefoon op	tele**foh**n op
the room	de kamer	duh **kah**mer
payphone in	publieke telefoon	p∞**blee**kuh tele**foh**n
the lobby	in de lobby	in duh lobby

▶ Do you have any rooms?
Heeft u nog kamers vrij?
hayft ∞ noкн **kah**mers vrī

▶▶ For how many people?
Voor hoeveel personen?
vohr **hoo**vayl per**soh**nuh

▶ For one/for two.
Voor één persoon/voor twee personen.
vohr ayn per**soh**n/vohr tvay per**soh**nuh

▶▶ Yes, we have rooms free.
Ja, wij hebben nog kamers vrij.
yah vī **he**bbuh noкн **kah**mers vrī

▶▶ For how many nights?
Voor hoe lang?
vohr hoo lang

▶ Just for one night.
Voor maar één nacht.
vohr mahr ayn naкнt

▶ How much is it?
Wat kost het?
vat kost uht

▶▶ 90 euros with bathroom and 70 euros without bathroom.
Negentig euro met badkamer en zeventig euro zonder
badkamer.
nayKHentiKH **ur**roh met b**a**t-kahmer en z**ay**ventikH **ur**roh z**o**nder
b**a**t-kahmer

▶ Does that include breakfast?
Is dat inclusief het ontbijt?
is dat **i**nkl**oo**seef uht ontb**ī**t

▶ Can I see a room with bathroom?
Zou ik een kamer met een badkamer kunnen zien?
z**ow** ik uhn k**ah**mer met uhn b**a**tkahmer k**oo**nnuh zeen

▶ OK, I'll take it.
Okay, ik neem hem.
okay ik naym uhm

▶ When do I have to check out?
Hoe laat moet ik de kamer verlaten?
hoo laht moot ik duh k**ah**mer verl**ah**tuh

▶ Is there anywhere I can leave luggage?
Kan ik mijn bagage ergens laten?
kan ik mīn bak**ah**Juh **air**KHens l**ah**tuh

4. Car hire

automatic	automaat	owtom**ah**t
full tank	volle tank	**vo**lluh tank
manual	met versnellingen	met versn**e**llinguh
rented car	huurauto	hoor-**ow**toh

▶ I'd like to rent a car.
Ik wil graag een auto huren.
ik vil KHrahKH uhn **ow**to h**oo**ren

> ▶▶ For how long?
> **Voor hoe lang?**
> vohr hoo lang

▶ Two days.
Twee dagen.
tvay d**ah**KHuh

▶ I'll take the…
Ik neem de…
ik naym duh

▶ Is that with unlimited mileage?
Is dat zonder kilometerbeperking?
is dat z**o**nder k**ee**lomaytuh-buhp**ai**rking

> ▶▶ Yes.
> **Ja.**
> yah

> ▶▶ Can I see your driving licence please?
> **Mag ik uw rijbewijs even zien?**
> maKH ik oo r**ī**bevis **ay**vuh zeen

> ▶▶ And your passport.
> **En uw paspoort.**
> en oo p**a**spohrt

▶ Is insurance included?
Is de verzekering erbij inbegrepen?
is duh verz**ay**kering erbī **i**nbegraypuh

> ▶▶ Yes, but you have to pay the first 100 euros.
> **Ja, maar de eerste honderd euro moet u zelf betalen.**
> yah mahr duh **ay**rstuh h**o**nderd **ur**roh moot oo zelf bet**ah**luh

▶▶ Can you leave a deposit of 100 euros?
Kunt u een borgsom van honderd euro betalen?
k00nt 00 uhn borkHsom van honderd urroh betahluh

▶ And if this office is closed, where do I leave the keys?
Waar laat ik de sleutel als dit kantoor gesloten is?
vahr laht ik duh slurtel als dit kantohr geslohtuh is

▶▶ You drop them in that box.
U kunt ze in die bus stoppen.
00 k00nt zuh in dee b00s stoppuh

5. Car problems

brakes	de remmen	remmuh
to break down	kapotgaan	kahpot-KHahn
clutch	de koppeling	koppuhling
diesel	de diesel	deesel
flat battery	de lege accu	laykHuh akk00
flat tyre	de lekke band	lekkuh bant
petrol	de benzine	benzeenuh

▶ Excuse me, where is the nearest petrol station?
Pardon, waar is het dichtstbijzijnde benzinestation?
pardon vahr is uht dikHtstbizinduh benzeenuh-stahshon

▶▶ In the next town, about 5km away.
In de volgende stad, ongeveer vijf kilometer verderop.
in duh volkHenduh stat onkHevayr vif keelomayter vairder-op

▶ The car has broken down.
Ik heb autopech.
ik hep owtoh-pekH

▶▶ Can you tell me what happened?
Kunt u me vertellen wat er gebeurd is?
k00nt 00 mï vertelluh vat air kHeboort is

▶ I've got a flat tyre.
Ik heb een lekke band.
ik hep uhn lekkuh bant

▶ I think the battery is flat.
Ik denk dat de accu leeg is.
ik denk dat duh akk00 laykH is

>> Can you tell me exactly where you are?
Kunt u me vertellen waar u precies bent?
koont oo mī vertelluh vahr oo presees bent

▶ I'm about 2km outside of Hilversum on the A1.
Ik sta ongeveer twee kilometer van Hilversum aan de A1.
ik stah onKHevayr tvay keelomayter van hilversum ahn duh ah-ayn

>> What type of car? What colour?
Welk type auto? Welke kleur?
velk teepuh owtoh, velkuh klur

▶ Can you send a tow truck?
Wilt u een sleepwagen sturen?
vilt oo uhn slayp-vahKHuh stooruh

6. Children

baby	de baby	baby
boy	de jongen	yonguh
child	het kind	kint
children	de kinderen	kinderuh
cot	het ledikantje	laydeekant-yuh
formula	de flesvoeding	fles-vooding
girl	het meisje	mīshuh
highchair	de hoge kinderstoel	hohKHuh kinder-stool
nappies (diapers)	de luiers	low-ers

▶ We need a babysitter for tomorrow evening.
We hebben een oppas nodig voor morgenavond.
vuh hebbuh uhn oppas nohdiKH vohr morKHuh-ahvont

>> For what time?
Voor hoe laat?
vohr hoo laht

▶ From 7.30 to 11.00.
Van half acht tot elf.
van hal-f aKHt tot elf

>> How many children? How old are they?
Voor hoeveel kinderen? Hoe oud zijn ze?
vohr hoovayl kinderuh, hoo owt zin zuh

▶ **Two children, aged four and eighteen months.**
Twee kinderen, van vier en anderhalf.
tvay kinderuh van feer en ander-hal-f

▶ **Where can I change the baby?**
Waar kan ik de baby verschonen?
vahr kan ik duh baby versKH**oh**nuh

▶ **Could you please warm this bottle for me?**
Wilt u dit flesje voor me opwarmen?
vilt ∞ dit fles-yuh vohr muh **o**pvarmuh

▶ **Can you give us a child's portion?**
Kunt u ons een kinderportie geven?
k**∞**nt ∞ ons uhn k**i**nderpors**ee** KH**ay**vuh

▶ **We need two child seats.**
We hebben twee kinderzitjes nodig.
vuh h**e**bbuh tvay k**i**nder-zit-yus n**oh**dikH

▶ **Is there a discount for children?**
Is er een kinderkorting?
is air uhn k**i**nder-k**o**rting

7. Communications: Internet

@, at sign	het apenstaartje	**ah**puh-stahrt-yuh
computer	de computer	computer
email	de e-mail	email
Internet	het internet	internet
keyboard	het toetsenbord	**too**tsuhbort
mouse	de muis	m**o**ws

▶ **Is there somewhere I can check my emails?**
Kan ik hier ergens mijn e-mail lezen?
kan ik heer **air**KHens mīn email l**ay**zuh

▶ **Do you have Wi-Fi?**
Heeft u wifi?
hayft ∞ w**i**fee

▶ **Is there an Internet café around here?**
Is hier een internetcafé in de buurt?
is heer uhn **i**nternet-kafay in duh b**∞**rt

▶▶ Yes, there's one in the shopping centre.
Ja, er is er een in het winkelcentrum.
yah air is air ayn in uht **vi**nkel-sentrum

▶▶ Do you want fifteen minutes, thirty minutes or one hour?
Wilt u een kwartier, een halfuur of een uur?
vilt ∞ uhn kwart**eer** uhn h**a**l-f-∞r of uhn ∞r

▶ Thirty minutes please. Can you help me log on?
Een halfuur graag. Kunt u mij helpen met inloggen?
uhn h**a**l-f-∞r **KH**rah**KH**, k∞nt ∞ muh **he**lpuh met **i**n-logguh

▶▶ OK, here's your password.
Oké, dit is uw wachtwoord.
ok**ay** dit is ∞ va**KH**t-vohrt

▶ Can you change this to an English keyboard?
Kunt u dit in een Brits toetsenbord veranderen?
k∞nt ∞ dit in uhn brits t**oo**tsuh-bort ver**a**nderuh

▶ I'll take another quarter of an hour.
Ik wil graag een kwartier langer internetten.
ik vil **KH**rah**KH** uhn kwart**eer** l**a**nger **i**nternettuh

▶ Is there a printer I can use?
Kan ik hier ook printen?
kan ik heer ohk **pri**ntuh

8. Communications: phones

mobile phone (cell phone)	de mobiele telefoon	mob**ee**luh telef**oh**n
payphone	de telefooncel	telef**oh**n-sel
phone call	het telefoontje	telef**oh**n-tyuh
phone card	de telefoonkaart	telef**oh**n-kahrt
phone charger	de telefoonoplader	telef**oh**n-oplahder
SIM card	de simkaart	**si**mkahrt

▶ Can I call abroad from here?
Kan ik hiervandaan naar het buitenland bellen?
kan ik h**ee**rvan-dahn nahr uht b**ow**tuhlant b**e**lluh

▶ How do I get an outside line?
Hoe krijg ik een buitenlijn?
hoo kr**ī**k**H** ik uhn b**ow**tuh-līn

► What's the code to call the UK/US from here?

Wat is de code om hiervandaan naar Groot-Brittannië/de Verenigde
Staten te bellen?

vat is duh **koh**duh om **hee**rvan-dahn nahr кнroht-brittanni-uh/duh ver**ay**nікнduh
sta**h**tuh tuh **be**lluh

► Hello, can I speak to Miss Jansen?

Dag, mag ik mevrouw Jansen spreken?

daкн, maкн ik mevr**ow** ya**n**suh spr**ay**kuh

zero	nul	nool
one	een	ayn
two	twee	tvay
three	drie	dree
four	vier	feer
five	vijf	vif
six	zes	zes
seven	zeven	**zay**vuh
eight	acht	aкнt
nine	negen	**nay**кнuh

►► Yes, that's me speaking.

Daar spreekt u mee.

dahr spraykt оо may

► Do you have a charger for this?

Heeft u hier een oplader voor?

hayft оо heer uhn **o**plahder vohr

► Can I buy a SIM card for this phone?

Kan ik een simkaart voor deze telefoon kopen?

kan ik uhn **si**mkahrt vohr **day**zuh telef**oh**n **ko**puh

9. Directions

turn off	afslaan	**a**fslahn
over there	daar	dahr
just after	even voorbij	**ay**vuh **voh**rbī
on the left	links	
on the right	rechts	reкнts
straight ahead	rechtuit	reкнt-owt
street	straat	straht
opposite	tegenover	tayкнen-**oh**ver
back	terug	terоoкн
further	verder	**vair**der
near	vlakbij	vlakbī
next	volgende	**vo**lкнenduh

► Hi, I'm looking for the Leidseplein.

Dag, ik ben op zoek naar het Leidseplein.

daкн ik ben op zook nahr uht **lī**dsuhplīn

► Hi, the Leidseplein, do you know where it is?

Dag, weet u waar het Leidseplein is?

daкн vayt оо vahr uht **lī**dsuhplīn is

▶▶ Sorry, never heard of it.
Sorry, nooit van gehoord.
sorry noyt van ᴋʜeh**oh**rt

▶ Hi, can you tell me where the Leidseplein is?
Dag, kunt u me zeggen waar het Leidseplein is?
daᴋʜ koont oo muh ze**ᴋʜ**uh vahr uht lɪ̄dsuhplɪ̄n is

▶▶ I'm a stranger here too.
Ik ben hier ook vreemd.
ik ben heer ohk vraymt

▶ Where?   ▶ Which direction?
Waar?   Welke richting?
vahr   **ve**lkuh ri**ᴋʜ**ting

▶▶ Left at the second traffic lights.
Bij het tweede stoplicht linksaf.
bī uht tv**ay**duh st**o**plikʜt linksaf

▶▶ Around the corner.
Om de hoek.
om duh hook

▶▶ Then it's the first street on the right.
Daarna is het de eerste straat rechts.
dahrn**ah** is uht duh **ay**rstuh straht reᴋʜts

10. Emergencies

accident	ongeluk	**o**nкHelook
ambulance	ambulance	amboolansuh
consul	consul	konsul
embassy	ambassade	ambass**ah**duh
fire brigade	brandweer	br**a**ntvayr
police	politie	pol**ee**tsee

▶ Help!
Help!

▶ Can you help me?
Kunt u me helpen?
koont oo muh h**e**lpuh

▶ Please come with me! It's really very urgent.
Komt u alstublieft mee! het is erg dringend.
komt oo alstoobl**ee**ft may! uht is airkH dr**i**ngent

▶ I've lost my keys.
Ik ben mijn sleutels verloren.
ik ben muhn sl**ur**tels verl**oh**ruh

▶ My car is not working.
Mijn auto doet het niet.
muhn **ow**to doot uht neet

▶ My purse has been stolen.
Mijn portemonnee is gestolen.
muhn portuhmohn**ay** is кHest**oh**luh

▶ I've been mugged.
Ik ben beroofd.
ik ben ber**oh**ft

▶▶ What's your name?
Hoe heet u?
hoo hayt oo

▶▶ I need to see your passport.
Ik moet uw paspoort even zien.
ik moot oo p**a**spohrt **ay**vuh zeen

▶ I'm sorry, all my papers have been stolen.
Sorry, al mijn papieren zijn gestolen.
sorry al muhn pap**ee**ruh zīn кHest**oh**luh

11. Friends

▶ Hi, how're you doing?
Hallo, hoe is het?
hallo hoo is uht

▶▶ OK, and you?
Goed, en met jou?
KHoot en met yOW

▶ Yeah, fine.   ▶ Not bad.
Prima.   Best.
preemah

▶ D'you know Mark?
Ken je Mark?
ken yuh mark

▶ And this is Hannah.
En dit is Hannah.

▶▶ Yeah, we know each other.
Ja, wij kennen elkaar.
yah vī kennuh elkahr

▶ Where do you know each other from?
Hoe kennen jullie elkaar?
hoo kennuh yOOllee elkahr

▶▶ We met at Thijs' place.
We hebben elkaar bij Thijs ontmoet.
vuh hebbuh elkahr bī tīs ontmoot

▶ That was some party, eh?
Dat was nog eens een feest hè?
dat vas noKH ayns uhn fayst hay

▶▶ The best.
Geweldig.
KHeveldiKH

▶ Are you guys coming for a beer?
Gaan jullie mee een biertje drinken?
KHahn yOOllee may uhn beertyuh drinkuh

▶▶ Cool, let's go.   ▶▶ No, I'm meeting Sanne.
Okay, laten we gaan.   Nee, ik heb een afspraak met Sanne.
okay lahtuh vuh KHahn   nay ik hep uhn afsprahk met sannuh

▶ See you at Thijs' place tonight.
Ik zie je bij Thijs vanavond.
ik zee yuh bī tis vanahvont

▶▶ See you.
Tot dan.

12. Health

antibiotics	antibiotica	antee-bee**oh**teeka
antiseptic ointment	antiseptische zalf	antee-se**p**teesuh zalf
cystitis	blaasontsteking	bla**h**s-ontstayking
dentist	tandarts	ta**n**tarts
diarrhoea	diarree	dee-ahra**y**
doctor	dokter	
hospital	ziekenhuis	ze**e**kuh-hows
ill	ziek	zeek
medicine	medicijn	maydees**ī**n
painkillers	pijnstillers	p**ī**nstillers
pharmacy	apotheek	ahpota**y**k
to prescribe	voorschrijven	v**oh**rsKH**r**īvuh
thrush	vaginale infectie	vaK**H**ina**h**luh infektee

▶ I'm not feeling very well.
Ik voel me niet lekker.
ik vool muh neet le**k**ker

▶ Can you get a doctor?
Kunt u een dokter halen?
k**ōō**nt **ōō** uhn d**o**kter ha**h**luh

▶▶ Where does it hurt?
Waar doet het pijn?
vahr doot uht pīn

▶ It hurts here.
Hier doet het pijn.
heer doot uht pīn

▶▶ Is the pain constant?
Is het een constante pijn?
is uht uhn konst**a**ntuh pīn

▶ It's not a constant pain
Het is geen constante pijn.
uht is кнayn konstantuh pin

▶ Can I make an appointment?
Kan ik een afspraak maken?
kan ik uhn afsprahk mahkuh

▶ Can you give me something for...?
kunt u me iets voor... geven?
kOOnt OO muh eets vohr... кнayvuh

▶ Yes, I have insurance.
Ja, ik ben verzekerd.
yah ik bin verzaykert

13. Hotels

maid	het kamermeisje	kahmer-mishuh
manager	de manager	manager
room service	de roomservice	room service

▶ Hello, we've booked a double room in the name of Cameron.
Hallo, we hebben een tweepersoonskamer gereserveerd op naam van Cameron.
hallo vuh hebbuh uhn tvay-persohns-kahmer кнeraysairvayrt op nahm van Cameron

▶▶ That was for four nights, wasn't it?
Voor vier nachten, klopt dat?
vohr feer naкнtuh klopt dat

▶ Yes, we're leaving on Saturday.
Ja, we vertrekken op zaterdag.
yah vuh vertrekkuh op zahterdaкн

▶▶ Can I see your passport please?
Mag ik uw paspoort zien?
maкн ik OO paspohrt zeen

▶▶ There you are, room 321 on the third floor.
Alstublieft, kamer driehonderdééénentwintig op de derde verdieping.
alstOObleeft kahmer dree-hondert-ayn-uhn-tvintiкн op duh dairduh verdeeping

▶ I can't get this keycard to work.
Deze sleutelkaart werkt niet.
dayzuh slurtelkahrt vairkt neet

>> Sorry, I need to reactivate it.
Sorry, ik moet hem reactiveren.
sorree ik moot uhm ray-aktivayruh

▶ What time is breakfast?
Hoe laat is het ontbijt?
hoo laht is uht ontbīt

▶ There aren't any towels in my room.
Er zijn geen handdoeken in mijn kamer.
air zīn KHayn handookuh in mīn kahmer

▶ My flight isn't until this evening, can I keep the room a bit longer?
Mijn vlucht is pas vanavond. Mag ik wat langer gebruik maken van de kamer?
mīn vlooKHt is pas vanahvont, maKH ik vat langer KHebrowk mahkuh van duh kahmer

▶ Can I settle up? Is this card ok?
Kan ik de rekening betalen? Kan ik met deze kaart betalen?
kan ik duh **ray**kening bet**ah**luh, kan ik met d**ay**zuh kahrt bet**ah**luh

14. Language difficulties

a few words	een paar woorden	uhn pahr **vohr**duh
interpreter	tolk	
to translate	vertalen	ver**tah**luh

▶▶ Your credit card has been refused.
Uw creditcard is geweigerd.
oo **kray**ditkard is книh-v**ī**кнert

▶ What, I don't understand; do you speak English?
Wat? ik begrijp het niet, spreekt u Engels?
vat? ik beкнr**ī**p uht neet spraykt oo **e**ngels

▶▶ This isn't valid.
Deze is niet geldig.
d**ay**zuh is neet **кне**ldiкн

▶ Could you say that again?   ▶ Slowly.
Wilt u dat nog eens zeggen?   Langzaam.
vilt oo dat noкн ayns z**e**кнuh   l**a**ngzahm

▶ I understand very little Dutch.
Ik begrijp niet zoveel Nederlands.
ik beкнr**ī**p neet zov**ay**l **nay**derlants

▶ I speak Dutch very badly.
Ik spreek slecht Nederlands.
ik sprayk sleкнt **nay**derlants

▶▶ You can't use this card to pay.
U kunt met deze kaart niet betalen.
oo k**oo**nt met d**ay**zuh kahrt neet bet**ah**luh

▶▶ Do you understand?
Begrijpt u het?
beкнr**ī**pt oo uht

▶ Sorry, no.
Nee, sorry.
nay sorry

▶ Is there someone who speaks English?
Is er iemand die Engels spreekt?
is er **ee**mant dee **e**ngels spraykt

▶ Oh, now I understand.
O, nu begrijp ik het.
oh nOO beKHrip ik uht.

▶ Is that OK now?
Is het zo goed?
is uht zoh KHoot

15. Meeting people

▶ Hello.
Hallo.

▶▶ Hello, my name's Annemarie.
Hallo, ik heet Annemarie.
hallo ik hayt **a**nnuh-mah**ree**

▶ Graham, from England, Thirsk.
Ik ben Graham, ik kom uit Thirsk in Engeland.
ik ben graham ik kom Owt thirsk in **e**nguhlant

▶▶ Don't know that, where is it?
Dat ken ik niet, waar is dat?
dat ken ik neet vahr is dat

▶ Not far from York, in the North; and you?
Niet ver van York, in het noorden; en u?
neet vair van york in uht n**oh**rduh; en OO

▶▶ I'm from Amsterdam; here by yourself?
Ik kom uit Amsterdam; bent u hier alleen?
ik kom Owt amsterd**a**m; bent OO heer all**ay**n

▶ No, I'm with my wife and two kids.
Nee, ik ben met mijn vrouw en twee kinderen.
nay ik ben met min vrOw en tvay k**i**nderuh

▶ What do you do?
Wat doet u?
vat doot OO

▶▶ I'm in computers.
Ik werk met computers.
ik vairk met computers

▶ Me too.
Ik ook.
ik ohk

▶ Here's my wife now.
Daar komt mijn vrouw.
dahr komt min vrow

▶▶ Nice to meet you.
Leuk u ontmoet te hebben.
lurk oo ontm**oo**t tuh h**e**bbuh

16. Nightlife

electro	electro	electro
folk	folkmuziek	f**o**lkm∞zeek
heavy metal	heavy metal	heavy metal
hip-hop	hiphop	hip hop
jazz	jazz	jazz
rock	rockmuziek	r**o**km∞zeek

▶ What's a good club for…?
Naar welke club kan ik het best voor…?
nahr v**e**lkuh kl∞b kan ik uht best vohr…

▶▶ There's going to be a great gig at the Melkweg tomorrow night.
Morgenavond is er een goed concert in de Melkweg.
morkHen**ah**vont is air uhn kHoot kons**ai**rt in duh m**e**lkwekH

▶ Where can I hear some Dutch music?
Waar kan ik Nederlandse muziek horen?
vahr kan ik n**ay**derlantsuh m∞z**ee**k h**oh**ruh

▶ What's a good place for dancing?
Waar kan ik het best naartoe om te dansen?
vahr kan ik uht best nahrt**oo** om tuh d**a**nsuh

▶ Can you write down the names of the best bars around here?
Wilt u de namen opschrijven van de beste cafés hier in de buurt?
vilt ∞ duh n**ah**muh o**p**skHrïvuh van duh b**e**stuh kaf**ays** heer in duh b∞rt

▶▶ That depends what you're looking for.
Dat hangt ervan af wat u zoekt.
dat hangt air**va**n af vat ∞ z∞kt

▶ The place where the locals go.
Het café waar de mensen hier uit de buurt heengaan.
uht kaf**ay** vahr duh m**e**nsuh heer Owt duh bOOrt h**ay**nkHahn

▶ A place for a quiet drink.
Een rustig café.
uhn r**OO**stikH kaf**ay**

▶▶ The casino across the canal is very good.
Het casino aan de overkant van de gracht is heel goed.
uht kaz**ee**noh ahn duh **oh**verkant van duh KHraKHt is hayl KHoot

▶ I suppose they have a dress code?
Ze hebben daar vast een kledingvoorschrift?
zuh h**e**bbuh dahr vast uhn kl**ay**ding-vohrsKHrift?

▶▶ You can wear what you like.
U kunt zich kleden zoals u wilt.
OO kOOnt ziKH kl**ay**duh z**oh**-als OO vilt

▶ What time does it close?
Hoe laat sluit het?
hoo laht slOwt uht

17. Post offices

airmail	luchtpost	lu<small>KH</small>tposst
post card	ansichtkaart	anzicht-kahrt
post office	postkantoor	posstkantohr
stamp	postzegel	posstzay<small>KH</small>el

▶ What time does the post office close?
Hoe laat sluit het postkantoor?
hoo laht slowt uht posstkantohr

> ▶▶ Five o'clock weekdays.
> **Door de week om vijf uur.**
> dohr duh vayk om vīf oor

▶ Is the post office open on Saturdays?
Is het postkantoor op zaterdag open?
is uht postkantohr op zahterda<small>KH</small> open

> ▶▶ Till midday.
> **Tot twaalf uur.**
> tot tvahlf oor

▶ I'd like to send this registered to England.
Ik wil dit graag aangetekend naar Engeland versturen.
ik vil dit <small>KH</small>rah<small>KH</small> **ah**n<small>KH</small>etaykent nahr **e**nguhlant verst**uh**ruh

> ▶▶ Certainly, that will cost 10 euros.
> **Jazeker, dat is dan tien euro.**
> yah**zay**ker dat is dan teen **u**rroh

▶ And also two stamps
for England, please.
En ook twee postzegels
voor Engeland, alstublieft.
en ohk tvay p**o**sstzay<small>KH</small>els vohr
enguhlant alstoobl**ee**ft

BINNENLAND	**domestic**
BRIEVEN	**letters**
BUITENLAND	**international**
PAKKETJES	**parcels**

▶ Do you have some airmail stickers?
Heeft u een paar airmailstickers voor me?
hayft oo uhn pahr **ai**rmailstickers vohr muh

▶ Do you have any mail for me?
Is er post voor mij?
is air posst vohr mī

18. Restaurants

bill	rekening	**ray**kuhning
menu	menukaart	muh**noo**-kahrt
table	tafel	**tah**fel

▶ Can we have a non-smoking table?
Mogen we een niet-roken tafel hebben?
moh**KH**uh vuh uhn n**ee**t-rohkuh t**ah**fel h**e**bbuh

▶ There are two of us.
We zijn met zijn tweeën.
vuh zin met zuhn t**vay**uh

▶ There are four of us.
We zijn met zijn vieren.
vuh zin met zuhn v**ee**ruh

▶ What's this?
Wat is dit?
vat is dit

▶▶ It's a type of fish.
Dat is vis.

▶▶ It's a local speciality.
Het is een plaatselijke specialiteit.
uht is uhn pl**ah**tsuh-luhkuh spay-shah-leet**i**t

▶▶ Come inside and I'll show you.
Kom maar mee, dan laat ik het u zien.
kom mahr may dan laht ik uht oo zeen

▶ We would like two of these, one of these, and one of those.
We willen graag twee van deze, één van deze en één van die.
vuh v**i**lluh KHrahKH tvay van d**ay**zuh ayn van d**ay**zuh en ayn van dee

▶▶ And to drink?
En te drinken?
en tuh dr**i**nkuh

▶ Red wine.
Rode wijn.
rohduh vin

▶ White wine.
Witte wijn.
v**i**ttuh vin

▶ A beer and two orange juices.
Eén bier en twee sinaasappelsap.
ayn beer en tvay s**ee**nas-appelsap

▶ Some more bread please.
Nog wat brood, alstublieft.
no**KH** vat broht **a**lst**oo**bleeft

▶▶ How was your meal?
Heeft het gesmaakt?
hayft uht KHesma**h**kt

▶ Excellent!, very nice!
Uitstekend! heerlijk!
owtsta**y**kent! ha**y**rlik

▶▶ Anything else?
Wilt u nog iets anders?
vilt ∞ noKH eets **a**nders

▶ Just the bill thanks.
Alleen de rekening graag.
all**ay**n duh r**ay**kuhning KHrahKH

19. Self-catering accommodation

air-conditioning	de airconditioning	airconditioning
apartment	het appartement	apartuh**ment**
cooker	het fornuis	forn**ows**
fridge	de koelkast	k**oo**lkast
heating	de verwarming	ver**war**ming
hot water	warm water	varm va**h**ter
lightbulb	de gloeilamp	KHl**oo**-ee-lamp
toilet	het toilet	twal**e**t

▶ The toilet's broken, can you get someone to fix it?
Het toilet is defect. Kunt u iemand sturen om het te maken?
uht twal**e**t is duhf**e**kt, k∞nt ∞ **ee**mant st**oo**ruh om uht tuh m**ah**kuh

▶ There's no hot water.
Er is geen warm water.
air is KHayn varm va**h**ter

▶ Can you show me how the air-conditioning works?
Wilt u me laten zien hoe de airconditioning werkt?
vilt ∞ muh l**ah**tuh zeen hoo duh airconditioning vairkt

▶▶ OK, what apartment are you in?
Ja, hoor. In welk appartement zit u?
yah, hohr, in velk apartuh**ment** zit ∞

▶ We're in number five.
We zitten in nummer vijf.
vuh z**i**ttuh in n**oo**mer vīf

▶ Can you move us to a quieter apartment?
Heeft u een rustiger appartement voor ons?
hayft oo uhn **roo**s-tikHer apartuh**ment** vohr ons

▶ Is there a supermarket nearby?
Is er een supermarkt in de buurt?
is air uhn s**oo**per-markt in duh b**oo**rt

▶▶ Have you enjoyed your stay?
Heeft u het naar uw zin gehad?
hayft oo uht nahr oo zin кнehat

▶ Brilliant holiday, thanks!
Een geweldige vakantie, dank u!
uhn кнe**vel**dikнuh vak**an**see, dank oo

20. Shopping

▶▶ Can I help you?
Kan ik u helpen?
kan ik oo **hel**puh

▶ Can I just have a look around?
Mag ik even rondkijken?
maкн ik **ay**vuh **ront**-kīkuh

▶ Yes, I'm looking for…
Ja, ik zoek een…
yah ik **zook** uhn…

GESLOTEN	closed
KASSA	cash desk
OMWISSELEN	to exchange
UITVERKOOP	sale

▶ How much is this?
Wat kost dit?
vat kost dit

▶▶ Thirty-two euros.
Tweeëndertig euro.
tvay-uhn-d**ai**rtiкн **ur**roh

▶ OK, I think I'll have to leave it; it's a little too expensive for me.
Dankuwel; laat dan maar, dat is iets te duur voor mij.
dankoovel; laht dan mahr dat is eets tuh d**oo**r vohr mī

▶▶ How about this?
Wat vindt u hiervan?
vat vint oo **heer**van

▶ Can I pay by credit card?
Kan ik met een creditcard betalen?
kan ik met uhn k**ray**ditkard bet**ah**luh

▶ It's too big.
Het is te groot.
uht is tuh groht

▶ It's too small.
Het is te klein.
uht is tuh klīn

▶ It's for my son – he's about this high.
Het is voor mijn zoon; hij is ongeveer zo lang.
uht is vohr muhn zohn; hī is **o**nKHevayr zoh lang

> ▶▶ Will there be anything else?
> **Kan ik u nog met iets anders helpen?**
> kan ik OO noKH met eets **a**nders h**e**lpuh

▶ That's all thanks.
Nee, dat is alles, dankuwel.
nay dat is **a**lles dankOOvel

▶ Make it twenty euros and I'll take it.
Kunt u er twintig euro van maken? Dan neem ik het.
kOOnt OO er tv**i**ntiKH **u**rroh van m**a**hkuh dan naym ik uht

▶ Fine, I'll take it.
Goed, ik neem het.
KHoot ik naym uht

21. Shopping for clothes

to alter	vermaken	vermahkuh
bigger	groter	KHrohter
just right	precies goed	presees KHoot
smaller	kleiner	klīner
to try on	aanpassen	ahnpassuh

▶▶ Can I help you?
Kan ik u helpen?
kan ik oo helpuh

▶ No thanks, I'm just looking.
Nee, dank u. Ik wil alleen even rondkijken.
nay dank oo, ik vil allayn ayvuh ront-kīkuh

▶▶ Do you want to try that on?
Wilt u dat aanpassen?
vilt oo dit ahnpassuh

▶ Yes, and I'll try this one too.
Ja, en ik wil dit ook passen.
yah en ik vil dit ohk passuh

▶ Do you have it in a bigger size?
Heeft u dit in een grotere maat?
hayft oo dit in uhn KHrohteruh maht

▶ Do you have it in a different colour?
Heeft u dit in een andere kleur?
hayft oo dit in uhn anderuh klur

▶▶ That looks good on you.
Dat staat u goed.
dat staht oo KHoot

▶ Can you shorten this?
Kunt u dit korter maken?
koont oo dit korter mahkuh

▶▶ Sure, it'll be ready on Friday, after 12.00.
Ja, hoor. Het is vrijdag na twaalf uur klaar.
yah hohr, uht is vrīdaKH nah tvahlf oor klahr

22. Sightseeing

art gallery	gallerie	gal̲luhree
bus tour	bustocht	b̲oostoKHt
city centre	centrum	sentr̲oom
closed	gesloten	KHeslo̲htuh
guide	gids	KHids
museum	museum	m̲oosay-uhm
open	open	o̲pen

▶ I'm interested in seeing the old town.
Ik zou graag het oude deel van de stad willen zien.
ik zow KHrahKH uht o̲wduh dayl van duh stad vi̲lluh zeen

▶ Are there guided tours?
Worden er rondleidingen gehouden?
vo̲rduh er ro̲ndlīdinguh KHuh-ho̲wduh

　　　▶▶ I'm sorry, it's fully booked.
　　　Het spijt me, het is volgeboekt.
　　　uht spīt muh uht is vo̲l-KHuhbookt

▶ How much would you charge to drive us around for four hours?
Hoeveel rekent u om ons vier uur lang rond te rijden?
ho̲ovayl ra̲ykent oo om ons feer ōor lang rond tuh rī̲duh

▶ Can we book tickets for the concert here?
Kunnen we hier kaartjes voor het concert reserveren?
k̲oonnuh vuh heer ka̲hrtyuhs vohr uht konsa̲irt rayserva̲yruh

　　　▶▶ Yes, in what name?　　　▶▶ Which credit card?
　　　Ja, op welke naam?　　　**Welke creditcard?**
　　　yah op ve̲lkuh nahm　　　ve̲lkuh kra̲yditkard

▶ Where do we get the tickets?
Waar kunnen we de kaartjes krijgen?
vahr k̲oonnuh vuh duh ka̲hrtyuhs krī̲KHuh

　　　▶▶ Just pick them up at the entrance.
　　　Die kunt u bij de ingang afhalen.
　　　dee k̲oont oo bī duh i̲nKHang a̲f-hahluh

▶ Is it open on Sundays?
Is het zondag open?
is uht zo̲ndaKH o̲pen

▶ How much is it to get in?
Wat kost een toegangskaartje?
vat kost uhn tooKHangs-kahrtyuh

▶ Are there reductions for groups of six?
Wordt er korting gegeven aan groepen van zes?
vort er korting KHeKHayvuh ahn KHroopuh van zes

▶ That was really impressive!
Dat was heel indrukwekkend!
dat vas hayl indrookvekkend

23. Taxis

▶ Can you get us a taxi?
Wilt u een taxi voor ons bellen?
vilt oo uhn taksee vohr ons belluh

>> For now? Where are you going?
Voor nu? Waar wilt u heen?
vohr noo, vahr vilt oo hayn

▶ To the town centre.
Naar het centrum.
nahr uht sentrum

▶ I'd like to book a taxi to the airport for tomorrow.
Ik wil graag een taxi voor morgen naar het vliegveld reserveren.
ik vil кнгакн uhn taksee vohr morкнuh nahr uht vleeкнvelt raysairvayruh

>> Sure, at what time? How many people?
Zeker. Voor hoe laat? Met hoeveel mensen bent u?
zayker, vohr hoo laht?, met hoovayl mensuh bent oo

▶ How much is it to Leidseplein?
Wat kost een taxi naar het Leidseplein?
vat kost uhn taksee nahr uht lïdsuhplïn

▶ Right here is fine, thanks.
Hier is goed, dank u wel.
heer is кнoot, dank oo vel

▶ Can you wait here and take us back?
Kunt u hier wachten en ons terugbrengen?
koont oo heer vaкнtuh en ons terooкнbrenguh

>> How long are you going to be?
Hoe lang gaat het duren?
hoo lang кнaht uht doohruh

24. Trains

to change trains	overstappen	ohver-stappuh
platform	perron	perron
return	retour	retoor
single	enkele reis	enkeluh rïs
station	station	stahtshon
stop	station	stahtshon
ticket	kaartje	kahrtyuh

▶ How much is...?
Wat kost...?
vat kost...

▶ A single, second class to...
Een enkele reis, tweede klas naar...
ayn enkeluh rïs tvayduh klas nahr...

▶ Two returns, second class to...
Twee retourtjes, tweede klas naar...
tvay retoortyuhs tvayduh klas nahr...

▶ **For today.**
Voor vandaag.
vohr vand**ah**KH

▶ **For tomorrow.**
Voor morgen.
vohr m**o**rKHuh

▶ **For next Tuesday.**
Voor aanstaande dinsdag.
vohr **ah**nstahnduh d**i**nsdaKH

▶▶ **There's a supplement for the ICE International.**
Voor de ICE International moet u toeslag betalen.
vohr duh i-c-e international moot oo t**oo**slaKH bet**ah**luh

▶▶ **Do you want to make a seat reservation?**
Wilt u een stoel reserveren?
vilt oo uhn stool rayserv**ay**ruh

▶▶ **You have to change at Utrecht.**
U moet overstappen in Utrecht.
oo moot **oh**ver-stappuh in **oo**treKHt

▶ **Is this seat free?**
Is deze plaats vrij?
is d**ay**zuh plahts vrī

▶ **Excuse me, which station are we at?**
Pardon, op welk station zijn we?
pard**o**n op velk stahtsh**o**n zīn vuh

▶ **Is this where I change for Maastricht?**
Moet ik hier overstappen voor Maastricht?
moot ik heer **oh**ver-stappuh vohr mahstri**KH**t

ENGLISH
→ DUTCH

A

a, an een uhn, 'n

about: about 20 ongeveer twintig onkHevayr

it's about 5 o'clock het is ongeveer vijf uur oor

a film about Holland een film over Nederland ohver

above boven bohvuh

abroad het buitenland bowtuhlant

absolutely! (I agree) zeker! zayker

absorbent cotton de watten vattuh

accelerator het gaspedaal KHaspedahl

accept accepteren akseptayruh

accident het ongeluk onkHelook

there's been an accident er is een ongeluk gebeurd KHeburt

accommodation de kamers kahmers

> **Travel tip** If you're looking for a place to stay after a day's cycling, visit a member of Vrienden op de Fiets (Friends of the Bicycle), who will put you up for the night in their home for a modest fee and feed you a princely breakfast the next morning. Hosts are usually wonderfully hospitable, as well as experts on cycling in their own country.

accurate precies presees

ache de pijn pin

my back aches mijn rug doet

pijn muhn rooKH doot

across: across the road aan de overkant van de straat ahn duh ohverkant van duh straht

adapter de adapter

address het adres

what's your address? wat is uw adres? vat is oo

address book het adresboek adresbook

adhesive tape het plakband plakbant

admission charge de toegangsprijs tooKHangsprïs

adult de volwassene volvassenuh

advance: in advance vooruit vohrowt

aeroplane het vliegtuig vleeKHtowKH

after na

after you na u oo

after lunch na het middageten middaKH-aytuh

afternoon de middag middaKH

in the afternoon 's middags smiddaKHs

this afternoon vanmiddag vanmiddaKH

aftershave de aftershave

aftersun cream de aftersun crème aftersoon krem

afterwards naderhand nahderhant

again opnieuw opnew

against tegen tayKHuh

age de leeftijd layftït

ago: a week ago een week

geleden uhn vayk KHel**ay**duh

an hour ago een uur geleden
oor

agree: I agree ik ben het er mee
eens may ayns

AIDS de AIDS

air de lucht lOOKHt

by air per vliegtuig vleeKHt0WKH

air-conditioning
de air-conditioning

airmail: by airmail per luchtpost
lOOKHtposst

airmail envelope de luchtpost-
enveloppe –envel**o**p

airplane het vliegtuig vleeKHt0WKH

airport het vliegveld vleeKHvelt

to the airport, please
naar het vliegveld, alstublieft
nahr – alst00bleeft

airport bus de bus naar het
vliegveld b00s

aisle seat de plaats bij het
middenpad plahts bī uht
m**i**dduhpat

alarm clock de wekker v**e**kker

alcohol **a**lcohol

alcoholic: is it alcoholic?
bevat het **a**lcohol? bev**a**t

all alle **a**lluh

all of it **a**lles

all of them allemaal **a**llemahl

that's all, thanks dat is alles,
dank u wel 00 vel

allergic: I'm allergic to…
ik ben allergisch voor…
all**ai**rKHees vohr

allowed: is it allowed? is het

toegestaan? t00KHestahn

all right goed KH00t

I'm all right met mij gaat het
goed mī KHaht uht KH00t

are you all right? gaat het?
KHaht uht

almond de am**a**ndel

almost bijna bīna

alone alleen all**ay**n

alphabet het **a**lfabet

a ah	j yay	s es
b bay	k ka	t tay
c say	l el	u 00
d day	m em	v vay
e ay	n en	w way
f ef	o 0	x ix
g KHay	p pay	y ī
h ha	q k00	z zet
i ee	r air	

already al

also ook ohk

although hoewel hoov**e**l

altogether helemaal h**ay**lemahl

always altijd alt**ī**t

am: I am ik ben

am: at 7am 's morgens om zeven
uur sm**o**rKHuhs – z**ay**vuh oor

amazing (very good)
verbazingwekkend verbazing-
v**e**kkent

that's amazing! (surprising)
hoe is het mogelijk! hoo is uht
m**oh**KHelik

ambulance de ziekenwagen

zeekuh-vaKHuh

call an ambulance! bel een
ziekenwagen!

America Amerika am**ay**rika

American Amerikaans
am**ay**rik**ah**ns

I'm American ik kom uit
Amerika owt

among **o**nder

amount de hoeveelheid hoov**ay**lhīt
(money) het bedrag bedr**a**KH

amp: a 13-amp fuse een stop
van dertien ampère d**ai**rteen
amp**ai**ruh

and en

angry boos bohs

animal het dier deer

ankle de **e**nkel

anniversary (wedding)
de trouwdag tr**ow**daKH

**annoy: this man's annoying
me** deze man valt me lastig
d**ay**zuh man valt muh l**a**stiKH

annoying vervelend verv**ay**lent

another (a different one) een **a**nder
(one more) nog een noKH ayn

  **can we have another
room?** kunnen we een andere
kamer krijgen? k**oo**nnuh vuh uhn
anderuh k**ah**mer krī**KH**uh

  another beer, please
nog een bier, alstublieft noKH
uhn beer alst**oo**bleeft

antibiotics antibiotica
antibi-**oh**tica

antifreeze het antivriesmiddel
antivr**ee**smiddel

antihistamine tablets
de antihistamine-tabletten
antihistam**ee**nuh-tabl**e**ttuh

antique: is it an antique?
is het antiek? ant**eek**

antique shop de antiekwinkel
ant**eek**vinkel

antiseptic antiseptisch
antis**e**ptees

**any: have you got any bread/
tomatoes?** heeft u ook brood/
tomaten? hayft oo ohk

  sorry, I don't have any…
het spijt me, ik heb geen…
spīt muh ik hep KHayn

anybody iemand **ee**mant

  **does anybody speak
English?** spreekt er iemand
Engels? spraykt

  there wasn't anybody there
er was niemand vas n**ee**mant

anything iets eets

DIALOGUE

  anything else? nog iets
(**a**nders)? noKH

  nothing else, thanks
nee dat is alles, dank u wel
nay das **a**lles dank oo vel

  **would you like anything to
drink?** wilt u iets drinken?
vilt oo eets

  **I don't want anything,
thanks** nee, dank u wel

apart from afgezien van
afKHezeen

apartment de flat

apartment block
het flatgebouw flet**kh**eb**ow**

aperitif de aperitief apayrit**ee**f

apology de verontschuldiging
veront-skh**oo**ldik**h**ing

appendicitis
de blindedarmontsteking
bl**i**nduh-d**ar**montstayking

appetizer het voorgerecht
v**oh**r**kh**ere**kh**t

apple de appel

appointment de afspraak
afsprahk

DIALOGUE

**good morning, how can I
help you?** goedemorgen,
waar kan ik u mee van dienst
zijn? **kh**oodem**or**k**h**uh vahr kan
ik **oo** may van deenst zin

**I'd like to make an
appointment** ik wil graag
een afspraak maken vil
khrah**kh** uhn **a**fsprahk m**ah**kuh

what time would you like?
hoe laat wilt u komen?
hoo laht vilt **oo**

three o'clock om drie
uur **oo**r

**I'm afraid that's not
possible, is four o'clock
all right?** dat is helaas niet
mogelijk, is vier uur goed?
hel**ah**s neet m**oh**k**h**elik is veer
oor **kh**oot

yes, that will be fine ja, dat
is goed ya

the name was...? en uw
naam was...? **oo** nahm vas

apricot de abrikoos abrik**oh**s

April april ahpr**i**l

are: we are wij zijn vī zin

you are (*pol*) u bent **oo**
(*sing, fam*) jij bent yī

they are zij zijn zī zin

area het gebied **kh**eb**ee**t

area code het netnummer
n**e**tnoommer

arm de arm

**arrange: will you arrange it
for us?** regelt u het voor ons?
r**ay**k**h**elt **oo** uht vohr

arrival de aankomst **ah**nkomst

arrive aankomen **ah**nkomuh

when do we arrive?
wanneer komen we aan?
v**a**nnayr k**oh**muh vuh ahn

has my fax arrived yet?
is mijn fax al gearriveerd?
mīn fax al **kh**uh-arriv**ay**rt

we arrived today wij zijn
vandaag aangekomen vī zin
vand**ah**k**h** **ah**nk**h**ekomuh

art de kunst k**oo**nst

art gallery de kunstgalerij
k**oo**nst-k**h**ahlerī

artist (*male/female*)
de kunstenaar/kunstenares
k**oo**nstenahr/k**oo**nstenar**e**s

as: as big as zo groot als **kh**roht

as soon as possible zo snel
mogelijk m**oh**k**h**elik

ashtray de asbak

ask vragen vr**a**k**h**uh

I didn't ask for this ik heb
hier niet om gevraagd hep heer

neet om кнеvrah кнt

could you ask him to...?
kunt u hem vragen of hij...?
koont ∞ uhm vrah кнuh of ee

asleep: she's asleep ze slaapt
zuh slahpt

aspirin de aspirine aspir**ee**nuh

asthma a**s**tma

astonishing verbazingwekkend
verbazing-v**e**kkent

at: at the hotel in het hotel

at the station op het station
stash**o**n

at six o'clock om zes uur ∞r

at Jan's bij Jan bï

athletics atletiek atlet**ee**k

ATM de ATM ah-tay-**e**m

@, at sign het apenstaartje
ahpuh-stahrt-yuh

attractive aantrekkelijk
ahnt**re**kkelik

aubergine de aubergine
ohberJ**ee**nuh

August augustus ow**кн∞**st∞s

aunt de tante t**a**ntuh

Australia Australië owstr**ah**li-uh

Australian Australisch owstr**ah**lees

I'm Australian ik kom uit
Australië owt owstr**ah**li-uh

automatic (*adj*) automatisch
owtom**ah**tees

(*noun:* car) de automaat
owtom**ah**t

autumn de herfst

in the autumn in de herfst

avenue de laan lahn

average (ordinary) gemiddeld
кнem**i**ddelt

(not good) middelmatig
middelm**ah**tiкн

on average gemiddeld
кнem**i**ddelt

avocado de avocado

awake: is he awake? is hij al wakker? is-ee al vakker

away: go away! ga weg! KHa veKH

is it far away? is het ver weg? vair

awful afschuwelijk afsKH00-uhlik

axle de as

B

baby de baby

baby food babyvoedsel babyvoodsel

baby-sitter de babysit

back (of body) de rug r00KH

(back part) de achterkant aKHterkant

at the back aan de achterkant

can I have my money back? kan ik mijn geld terugkrijgen? muhn KHelt ter00KH-krīKHuh

to come back terugkomen ter00KH-kohmuh

to go back teruggaan ter00KH-KHahn

backache rugpijn r00KHpīn

bacon het spek

bad slecht sleKHt

not bad niet slecht neet

a bad headache een zware hoofdpijn uhn zvaruh hohftpīn

badly slecht sleKHt

(injured, damaged) zwaar zvahr

bag de tas

(handbag) de hant-tas

baggage de bagage baKHahJuh

baggage checkroom het bagagedepot baKHahJuh-depoh

baggage claim de bagage-afhaalruimte baKHahJuh-afhahlrowmtuh

bakery de bakkerij bakkerī

balcony het balkon

a room with a balcony een kamer met een balkon uhn kahmer

bald kaal kahl

ball de bal

ballet het ballet ballet

ballpoint pen de balpen

banana de banaan banahn

band (musical) de band bent

Bandaid de pleister plīster

bandage het verband verbant

bank (money) de bank

bank account de bankrekening

bar de bar

a bar of chocolate een reep chocolade uhn rayp shokolahduh

barber's de herenkapper hayruhkapper

barge (house boat) de woonboot vohnboht

basket de mand mant

(in shop) het mandje mant-yuh

bath het bad bat

can I have a bath? kan ik een bad nemen? naymuh

bathroom de badkamer batkahmer

with a private bathroom met eigen badkamer īKHuh

bath towel de badhanddoek bathandook

bathtub de badkuip batkowp

battery (for radio etc) de batterij batterī

(for car) de accu akkoo

bay de baai bī

be zijn zin

beach het strand strant

on the beach op het strand

beans de bonen bohnuh

French beans de prinsessenbonen

runner beans de pronkbonen

broad beans de tuinbonen townbohnuh

beard de baard bahrt

beautiful mooi moy

because omdat

because of... vanwege... vanvayкниh

bed het bed bet

I'm going to bed now ik ga nu naar bed кнa noo nahr

bed and breakfast logies en ontbijt lojees en ontbīt

bedroom de slaapkamer slahpkahmer

beef het rundvlees roontvlays

beer het bier beer

two beers, please twee pils, alstublieft alstoobleeft

before voor vohr

begin beginnen beкнinnuh

when does it begin? wanneer begint het? vannayr beкнint

beginner de beginneling beкнinneling

beginning: at the beginning in het begin beкнin

behind achter aкнter

behind me achter me muh

beige beige

Belgian Belgisch belкнees

Belgium België belкні-uh

believe geloven кнelohvuh

below onder

belt de riem reem

bend (in road) de bocht boкнt

berth (on ship) de hut hoot

beside: beside the... naast de... nahst duh

best best

better beter bayter

are you feeling better? (pol) voelt u zich nu beter? voolt oo ziкн noo

(fam) voel je je nu beter? vool yuh yuh

between tussen toossuh

beyond verder dan vairder

bicycle de fiets feets

Travel tip No country in Europe is as kindly disposed towards the bicycle as the pancake-flat Netherlands: you'll find well-marked cycle paths in and around all the towns, plus long-distance touring routes that allow you to reach beaches, forests and moorland that might other-wise be inaccessible.

---

big groot KHroht

  too big te groot tuh

  it's not big enough het is niet groot genoeg neet KHroht KHenooKH

bike de fiets feets

  (motorbike) de motorfiets

bikini de bikini bikini

bill de rekening raykening

  (banknote) het bankbiljet bankbil-yet

  could I have the bill, please? kan ik afrekenen, alstublieft? alstoobleeft

bin de afvalbak

bin liners de afvalzakken afvalzakkuh

bird de vogel vohKHel

birthday de verjaardag ver-yahrdaKH

  happy birthday! hartelijk gefeliciteerd! hartelik KHefelisitayrt

biscuit het koekje kook-yuh

bit: a little bit een klein beetje uhn klīn bayt-yuh

  a big bit een groot stuk KHroht stook

  a bit of… een beetje… bayt-yuh

  (a piece) een stukje… stook-yuh

  a bit expensive vrij duur vrī door

bite (by insect) de insectenbeet insektuhbayt

  (by dog) de beet bayt

bitter (taste etc) bitter

black zwart zvart

blanket de deken daykuh

bleach (for toilet) het bleekmiddel blaykmiddel

bless you! gezondheid! KHezont-hīt

blind blind blint

blinds de rolgordijnen rolKHordīnuh

blister de blaar blahr

blocked (road) versperd verspairt

  (pipe, sink) verstopt verstopt

blond blond blont

blood bloed bloot

  high blood pressure de hoge bloeddruk hohKHuh bloot-drook

blouse de bloes bloos

blow-dry föhnen furnuh

  I'd like a cut and blow-dry ik wil graag geknipt en geföhnd worden vil KHrahKH KHek-nipt en KHefurnt vorduh

blue blauw blow

blusher de rouge

boarding pass de instapkaart instapkahrt

boat de boot boht

boat trip de boottocht bohttoKHt

body het lichaam liKHahm

boiled egg het gekookt ei KHekohkt ī

boiler de boiler

bone het bot

bonnet (of car) de motorkap

book het boek book

  (verb: transport) reserveren raysairvayruh

(table, tickets etc) bespreken besp**ray**kuh

can I book a seat? kan ik een zitplaats reserveren? uhn z**i**tplahts

I'd like to book a table for two ik wil graag een tafel voor twee personen bespreken vil KHrahKH uhn t**ah**fel vohr tvay pers**oh**nuh besp**ray**kuh

for what time? voor hoe laat? vohr hoo laht

half past seven half acht

that's fine dat kan

and your name? en wat is uw naam? vat is ∞ nahm

bookshop, bookstore de boekwinkel b**oo**kvinkel

boot (footwear) de laars lahrs

(of car) de k**o**fferbak

border (of country) de grens KHrens

bored: I'm bored ik verveel me verv**ay**l muh

boring saai s**ī**

born: I was born in Manchester/1960 ik ben in Manchester/1960 geboren KHeb**oh**ruh

borrow lenen l**ay**nuh

may I borrow…? kan ik… lenen?

both beide b**ī**duh

bother: sorry to bother you het spijt me dat ik u lastig val sp**ī**t muh dat ik ∞ l**a**stiKH val

bottle de fles

a bottle of house red een fles rode huiswijn uhn fles r**oh**duh h**ow**svin

bottle-opener de fl**e**sopener

bottom (of person) de bips

at the bottom of… (hill) aan de voet van… ahn duh voot

(road) aan het eind van… int

bowl het bord bort

box de doos dohs

box office het lok**e**t

boy de jongen y**o**nguh

boyfriend de vriend vreent

bra de b.h. bay-h**ah**

bracelet de armband **a**rmbant

brake de rem

brandy de cognac

bread het brood broht

white bread het wittebrood v**i**ttebroht

brown bread het bruinbrood br**ow**nbroht

wholemeal bread het volkorenbrood volk**oh**ruhbroht

rye bread het roggebrood r**o**KHuhbroht

break breken br**ay**kuh

I've broken the… ik heb de… gebroken hep duh… KHebr**oh**kuh

I think I've broken my wrist ik geloof dat ik mijn pols gebroken heb KHel**oh**f dat ik muhn pols KHebr**oh**kuh heb

break down kap**o**t gaan KH**ah**n

I've broken down ik heb autopech hep **ow**topeKH

breakdown autopech

breakdown service
de wegenwacht vay**KH**uhvak**KH**t

breakfast het ontbijt ont**bī**t

break-in: I've had a break-in
er is bij mij ingebroken
bī mī **in**KHebrokuh

breast de borst

breathe ademen a**h**demuh

breeze de bries brees

bridge (over river) de brug br**OO**KH

brief kort

briefcase de aktentas a**k**tuhtas

bright (light etc) fel

bright red felrood felr**oh**t

brilliant (great) geweldig
KHev**e**ldiKH

(idea) heel goed hayl KH**oo**t

(person) briljant bril-y**a**nt

bring meebrengen **may**brenguh

I'll bring it back later
ik breng het terug ter**OO**KH

Britain Groot-Brittannië
KHr**oh**t-britt**a**nnee-uh

British Brits

brochure de brochure brosh**OO**ruh

broken kap**o**t

(leg etc) gebroken KHebr**oh**kuh

brooch de broche br**o**sh

brother de broer broor

brother-in-law de zwager
zv**ah**KHer

brown bruin br**ow**n

bruise de blauwe plek bl**ow**uh

brush de borstel

(artist's) het penseel pens**ay**l

bucket de **e**mmer

buffet car de restauratiewagen
resto**w**r**ah**tsee-v**ah**KHuh

buggy (for child) de wandelwagen
v**a**ndelv**ah**KHuh

building het gebouw KHeb**ow**

bulb (flower) de bloembol
bl**oo**mbol

(light bulb) de gloeilamp
KHl**oo**-eelamp

bulb fields de bollenvelden
b**o**lluhvelduh

bumper de bumper b**oo**mper

bunk (on train) de couchette

(on ship) de kooi koy

bureau de change het
wisselkantoor v**i**sselkantohr

burglary de inbraak **i**nbrahk

burn de brandwond br**a**ntvont

(verb) verbranden verbr**a**nduh

burnt: this is burnt dit is
aangebrand **ah**nKHebrant

burst: a burst pipe
een gesprongen leiding
uhn KHespr**o**nguh l**ī**ding

bus de bus b**OO**s

**what number bus is it
to…?** wat is het busnummer
van de bus naar…? vat is uht
b**OO**snoommer van duh b**OO**s nahr

when is the next bus to…?
hoe laat gaat de volgende
bus naar…? hoo laht KH**ah**t duh
v**o**lkHenduh

what time is the last bus?
hoe laat vertrekt de laatste bus?
vertr**e**kt duh l**ah**tstuh

does this bus go to…?
is dit de bus naar…? duh
boos nahr

no, you need a number…
nee, u moet met bus
nummer… nay oo moot met
boos noommer

business zaken za**h**kuh

bus station het busstation
b**oo**s-stashon

bus stop de bushalte
b**oo**s-haltuh

bust het borstbeeld b**o**rstbaylt

busy druk dr**oo**k

I'm busy tomorrow
morgen kan ik niet
m**o**rk**h**uh kan ik neet

but maar mahr

butcher's de slager sl**ah**k**h**er

butter de boter

button de knoop k-nohp

buy kopen k**oh**puh

where can I buy…?
waar kan ik… kopen? vahr

by: by bus/car per bus/auto
b**oo**s/**o**wto

written by… geschreven
door… k**h**esk**h**r**ay**vuh dohr

by the window bij het raam
bī uht rahm

by the sea aan zee ahn zay

by Thursday voor donderdag
vohr d**o**nderdak**h**

bye tot ziens zeens

C

cabbage de kool kohl

cabin (on ship) de hut h**oo**t

café het café kaf**ay**

cagoule de anorak

cake de taart tahrt

cake shop de banketbakkerij
bank**e**tbakker**ī**

call het telefoongesprek
telef**oh**n-k**h**esprek

(*verb*: to phone) bellen b**e**lluh

what's it called?
hoe heet het? hoo hayt

he/she is called…
hij/zij heet… hī/zī

please call the doctor
zou u de dokter willen bellen?
zow oo duh dokter v**i**lluh

**please give me a call
at 7.30am tomorrow**
zou u me morgen om half acht
kunnen wekken?
zow oo muh m**o**rk**h**uh om hal-f
ak**h**t k**oo**nnuh v**e**kkuh

please ask him to call me
zou u hem willen vragen om
mij te bellen?
v**i**lluh vr**ah**k**h**uh om mī tuh

call back: I'll call back later
ik kom straks wel terug
vel ter**oo**k**h**

(phone back) ik bel later wel
terug l**ah**ter

**call round: I'll call round
tomorrow** ik kom morgen
even langs m**o**rk**h**uh **ay**fvuh

camcorder de camcorder

camera de camera, het fototoestel **fo**totoostel

camera shop de fotowinkel **fo**tovinkel

camp kamperen kamp**ay**ruh

  can we camp here? kunnen we hier kamperen? k**oo**nnuh vuh heer

camping gas de camping gas gahs

campsite de camping

can het blik

  a can of beer een blikje bier uhn bl**i**k-yuh beer

can: can you...? (*pol*) kunt u...? k**oo**nt **oo**

  (*fam*) kun je...? k**oo**n yuh

  can I have...? mag ik... h**e**bben? maкн ik

  I can't... ik kan niet... neet

Canada Canada

Canadian Canadees kanad**ay**s

  I'm Canadian ik kom uit Canada **ow**t

canal (in city) de gracht кнraкнt

  (shipping) het kanaal kan**ah**l

canal bus de rondvaartboot r**o**ntvahrtboht

canal trip de tocht met de rondvaartboot t**o**кнt met duh

cancel annuleren ann**oo**layruh

candies het snoepgoed sn**oo**pкн**oo**t

candle de kaars kahrs

cannabis de marihuana mar**oo**w**ah**na

> **Travel tip** Thousands of visitors come to the Netherlands just to get stoned, but the government's attitude to soft drugs is more complex than you might think: the use of cannabis is tolerated but not condoned, which means very small amounts for personal use only. Never, ever buy dope on the street and don't try to take any form of cannabis out of the country.

canoe de kano k**ah**no

canoeing kanoën k**ah**nowuh

can-opener de blikopener

cap (hat) de pet

  (of bottle) de dop

car de auto **ow**to

  by car met de auto

carafe de karaf

  a carafe of house white, please een karaf witte huiswijn, alstublieft v**i**ttuh h**ow**svin alst**oo**bleeft

caravan de caravan

caravan site de camping

carburettor de carburateur karb**oo**rat**urr**

card (birthday etc) de kaart kahrt

  here's my (business) card hier is mijn visitekaartje heer is muhn vis**ee**tuh-kahrt-yuh

cardigan het vest

cardphone de kaarttelefoon k**ah**rt-telefohn

careful voorzichtig vohrzi**K**Hti**K**H

  be careful! wees voorzichtig!
vays vohrzi**K**Hti**K**H

caretaker (*male/female*)
de toezichthouder/toezicht-
houdster t**oo**zi**K**Ht-h**o**wder/
t**oo**zi**K**Ht-h**o**wtster

car ferry het autoveer **o**wtovayr

carnation de anjer **a**nyer

car park het parkeerterrein
park**ay**r-terr**i**n

carpet het tapijt tap**i**t

car rental de autoverhuur
owtoverh**oo**r

carriage (of train) de wagon
va**K**H**o**n

carrier bag de plastic tas pl**e**stik

carrot de wortel v**o**rtel

carry dragen dra**K**H**u**h

carry-cot de reiswieg r**i**sveek**K**H

carton het pak

carwash de autowasserette
owtovasserett**u**h

case (suitcase) de koffer

cash (*noun*) het cont**a**nt geld **K**Helt

  will you cash this for me?
kunt u dit voor mij verzilveren?
k**oo**nt **oo** dit voh**r** m**i** verz**i**lver**u**h

cash desk de kassa

cash dispenser
de geldautomaat **K**Helt**o**wtomaht

cassette de cassette kass**e**ttuh

cassette recorder de cassetterecorder kass**e**ttuh–

castle het kasteel kast**ay**l

casualty department
de eerste hulpafdeling

ayrstuh h**oo**lpafdayling

cat de kat

catch vangen v**a**ngu**h**

  **where do we catch the bus
to...?** waar kunnen we de bus
nemen naar...? vahr k**oo**nnuh vuh
duh b**oo**s n**a**ymuh nah**r**

cathedral de kathedraal
kahtaydr**ah**l

Catholic katholiek kahtohl**ee**k

cauliflower de bloemkool
bl**oo**mkohl

cave de grot **K**Hrot

CD de CD say-d**ay**

ceiling het plafond plahf**o**n

celery de selderij s**e**lder**i**

cell phone de GSM **K**H**a**y-ess-em,
de mobiele telefoon
mob**ee**luh telef**oh**n

cemetery de begraafplaats
be**K**Hr**ah**fplahts

centigrade Celsius s**e**lsi-**oo**s

centimetre de centimeter
s**e**ntimayter

central centraal sentr**ah**l

central heating de centrale
verwarming sentr**ah**luh
verv**a**rming

centre het centrum s**e**ntr**oo**m

  **how do we get to the city
centre?** hoe komen we in het
centrum? h**oo** k**oh**muh vuh

certainly zeker z**a**yker

  certainly not beslist niet neet

chair de stoel stool

champagne de champagne
shamp**a**n-yuh

change (small change)
het kleingeld klīn-KHelt

(money back) het wisselgeld
vissel-KHelt

(*verb:* money) wisselen visseluh

can I change this for...? kan
ik dit ruilen voor...? rowluh vohr

I don't have any change
ik heb helemaal geen kleingeld
hep helemahl KHayn klīn-KHelt

**can you give me change
for a 100-euro note?**
kunt u een biljet van honderd
euro wisselen? koont oo uhn bil-
yet van hondert urroh visseluh

**do we have to change
(trains)?** moeten we
overstappen? mootuh vuh
ohverstappuh

**yes, change at Utrecht/
no, it's a direct train**
ja, u moet in Utrecht
overstappen/nee, de trein
gaat rechtstreeks ya oo moot
in ootreKHt– /nay duh trīn KHaht
reKHtstrayks

changed: to get changed
zich omkleden ziKH omklayduh

charge (cost) de prijs prīs
(*verb*) rekenen raykenuh

cheap goedkoop KHootkohp

**do you have anything
cheaper?** heeft u iets
goedkopers? hayft oo eets
KHootkohpers

check (US) de cheque shek
(bill) de rekening raykening

check (*verb*) nakijken naHkīkuh

**could you check the...,
please?** kunt u de... nakijken,
alstublieft? koont oo duh –
alstoobleeft

check book het chequeboek
shekbook

check card de betaalpas
betahlpas

check in (at hotel) zich melden
ziKH

(at airport) inchecken inchekuh

**where do we have to
check in?** waar moeten we
inchecken? vahr mootuh vuh
inchekuh

check-in de check-in-balie
check-in-bahlee

cheek de wang vang

cheerio! tot ziens! zeens

cheers! (toast) proost! prohst
(thanks) bedankt!

cheese de kaas kahs

cheese shop de kaaswinkel
kahsvinkel

chemist's de apotheek
ahpohtayk

(non-dispensing) de drogisterij
drohKHisterī

cheque de cheque shek

do you take cheques?
kan ik met een cheque betalen?
betahluh

cheque book het chequeboek
shekbook

cheque card de betaalpas
betahlpas

cherry de kers kairs

chess het schaakspel sKHahkspel

chest de borstkas borstkas

chewing gum de kauwgum kow-KHoom

chicken de kip

chickenpox de waterpokken vahterpokkuh

child het kind kint

children de kinderen kinderuh

child minder de kinderoppas

children's pool het kinderbad kinderbat

children's portion de kinderportie kinderporsee

chin de kin

china het porselein porselin

Chinese Chinees sheenays

chips de (patat) friet freet

(US) de chips ships

chocolate de chocolade shokolahduh

milk chocolate de melkchocolade melkshokolahduh

plain chocolate de pure chocolade poor

a hot chocolate de warme chocolademelk varmuh shokolahduh-melk

choose kiezen keezuh

Christian name de voornaam vohrnahm

Christmas kairstmis

Christmas Eve kerstnacht kairstnaKHt

merry Christmas! vrolijk kerstfeest! vrohlik kairstfayst

chrysanthemum de chrysant kreesant

church de kerk

cider de cider seeder

cigar de sigaar seeKHahr

cigarette de sigaret seeKHaret

cigarette lighter de aansteker ahnstayker

cinema de bioscoop bioskohp

cinnamon de kaneel kahnayl

circle de cirkel

(in theatre) het balkon

city de stad stat

city centre het stadscentrum stats-sentroom

clean (*adj*) schoon sKHohn

can you clean these for me? zou u deze voor me kunnen schoonmaken? zow oo dayzuh vohr muh koonnuh sKHohnmahkuh

cleaning solution (for contact lenses) de lensvloeistof lensvloo-eestof

cleansing lotion de reinigingsmelk rīnikHings-melk

clear helder

(obvious) duidelijk dowdelik

clever slim, knap k-nap

cliff de steile rots stīluh

cling film de vershoudfolie vairs-howtfohlee

clinic de kliniek kleeneek

cloakroom de garderobe KHarderobuh

clock de klok

clogs de klompen klompuh

close (*verb*) sluiten slowtuh

what time do you close? hoe laat sluit u? hoo laht slowt oo

we close at 8pm on weekdays and 6pm on Saturdays door de week sluiten we om acht uur en op zaterdag om zes uur dohr duh vayk slowtuh vuh om akHt oor en op zahterdakH

do you close for lunch? gaat u tussen de middag dicht? KHaht oo toossuh duh middakH dikHt

yes, between 1 and 3.30pm ja, tussen een en half vier ya

closed gesloten KHeslohtuh

cloth (fabric) de stof

(for cleaning etc) de doek dook

clothes de kleren klayruh

clothes line de drooglijn drohKHlin

clothes peg de wasknijper vask-nīper

cloud de wolk volk

cloudy bewolkt bevolkt

clutch de koppeling

coach (bus) de touringcar tooringkar

(on train) het rijtuig rītowKH

coach station het busstation boos-stashon

coach trip de bustocht boos-tokHt

coast de kust koost

on the coast aan de kust ahn

coat de jas yas

coathanger de kleerhanger klayrhanger

cockroach de kakkerlak

cocoa de warme chocolademelk varmuh shokolahduh-melk

coconut de kokosnoot kohkosnoht

code (for phoning) het netnummer netnoommer

what's the (dialling) code for Amsterdam? wat is het netnummer voor Amsterdam? vat – vohr

coffee de koffie koffee

two coffees, please twee koffie, alstublieft alstoobleeft

coin de munt moont

cold koud kowt

I'm cold ik heb het koud hep

I have a cold ik ben
verkouden verk**ow**duh

collapse: he's collapsed
hij is in elkaar gezakt
hī is in elk**ah**r KHez**a**kt

collar (on coat) de kraag
krahKH

(on shirt) het boord bohrt

collect ophalen **o**phahluh

I've come to collect...
ik kom... ophalen

collect call het coll**e**ct gesprek
KHesp**re**k

college de beroepsschool
ber**oo**ps-sKH**oh**l

colour de kleur klur

**do you have this in other
colours?** heeft u dit ook in
andere kleuren? hayft ∞ dit ohk
in **a**nderuh kl**u**ruh

colour film de kleurenfilm
kl**u**ruhfilm

comb de kam

come komen k**oh**muh

where do you come from?
waar komt u vandaan?
vahr komt ∞ vand**ah**n

I come from Edinburgh
ik kom uit Edinburgh ∞t

come back terugkomen
ter**oo**KH-kohmuh

I'll come back tomorrow
ik kom morgen terug m**o**rKHuh
ter**oo**KH

come in binnenkomen
b**i**nnenkohmuh

comfortable comfortabel
komfort**ah**bel

company (business) het bedrijf
bedr**ī**f

compartment (on train) de coupé
koop**ay**

compass het komp**a**s

complain klagen klahKHuh

complaint de klacht klaKHt

I have a complaint ik heb
een klacht hep uhn

completely helemaal haylem**ah**l

computer de computer

concert het concert kons**ai**rt

concussion de hersenschudding
hersuh-sKH**oo**ding

conditioner (for hair) de
crèmespoeling krem-spooling

condom het condoom kond**oh**m

conference de conferentie
konfer**e**nsee

confirm bevestigen bev**e**stiKHuh

congratulations! gefeliciteerd!
KHefaylisit**ay**rt

connecting flight
de aansluitende vlucht
ahnsl**ow**tenduh vl**oo**KHt

connection (travel) de aansluiting
ahnsl**ow**ting

conscious bij bewustzijn
bī bev**oo**stzīn

constipation de constipatie
konstip**ah**tsee

consulate het consulaat
kons∞l**ah**t

contact contact opnemen
opnaymuh

contact lens de contactlens

contraceptive
het voorbehoedsmiddel
vohrbehoots-middel

convenient gelegen кнelaykнuh

that's not convenient dat is
niet gelegen neet

cook koken kohkuh

not cooked niet gaar
neet кнahr

cooker het fornuis fornows

cookie het koekje kook-yuh

cooking utensils het kookgerei
kohk-кнerī

cool koel kool

cork de kurk kоork

corkscrew de kurkentrekker
kоorkuhtrekker

corner: on the corner op de
hoek duh hook

in the corner in de hoek

cornflakes de cornflakes

correct (right) correct

corridor de gang кнang

cosmetics de cosmetica
kosmaytika

cost: how much does it cost?
wat kost het? vat

cot het kinderbedje kinderbet-yuh

cotton het katoen katoon

cotton wool de watten vattuh

couch (sofa) de bank

couchette de slaapcoupé
slahpkoopay

cough de hoest hoost

cough medicine het
hoestdrankje hoostdrank-yuh

could: could you...? zou u...
kunnen? zоw оо... kоonnuh

could I have...? kan ik...
krijgen? krīkнuh

I couldn't... ik kon niet... neet

country het land lant

(countryside) het platteland
plattelant

countryside het platteland

couple (two people) het paar pahr
(married) het echtpaar eкнtpahr

a couple of... een paar... uhn

courgette de courgette

courier de koerier kooreer

course: of course natuurlijk
natоorlik

of course not natuurlijk niet
neet

cousin (male/female) de neef/
nicht nayf/nikнt

cow de koe koo

crab de krab

cracker (biscuit) de cracker

craft shop
de kunstnijverheidswinkel
kоonstnīverhīds-vinkel

crash de botsing

I've had a crash ik heb een
botsing gehad hep uhn botsing
кнehat

crazy gek кнek

cream (in cake) de room rohm
(lotion) de crème krem
(colour) roomkleurig rohmklurikн

whipped cream de slagroom
slaкн-rohm

crèche de crèche

credit card de creditcard

do you take credit cards?
kan ik met een creditcard
betalen? bet**ah**luh

can I pay by credit card?
kan ik met een creditcard
betalen?

**which card do you want
to use?** met welke kaart
wilt u betalen? v**e**lkuh kahrt
vilt oo

Access/Visa

yes, sir ja, meneer ya men**ay**r

what's the number?
wat is het nummer?
vat is uht n**oo**mmer

and the expiry date?
en de vervaldatum?
en duh verv**a**ldat**oo**m

credit crunch de kredietcrisis
kred**ee**t-kr**ee**sis

crisps de chips ships

crockery het aardewerk **ah**rdeverk

crocus de krokus kr**oh**k**oo**s

crossing (by sea) de overtocht
ohverto**KH**t

crossroads het kruispunt
kr**ow**sp**oo**nt

crowd de menigte m**ay**ni**KH**tuh

crowded druk dr**oo**k

crown (on tooth) de kroon krohn

crutches de krukken kr**oo**kkuh

cry huilen h**ow**luh

cucumber de komkommer
komk**o**mmer

cup de kop

a cup of..., please een
kop..., alstublieft alst**oo**bleeft

cupboard de kast

cure genezen **KH**en**ay**zuh

curly krullend kr**oo**llent

current de stroom strohm

curry de kerrie k**e**rree

curtains de gordijnen **KH**ord**ī**nuh

cushion het kussen k**oo**ssuh

custom de gewoonte
KHev**oh**ntuh

Customs de douane doow**ah**nuh

cut de snijwond sn**ī**vont

(verb) snijden sn**ī**duh

I've cut myself ik heb me
gesneden hep muh **KH**esn**ay**duh

cutlery het bestek

cycling fietsen f**ee**tsuh

cyclist de fietser f**ee**tser

D

dad pa, papa

daffodil de narcis n**a**rsis

daily dagelijks d**ah**K**H**eliks

damage beschadigen
bes**KHah**di**KH**uh

damaged beschadigd
bes**KHah**di**KH**t

**I'm sorry, I've damaged
this** neem me niet kwalijk, ik
heb dit beschadigd naym muh
neet kv**ah**lik ik hep

damn! verdomme! verd**o**mmuh

damp vochtig v**o**K**H**ti**KH**

dance de dans

(*verb*) dansen d**a**nsuh

would you like to dance?
wil je dansen? vil yuh

dangerous gevaarlijk KHev**ah**rlik

Danish Deens dayns

dark d**o**nker

it's getting dark het wordt
donker vort

date: what's the date today?
welke datum is het vandaag?
v**e**lkuh d**ah**t00m is uht vand**ah**KH

**let's make a date for next
Monday** laten we een afspraak
voor aanstaande maandag
maken l**ah**tuh vuh uhn **a**fsprahk
vohr **ah**nstahnduh m**ah**ndaKH
m**ah**kuh

dates (fruit) de dadels d**ah**dels

daughter de dochter d**o**KHter

daughter-in-law de
schoondochter sKH**oh**ndoKHter

dawn de zonsopgang
zons**op**KHang

at dawn bij zonsopgang bī

day de dag daKH

the day after de volgende dag
v**o**lKHenduh

the day after tomorrow
overmorgen **oh**vermorKHuh

the day before de dag ervoor
erv**oh**r

the day before yesterday
eergisteren ayrKH**i**steruh

every day iedere dag **ee**deruh

all day de hele dag h**a**yluh

in two days' time over twee
dagen **oh**ver tvay d**ah**KHuh

have a nice day! prettige dag!
pr**e**ttiKHuh

day trip de dagexcursie
daKH-exk**00**rsee

dead dood doht

deaf doof dohf

deal (business) de transactie
trans-**a**ksee

it's a deal dat is afgesproken
afkHesprohkuh

decaffeinated coffee
de cafeïnevrije koffie
kafay-**ee**nuh-vri-uh k**o**ffee

December dec**e**mber

decide besl**i**ssen besl**i**ssuh

we haven't decided yet
we hebben nog geen beslissing
genomen vuh h**e**bbuh noKH KHayn
besl**i**ssing KHen**oh**muh

decision de beslissing

deck (on ship) het dek

deckchair de dekstoel d**e**kstool

deep diep deep

definitely besl**i**st

definitely not beslist niet neet

degree (qualification) de graad
KHraht

delay de vertraging vertr**ah**KHing

deliberately opzettelijk
opz**e**ttelik

delicatessen
de delicatessenwinkel

delicious heerlijk h**a**yrlik

deliver bezorgen bez**or**KHuh

delivery (of mail) de best**e**lling

Denmark Denemarken
d**a**ynemarkuh

dental floss de tandzijde tantzīduh

dentist de tandarts

it's this one here het is deze
hier dayzuh heer

this one? deze?

no, that one nee, die nay dee

here hier

yes ja ya

dentures het kunstgebit koonstkнebit

deodorant de deodorant

department de afdeling afdayling

department store het warenhuis vahruh-hows

departure het vertrek vertrek

departure lounge de vertrekhal vertrekhal

depend: it depends het hangt ervan af airvan

it depends on... het hangt af van...

deposit (as security) de waarborgsom vahrborkнsom

(as part payment) de aanbetaling ahnbetahling

dessert het nagerecht nah-кнerекнt

destination de bestemming

develop ontwikkelen ontvikkeluh

diabetic de suikerpatient sowkerpahshent

diabetic foods de etenswaren voor diabetici aytensvaruh vohr diabaytici

dial draaien drah-yuh

dialling code het netnummer netnoommer

diamond de diamant

diaper de luier low-yer

diarrhoea de diarree dee-array

do you have something for diarrhoea? heeft u iets tegen diarree? hayft oo eets tayкнuh

diary (business etc) de agenda ahkнenda

(for personal experiences) het dagboek daкнbook

dictionary het woordenboek vohrduhbook

didn't see **not**

die sterven stairvuh

diesel de diesel

diet het dieet diayt

I'm on a diet ik ben op dieet

I have to follow a special diet ik volg een speciaal dieet volкн uhn spesiahl

difference het verschil versкнil

what's the difference? wat is het verschil? vat

different: they are different ze zijn verschillend zuh zīn versкнillent

this one is different deze is anders dayzuh

a different table een andere tafel uhn anderuh

difficult moeilijk moo-eelik

difficulty de moeilijkheid moo-eelik-hīt

dinghy (rubber) de rubberboot roobberboht

dining room de eetzaal **ay**tzahl

dinner (evening meal) het diner din**ay**

  to have dinner dineren din**ay**ruh

direct (adj) rechtstreeks re**KH**tstrayks

  is there a direct train? is er een rechtstreekse trein? uhn re**KH**tstrayksuh trīn

direction de richting r**i**k**H**ting

  which direction is it? in welke richting is het? v**e**lkuh

  is it in this direction? is het in deze richting? d**ay**zuh

directory enquiries inlichtingen **i**nlik**H**tinguh

dirt het vuil v**ow**l

dirty vuil

disabled gehandicapt **KH**eh**e**ndikept

  is there access for the disabled? is het voor gehandicapten toegankelijk? vohr **KH**eh**e**ndikeptuh too**KH**ankelik

disappear verdwijnen verd**vī**nuh

  it's disappeared ik ben het kwijt kvīt

disappointed teleurgesteld tel**u**r**KH**estelt

disappointing teleurstellend tel**u**rstellent

disaster de ramp

disco de disco

discount de korting

  is there a discount? zit er korting op?

Travel tip Concessionary rates are applied at almost every sight and attraction as well as on public transport. Rates vary, but usually seniors (65+) get in for free or for a discounted price, under 5s go free and kids over 5 and under 15/16 get a substantial discount; family tickets are common too.

disease de ziekte z**ee**ktuh

disgusting afschuwelijk afs**KH**00-uhlik

dish (meal) het gerecht **KH**er**e**k**H**t

  (bowl) het bord bort

dishcloth de vaatdoek v**ah**tdook

disinfectant het ontsmettingsmiddel

disk (for computer) de diskette disk**e**ttuh

disposable diapers/nappies de wegwerpluiers ve**KH**verp-l**ow**-yers

distance de afstand **a**fstant

  in the distance in de verte duh v**ai**rtuh

district het district

disturb storen st**oh**ruh

diversion (detour) de wegomlegging ve**KH**-omle**KH**Hing

diving board de duikplank d**ow**kplank

divorced gescheiden **KH**es**KH**īduh

dizzy: I feel dizzy ik ben duizelig d**ow**zelik**H**

do doen doon

what shall we do? wat zullen we doen? vat zoolluh vuh doon

how do you do it? (pol) hoe doet u het? hoo doot oo (fam) hoe doe je het? doo yuh

will you do it for me? wilt u het voor me doen? vilt oo uht vohr muh doon

how do you do? aangenaam, hoe maakt u het? ahnKHenahm hoo mahkt oo

nice to meet you aangenaam kennis te maken tuh mahkuh

what do you do? (work) wat doet u? vat doot oo

I'm a teacher, and you? ik ben leraar, en u? layrahr

I'm a student ik ben student

what are you doing this evening? wat doe je vanavond? vat doo yuh vanahvont

we're going out for a drink, do you want to join us? we gaan ergens iets drinken, ga je met ons mee? vuh KHahn erKHens eets drinkuh KHa yuh met ons may

do you want mayonnaise? wilt u mayonaise? vilt oo mahyohnaisuh

I do, but she doesn't ik wel, maar zij niet vel mahr zi neet

docks de haven hahvuh

doctor de dokter, de arts

we need a doctor we hebben een dokter nodig vuh hebbuh uhn dokter nohdiKH

please call a doctor zou u een dokter willen bellen? zow oo uhn dokter villuh

where does it hurt? waar doet het pijn? vahr doot uht pin

right here hier heer

does that hurt now? doet dat pijn? doot

yes ja ya

take this to the chemist ga hiermee naar de apotheek KHa heermay nahr duh apotayk

document het document dokooment

dog de hond hont

doll de pop

domestic flight de binnenlandse vlucht binnuhlantsuh vlooKHt

don't! niet doen! neet doon

don't do that! dat moet je niet doen! moot yuh

see **not**

door de deur durr

doorman de portier porteer

double dubbel doobbel

double bed het tweepersoonsbed tvaypersohns-bet

double room de tweepersoonskamer tvaypersohns-kahmer

doughnut de doughnut

down neer nayr

down here hier beneden heer ben**ay**duh

put it down over there zet hier neer

it's down there on the right het is daar rechts dahr reKHts

it's further down the road het is verderop verder**op**

download (*verb*) downloaden download-uh

downmarket (restaurant etc) heel eenvoudig hayl aynv**ow**diKH

downstairs beneden ben**ay**duh

downstream stroomafwaarts strohm**a**fvahrts

dozen het dozijn doz**ī**n

half a dozen zes

drain (in sink) de afvoerbuis **a**fvoorb**ow**s

(in road) het afvoerkanaal **a**fvoorkanahl

draught beer bier van het vat beer van uht vat

draughty: it's draughty het is tochtig to**KH**tiKH

drawer de lade l**ah**duh

drawing de tekening t**ay**kening

dreadful afschuwelijk afsKH**oo**-uhlik

dream de droom drohm

dress de jurk y**oo**rk

dressed: to get dressed zich aankleden ziKH **ah**nklayduh

dressing (for cut) het verband verb**a**nt

salad dressing de dr**e**ssing

dressing gown de kamerjas k**ah**mer-yas

drink (alcoholic) de b**o**rrel

(non-alcoholic) de drank

(*verb*) drinken dr**i**nkuh

a cold drink iets kouds te drinken eets k**ow**ts tuh

can I get you a drink? wil je iets drinken? vil yuh

what would you like (to drink)? wat wilt u (drinken)? vat vilt **oo**

no thanks, I don't drink nee dank u, ik drink niet nay dank **oo** ik drink neet

I'll just have a drink of water ik wil graag een glas water vil KHrahKH uhn KHlas v**ah**ter

drinking water drinkwater dr**i**nkvahter

is this drinking water? is dit drinkwater?

drive rijden r**ī**duh

we drove here we zijn met de auto vuh z**ī**n met duh **ow**to

I'll drive you home ik zal je naar huis rijden yuh nahr h**ow**s

driver de bestuurder best**oo**rder

driving licence het rijbewijs r**ī**bevis

drop: just a drop, please (of drink) een klein beetje maar, alstublieft uhn kl**ī**n b**ay**t-yuh mahr alst**oo**bleeft

drug (medicine) het medicijn medis**ī**n

drugs (narcotics) de drugs dr**oo**gs

drunk dronken dr**o**nkuh

drunken driving dronken achter het stuur a**k**Hter uht st**oo**r

dry (*adj*) droog drohKH

dry-cleaner de stomerij stohmer**ī**

duck de eend aynt

due: he is due on Sunday hij komt op z**o**ndag aan h**ī** – ahn

when is the train due? hoe laat komt de trein aan? hoo laht komt duh tr**ī**n

he was due to arrive yesterday hij had gisteren aan moeten k**o**men hat KH**i**steruh ahn m**oo**tuh

dull (pain) vaag vahKH

(weather) saai s**ī**

dummy (baby's) de fopspeen f**o**pspayn

during tijdens t**ī**dens

dust het stof

dustbin de vuilnisbak v**ow**lnisbak

dusty stoffig st**o**ffikH

Dutch Nederlands n**ay**derlants

the Dutch de Nederlanders n**ay**derlanders

Dutchman de Nederlander n**ay**derlander

Dutchwoman de Nederlandse n**ay**derlantsuh

duty-free (goods) belastingvrij belastingvr**ī**

duty-free shop de tax-free-winkel tax-free-vinkel

duvet het dekbed d**e**kbet

DVD de dvd dayvayd**ay**

dyke de dijk d**ī**k

E

each (*with nouns with de*) elk
(*with nouns with het*) elke **e**lkuh

each book elk boek

each time elke keer kayr

each of them (people)
ieder van hen

how much are they each?
hoeveel zijn ze per stuk?
hoovayl zīn zuh puhr stook

ear het oor ohr

earache: I have earache
ik heb oorpijn hep **oh**rpīn

early vroeg vrooKH

early in the morning
's morgens vroeg smorKHens

I called by earlier ik ben een
poosje geleden langs geweest
uhn **poh**s-yuh KHel**ay**duh langs
KHev**ay**st

earrings de oorringen **oh**rringuh

east het oosten **oh**stuh

in the east in het oosten

Easter Pasen pa**h**suh

eastern oostelijk **oh**stelik

easy gemakkelijk KHem**a**kkelik

eat eten **ay**tuh

**we've already eaten,
thanks** bed**a**nkt, maar wij
hebben al gegeten mahr vuh
hebbuh al KHekH**ay**tuh

eau de toilette de eau de toilette

economy class economy-class

eel de aal ahl

egg het ei ī

eggplant de aubergine
ohber**J**eenuh

either: either... or... of... of...

either of them een van beide
ayn van b**ī**duh

elastic het elastiek aylast**ee**k

elastic band het elastiekje
aylast**ee**k-yuh

elbow de elleboog **e**llebohKH

electric elektrisch ayl**e**ktrees

electrical appliances
de elektrische apparaten
ayl**e**ktrishuh

electric fire de elektrische
kachel k**a**KHel

electrician de elektricien
aylektrish**ye**n

electricity de elektriciteit
aylektrisit**ī**t

elevator de lift

else: something else
iets anders eets

somewhere else
ergens anders **ai**rKHens

**would you like anything
else?** wilt u nog iets
anders? vilt oo noKH

no, nothing else, thanks
nee, dat is alles, dank u
nay – oo

e-mail de e-mail

e-mail (*verb*) e-mailen email-uh

embassy de ambassade
ambass**ah**duh

emergency het spoedgeval
sp**oo**tKHeval

this is an emergency!
dit is een spoedgeval!

emergency exit de nooduitgang
n**oh**t-owtKHang

empty leeg layKH

end het einde **ī**nduh

at the end of the street
aan het einde van de straat

when does it end?
wanneer is het afgelopen?
vann**ayr** is het **a**fk**H**elohpuh

engaged (toilet, telephone) bez**et**

(to be married) verloofd
verl**oh**ft

engine (car) de motor

England Engeland **e**nguh-lant

English Engels

I'm English ik kom uit
Engeland **O**wt

do you speak English?
spreekt u Engels? spraykt ∞

enjoy: to enjoy oneself
plezier h**e**bben plez**ee**r

> **DIALOGUE**
>
> **how did you like the film?**
> hoe vond je de film? hoo
> vont yuh duh
>
> **I enjoyed it very much, did
> you enjoy it?** ik heb ervan
> genoten, vond jij hem goed?
> hep airvan **KH**en**oh**tuh vont yï
> uhm **KH**oot

enjoyable aangenaam
ahnk**H**enahm

enlargement (of photo)
de vergroting ver**KH**r**oh**ting

enormous reusachtig
r**O**ws**a**k**H**tik**H**

enough genoeg **KH**en**oo**k**H**

there's not enough
er is niet genoeg neet

it's not big enough
het is niet groot genoeg **KH**roht

that's enough dat is genoeg

entrance de ingang **i**nk**H**ang

envelope de enveloppe
envel**o**p

epileptic de epilepticus
aypil**e**ptik∞s

equipment de uitrusting
Owt-r**oo**sting

eraser het gummetje
KH∞mmet-yuh

error de fout f**O**wt

especially vooral vohr**a**l

essential essentieel
essensh**a**yl

it is essential that...
het is essentieel dat...

EU de EU ay-∞

Eurocheque de Eurocheque
urroshek

Eurocheque card
de Eurochequekaart
urroshek-kahrt

Europe Europa urr**o**pa

European (adj) Europees
urrop**ays**

even zelfs

even if... zelfs als...

evening de avond **a**hvont

this evening vanavond
van**a**hvont

in the evening 's avonds
s**a**hvonts

evening meal de avondmaaltijd
ahvontmahlt**ï**t

eventually uiteindelijk
Owt-**ï**ndelik

ever ooit oyt

have you ever been to Maastricht? ben je ooit in Maastricht geweest? yuh oyt in mahstriKHt KHevayst

yes, I was there two years ago ja, ik ben er twee jaar geleden geweest ya – KHelayduh KHevayst

every (*with nouns with het*) ieder eeder

(*with nouns with de*) iedere eederuh

every hotel ieder hotel

every day iedere dag daKH

everyone iedereen eederayn

everything alles

everywhere overal ohveral

exactly! precies! presees

exam het examen

example het voorbeeld vohrbaylt

for example bijvoorbeeld bivohrbaylt

excellent uitstekend owtstaykent

(*food*) heel lekker hayl

excellent! prima!

except behalve behalvuh

excess baggage het overgewicht (van de bagage) ohverKHeviKHt (van duh baKHahJuh)

exchange rate de wisselkoers visselkoors

exciting (*day*) opwindend opvindent

(*holiday*) geweldig KHeveldiKH

(*film*) spannend spannent

excuse me (*to get past, to get attention*) pardon

(*to say sorry*) neemt u mij niet kwalijk naymt oo mi neet kvahlik

exhaust (*pipe*) de uitlaat owtlaht

exhausted (*tired*) uitgeput owtKHepoot

exhibition de tentoonstelling tentohnstelling

exit de uitgang owtKHang

where's the nearest exit? waar is de dichtstbijzijnde uitgang? vahr is duh diKHtstbizinduh

expect verwachten vervaKHtuh

expensive duur door

experienced ervaren ervahruh

explain uitleggen owtleKHuh

can you explain that? zou u dat uit kunnen leggen? zow oo dat owt koonnuh leKHuh

express (*mail*) expresse express

(*train*) de sneltrein sneltrin

extension (*telephone*) het toestel toostel

extension 221, please toestel twee, twee, een, alstublieft tvay tvay ayn alstoobleeft

extension lead het verlengsnoer verlengsnoor

extra: can we have an extra one? kunnen we er een extra krijgen? koonnuh vuh er ayn extra kriKHuh

do you charge extra for that? brengt u daar een extra bedrag voor in rekening? oo dahr uhn extra bedraKH vohr in raykening

extraordinary buitengewoon
bowtuhkHev**oh**n

extremely uiterst **ow**terst

eye het oog oh**KH**

**will you keep an eye on my
suitcase for me?** wilt u even
op mijn k**o**ffer l**e**tten? vilt oo
ayvuh op min

eyebrow pencil
het wenkbrauwpotlood
v**e**nkbr**ow**-potloht

eye drops de oogdruppels
ohKH-dr**oo**ppels

eyeglasses de bril

eyeliner de eyeliner

eye make-up remover de oog
make-up remover ohKH

eye shadow de oogschaduw
ohKH-sKH**ah**doo

F

face het gezicht KHezi**KH**t

factory de fabriek fahbr**ee**k

Fahrenheit F**ah**renheit

faint (*verb*) flauwvallen fl**ow**valluh

she's fainted
ze is flauwgevallen
zuh is fl**ow**KHevalluh

I feel faint ik voel me flauw
vool muh fl**ow**

fair (*funfair*) de k**e**rmis

(*trade*) de beurs boors

(*adj*) eerlijk **ay**rlik

fairly vrij vr**ee**

fake de verv**a**lsing

fall vallen v**a**lluh

she's had a fall zij is gevallen
z**ee** is KHev**a**lluh

fall (*autumn*) de herfst hairfst

in the fall in de herfst duh

false vals

family het gezin KHez**i**n

famous beroemd ber**oo**mt

fan (*electrical*) de ventilator
ventil**ah**tor

(*handheld*) de waaier v**ah**-yer

(*sports*) de supporter

fan belt de ventilatorriem
ventil**ah**tor-reem

fantastic fantastisch fant**a**stees

far ver vair

is it far from here?
is het ver hier vandaan?
heer vand**ah**n

no, not very far
nee, niet zo ver nay neet

well, how far?
hoe ver dan? hoo

it's about 20 kilometres
het is ongeveer twintig
kilometer onKHev**ay**r –
k**ee**lomayter

DIALOGUE

fare de (vervoer)prijs (verv**oo**r)pr**ee**s

farm de boerderij boorder**ee**

fashionable modieus modi-**ow**s

fast snel

fat (*person*) dik

(*on meat*) het vet

father de vader v**ah**der

father-in-law de schoonvader
sKH**oh**nvahder

faucet de kraan krahn

fault: sorry, it was my fault
sorry, het was mijn fout
vas mīn fowt

it's not my fault het is niet
mijn schuld neet mīn sкнооlt

faulty defect deh-fekt

favourite favoriet fahvoreet

fax de fax

(*verb*) faxen faxuh

February februari faybroo-ahri

feel voelen vooluh

I feel hot ik heb het warm
hep

I feel unwell ik voel me niet
goed vool muh neet кнoot

I feel like going for a walk
ik heb zin om een wandeling te
maken uhn vandeling

how are you feeling? hoe
voelt u zich? hoo voolt oo ziкн

I'm feeling better ik voel me
beter muh bayter

felt-tip (pen) de viltstift viltstift

fence de omheining omhīning

fender (of a car) de bumper
boomper

ferry de veerboot vayrboht

festival het festival

fetch halen hahluhl

I'll fetch him ik ga hem wel
halen кнa uhm vel

**will you come and fetch
me later?** kom je me straks
ophalen? yuh muh straks ophahluh

feverish koortsachtig
kohrtsaкнtiкн

few: a few een paar uhn pahr

a few days een paar dagen
dahкнuh

fiancé de verloofde verlohfduh

fiancée de verloofde

field het veld velt

fight het gevecht кнeveкнt

figs de vijgen vīкнuh

file het bestand bestant

fill in invullen invoolluh

do I have to fill this in?
moet ik dit invullen? moot

fill up vullen voolluh

fill it up, please kunt u
hem vol tanken, alstublieft
koont oo uhm vol tenkuh
alstoobleeft

filling (in tooth) de vulling
voolling

(in sandwich) het beleg beleкн

film de film

film processing
het ontwikkelen ontvikkeluh

filthy smerig smayriкн

find vinden vinduh

I can't find it ik kan het niet
vinden neet

I've found it ik heb het
gevonden hep het кнevonduh

find out er achter komen aкнter

could you find out for me?
zou u dat voor mij kunnen
uitzoeken? zow oo dat vohr mī
koonnuh owtzookuh

fine (weather) mooi moy

(punishment) de bekeuring
bekuring

how are you? hoe gaat het met u? hoo KHaht uht met oo

I'm fine, thanks uitstekend, dank u owtstaykent

is that OK? is dat goed? KHoot

that's fine, thanks zo is het goed, dank u wel oo vel

---

finger de vinger ving-er

finish aflopen aflohpuh

(completely) klaar zijn klahr zīn

I haven't finished yet ik ben nog niet klaar noKH neet

when does it finish? wanneer is het afgelopen? vannayr is het afKHelohpuh

fire het vuur voor

(blaze) de brand brant

fire! brand!

can we light a fire here? mogen we hier een vuur maken? mohKHuh vuh heer uhn voor mahkuh

it's on fire het staat in brand staht

fire alarm het brandalarm brantalarm

fire brigade de brandweer brantvayr

fire escape de brandtrap brant-trap

fire extinguisher het blusapparaat bloos-appahraht

first eerst ayrst

I was first ik was eerst vas

at first eerst

the first time de eerste keer ayrstuh kayr

first on the left de eerste straat links straht

first aid de eerste hulp ayrstuh hoolp

first-aid kit de verbanddoos verbant-dohs

first-class (travel etc) eerste klas ayrstuh

first floor de eerste verdieping verdeeping

(US) de begane grond beKHahnuh KHront

first name de voornaam vohrnahm

fish de vis

fishmonger's de viswinkel visvinkel

fit (attack) de aanval ahnval

(healthy) fit

fit: it doesn't fit me het past me niet muh neet

fitting room de paskamer

fix (arrange) regelen rayKHeluh

can you fix this? (repair) kunt u dit repareren? koont oo dit rayparayruh

fizzy bruisend browsent

fizzy orange de sinas met prik seenas

flag de vlag vlaKH

flannel het washandje vashant-yuh

flash (for camera) de flitser flitser

flat (apartment) de flat

(adj) plat

I've got a flat tyre ik heb een lekke band hep uhn lekkuh bant

flavour de smaak smahk

flea de vlo

Flemish Vlaams vlahms

flight de vlucht vl00кнt

flight number het vluchtnummer vl00кнt-noommer

flood de overstroming ohverst**roh**ming

floor (of room) de vloer vloor

(storey) de verdieping verd**ee**ping

on the floor op de grond duh кнront

florist de bloemist bloomist

flour het meel mayl

flower de bloem bloom

flu de griep кнreep

fluent: he speaks fluent Dutch hij spreekt vloeiend Nederlands hī spraykt vl**oo**-yent n**ay**derlants

fly de vlieg vleeкн

(verb) vliegen vlee**кн**uh

fog de mist

foggy: it's foggy het is mistig **mi**stiкн

folk dancing het volksdansen **vo**lksdansuh

folk music de volksmuziek **vo**lksm**oo**zeek

follow volgen **vo**lкнuh

follow me volg mij volкн mī

food het voedsel **voo**dsel

(in restaurant, at home) het eten **ay**tuh

(in shops) de levensmiddelen **lay**vuhs-middeluh

food poisoning de voedselvergiftiging **voo**dsel-verкнiftiкнing

food shop/store de levensmiddelenzaak **lay**vuhs-middeluhzahk

foot (of person, measurement) de voet voot

on foot te voet tuh

football het voetbal **voo**tbal

football match de voetbalwedstrijd **voo**tbal-vedstrīt

for: do you have something for...? (headache/diarrhoea etc) heeft u iets voor...? hayft 00 eets vohr

DIALOGUE

who's the pea soup for? voor wie is de erwtensoep? vohr vay

that's for me die is voor mij dee is vohr mī

and this? en dit?

that's for her dat is voor haar hahr

where do I get the bus for Artis? waar vandaan vertrekt de bus naar Artis? vahr vandahn vertrekt duh b00s nahr

the bus for Artis leaves from the central station de bus naar Artis vertrekt vanaf het centraal station van**af** het sentr**ah**l stah**shon**

how long have you been here? hoe lang bent u hier al? hoo lang bent ∞ heer

I've been here for two days, how about you? ik ben hier nu twee dagen, en u? heer n∞ – ∞

I've been here for a week ik ben hier nu een week vayk

forehead het voorhoofd **voh**rhohft

foreign buitenlands b**ow**tuhlants

foreigner de buitenlander b**ow**tuhlander

forest het bos

forget vergeten verkH**ay**tuh

I forget, I've forgotten ik ben het vergeten

fork de vork

(in road) de tweesprong t**vay**sprong

form (document) het formulier form∞l**eer**

formal (dress) formeel form**ay**l

fortnight twee weken tvay **vay**kuh

fortunately gelukkig kHel**oo**kkikH

forward: could you forward my mail? zou u mijn post kunnen doorsturen? z**ow** ∞ mīn posst koonnuh d**oh**rst∞ruh

forwarding address het adres voor het nazenden van de post vohr het n**ah**zenduh van duh posst

foundation (make-up) de basiscrème b**ah**siskrem

fountain de fontein font**īn**

foyer de foyer

fracture de breuk br**ow**k

France Frankrijk frankr**ī**k

free vrij vrī

(no charge) gratis кHr**ah**tis

is it free (of charge)? is het gratis?

freeway de (auto)snelweg (**ow**to) snelvekH

freezer de diepvries d**ee**pvrees

French Frans

French fries de patat friet freet

frequent vaak vahk

how frequent is the bus to Nijmegen? hoe vaak gaat de bus naar Nijmegen? hoo vahk кHaht duh b∞s nahr

fresh (air) fris

(fruit, milk etc) vers vairs

fresh orange juice vers sinaasappelsap **see**nahsappelsap

Friday de vrijdag vr**ī**dakH

fridge de koelkast k**oo**lkast

fried gebakken кHeb**a**kkuh

fried egg het gebakken ei ī

friend (*male/female*) de vriend/ vriendin vreent/vreend**in**

a friend of mine (*male/female*) een vriend/vriendin van mij mī

friendly vriendelijk vr**ee**ndelik

from van

when does the next train from Antwerp arrive? wanneer komt de volgende trein uit Antwerpen aan? v**a**nnayr komt duh v**o**lкHenduh trīn **ow**t **a**ntverpuh ahn

from Monday to Friday
van maandag tot vrijdag
mahndakH – vrīdakH

from this Thursday
vanaf donderdag vanaf

from next Thursday (a week
on Thursday) vanaf volgende
week donderdag volkHenduh
vayk

DIALOGUE

where are you from?
waar komt u vandaan?
vahr komt oo vandahn

I'm from Brighton
ik kom uit Brighton owt

front de voorkant vohrkant

in front vooraan vohrahn

in front of the hotel
voor het hotel vohr

at the front aan de voorkant
ahn duh

frost de vorst vorst

frozen bevroren bevrohruh

frozen food de diepvrieseten
deep-vreesaytuh

fruit het fruit frowt

fruit juice het vruchtensap
vrooKHtuhsap

fry bakken bakkuh

frying pan de koekenpan
kookuhpan

full vol

it's full of... het zit vol met...

I'm full ik heb genoeg gegeten
hep kHenooKH kHeKHaytuh

full board volpension
vol-penshon

fun: it was fun het was leuk
vas lurk

funeral de begrafenis
beKHrahfuhis

funny (strange) vreemd vraymt
(amusing) grappig KHrappikH

furniture het meubilair murbilayr

further verder vairder

it's further down the road
het is een eindje verderop
uhn īnt-yuh vairderop

DIALOGUE

**how much further is it to
Haarlem?** hoe ver is het
nog naar Haarlem hoo vair is
het noKH nahr

about 5 kilometres
ongeveer vijf kilometer
onkHevayr – keelomayter

fuse de zekering zaykering

the lights have fused
de zekeringen zijn gesprongen
zīn KHespronguh

fuse box de stoppenkast

fuse wire het smeltdraad
smeltdraht

future de toekomst tookomst

in future van nu af aan
noo af ahn

G

game (cards etc) het spelletje
spellet-yuh
(match) de partij partī
(meat) het wild vilt

garage (for fuel)
het benzinestation
benz**ee**nuh-stash**o**n

(for repairs, parking) de garage
KHahr**ah**Juh

garden de tuin t**o**wn

garlic het knoflook k-n**o**flohk

gas het gas KH**a**s

(petrol) de benzine benz**ee**nuh

gas cylinder (camping gas)
de gasfles KH**a**sfles

gasoline de benzine benz**ee**nuh

gas-permeable lenses
de poreuze l**e**nzen por**o**wzuh

gas station (for fuel)
het benzinestation
benz**ee**nuh-stash**o**n

gate het hek

(at airport) de gate

gay homo

gay bar het h**o**mocafé

gearbox de versnellingsbak
versn**e**llingsbak

gear lever de versnellingspook
versn**e**llings-pohk

gears de versnellingen
versn**e**llinguh

general algemeen alKH**e**m**ay**n

gents (toilet) het herentoilet
h**ay**ruh-twa-let

genuine (antique etc) echt **e**KHt

German Duits d**o**wts

Germany Duitsland d**o**wtslant

get (fetch) halen h**ah**luh

(find) krijgen kr**ī**KHuh

**could you get me another
one, please?** wilt u er nog
een voor mij halen, alstublieft?
vilt **oo** er n**o**KH ayn vohr m**ī** hahluh
alst**oo**bl**ee**ft

how do I get to…? hoe kom
ik in…? hoo

**do you know where I can
get them?** weet u waar ik ze
kan krijgen? vayt **oo** vahr ik zuh
kan kr**ī**KHuh

get back (return) terugkomen
ter**oo**KH-kohmuh

get in (arrive) aankomen
ahnkohmuh

get off uitstappen **o**wtstappuh

where do I get off? waar
moet ik uitstappen? vahr moot

get on (to train etc) instappen
instappuh

get out (of car etc) uitstappen
owtstappuh

get up (in the morning) opstaan
opstahn

gift het cadeau kahd**oh**

gift shop de cadeauwinkel
kahd**oh**-vinkel

gin de gin

(Dutch) de jenever yen**ay**ver

a gin and tonic, please
een gin en tonic, alstublieft
uhn – alstoobleeft

girl het meisje *mīshuh*

girlfriend de vriendin *vreendin*

give geven *KHayvuh*

can you give me some change? kunt u mij wat wisselgeld geven? koont oo mī vat *visselkHelt*

I gave it to him ik heb het aan hem gegeven hep uht ahn hem *KHekHayvuh*

will you give this to…? wil je dit aan… geven? vil yuh dit

DIALOGUE

how much do you want for this? hoeveel wilt u hiervoor hebben? hoovayl vilt oo heervohr

25 euros vijfentwintig euro urroh

I'll give you 10 euros ik geef u tien euro *KHayf oo*

give back teruggeven *terooKH-KHayvuh*

glad blij *blī*

glass (material) het glas *KHlas* (for drinking) het (drink)glas

a glass of wine een glas wijn *vīn*

glasses de bril

gloves de handschoenen *hantsKHoonuh*

glue de lijm *līm*

go gaan *KHahn*

we'd like to go to the Efteling we willen graag naar de Efteling vuh villuh KHrahKH nahr duh

where are you going? waar gaat u heen? vahr KHaht oo hayn

where does this bus go? waar gaat deze bus heen? vahr KHaht dayzuh boos

let's go! we gaan! vuh KHahn

she's gone (left) ze is weg zuh is veKH

where has he gone? waar is hij heen? vahr is hī hayn

I went there last week ik ben daar vorige week geweest dahr vohriKHuh vayk KHevayst

hamburger to go de hamburger om mee te nemen hamboorkHer om may tuh naymuh

go away weggaan veKH-KHahn

go away! ga weg! KHah veKH

go back (return) teruggaan
terooKH-KHahn

go down (the stairs etc)
naar beneden gaan nahr
ben**ay**duh KHahn

go in naar binnen gaan

go out (in the evening) uitgaan
owtKHahn

**do you want to go out
tonight?** heb je zin om
vanavond uit te gaan? hep yuh
zin om van**ah**vont owt tuh KHahn

go through meemaken
maymahkuh

go up (the stairs etc) naar boven
gaan nahr b**oh**vuh KHahn

goggles (for swimming)
de duikbril d**ow**kbril

gold het goud KHOWt

golf het golfen g**o**lfuh

golf course de golfbaan g**o**lfbahn

good goed KH**oo**t

good! goed zo!

it's no good daar heb ik niets
aan dahr hep ik neets ahn

goodbye tot ziens zeens

good evening goedenavond
KH**oo**yuh-**ah**vont

Good Friday Goede Vrijdag
KH**oo**duh vr**ī**daKH

good morning goedemorgen
KH**oo**yuh-m**o**rKHuh

good night goedenacht
KH**oo**yuh-n**a**KHt

goose de gans KHans

got: we've got to leave
we moeten nu weg vuh m**oo**tuh
noo veKH

have you got any…?
heeft u ook…? hayft oo ohk

government de regering
reKH**ay**ring

gradually geleidelijk KHel**ī**delik

grammar de grammatica
KHramm**ah**tika

gram(me) de gram KHram

granddaughter de kleindochter
kl**ī**ndoKHter

grandfather de grootvader
KHr**oh**tvahder

grandmother de grootmoeder
KHr**oh**tmooder

grandson de kleinzoon kl**ī**nzohn

grapefruit de grapefruit

grapefruit juice
het grapefruitsap

grapes de druiven dr**ow**vuh

grass het gras KHras

grateful dankbaar d**a**nkbahr

gravy de jus Joo

great (excellent) geweldig
KHev**e**ldiKH

that's great! dat is fantastisch!
fant**a**stees

a great success een groot
succes uhn KHr**o**ht s**oo**ksΘs

Great Britain Groot-Brittannië
KHr**o**ht-britt**a**nni-uh

Greece Griekenland KHr**ee**kuhlant

greedy gulzig KH**oo**lziKH

Greek Grieks KHr**ee**ks

green groen KHr**oo**n

green card (car insurance)
het verzekeringsbewijs
ver**zay**kerings-bewīs

greengrocer's de groentewinkel
KH**roo**ntevinkel

grey grijs KHrīs

grilled gegrild KHe**KH**rīlt

grocer's de kruidenier(swinkel)
kr**ow**duh**ee**r(svinkel)

ground de grond KHront

on the ground op de grond

ground floor de begane grond
be**KHah**nuh

group de groep KHroop

guarantee de garantie KHah**ran**see

is it guaranteed? is dat
gegarandeerd? KHe**KH**ahran-d**ayr**t

guest de gast KHast

guesthouse het pension pensh**on**

guide (person) de gids KHīts

guidebook de reisgids r**ī**sKHīts

guided tour de rondleiding
r**on**tlīding

guitar de gitaar KHi**tah**r

gum (in mouth) het tandvlees
t**an**tvlays

gun de revolver

gym de gymnastiekzaal
KHimnast**ee**k-zahl

H

Hague: the Hague Den Haag
hahKH

hair het haar hahr

hairbrush de haarborstel
h**ah**rborstel

haircut de coupe koop

hairdresser's (men's)
de herenkapper h**ay**ruhkapper

(women's) de dameskapper
d**ah**meskapper

hairdryer de haardroger
h**ah**rdrohKHer

hair gel de haargel hahrJel

hairgrips de haarspelden
h**ah**rspelduh

hair spray de haarlak h**ah**rlak

half half hal-f

half an hour een half uur
uhn hal-f oor

half a litre een halve liter
h**al**fvuh

about half that ongeveer de
helft daarvan onKHev**ay**r duh helft
d**ah**rvan

half board halfpension
hal-f-pensh**on**

half-bottle de halve literfles
h**al**fvuh

half fare de halve prijs prīs

half-price tegen de halve prijs
t**ay**KHuh

ham de ham

hamburger de hamburger
hamb**oo**rKHer

hammer de hamer h**ah**mer

hand de hand hant

handbag de handtas hant-tas

handbrake de handrem h**an**trem

handkerchief de zakdoek z**ak**dook

handle (on door) de deurknop
d**ur**-k-nop

(on suitcase etc) het handvat
hantvat

hand luggage de handbagage
hantbaKKHahJuh

hang-gliding het deltavliegen
deltavleeKHuh

hangover de kater kahter

I've got a hangover
ik heb een kater hep

happen gebeuren KHeburuh

what's happening?
wat gebeurd er allemaal?
vat KHeboort er allemahl

(what's on?) wat is er te doen?
tuh doon

what has happened?
wat is er gebeurd?

happy gelukkig KHelookkiKH

I'm not happy about this
ik ben hier niet erg blij mee
heer neet erkH blī may

harbour de haven hahvuh

hard hard hart

(difficult) moeilijk moo-eelik

hard-boiled egg het
hardgekookt ei hartKHekohkt ī

hard lenses de harde lenzen
harduh

hardly nauwelijks nOweliks

hardly ever haast nooit hahst
noyt

hardware shop de
ijzerwarenwinkel īzervaruhvinkel

hat de hoed hoot

hate haten hahtuh

have hebben hebbuh

can I have a...? mag ik een...
(hebben)? maKH

do you have...? heeft u...?
hayft oo

what'll you have? wat wil je
drinken? vat vil yuh

I have to leave now ik moet
nu weg moot noo vekH

do I have to...? moet ik...?

can we have some...?
kunnen we wat... krijgen?
koonnuh vuh vat... krīKHuh

hayfever de hooikoorts
hoykohrts

hazelnuts de hazelnoten
hahzelnohtuh

he hij hī

head het hoofd hohft

headache de hoofdpijn hohftpīn

headlights de koplampen
koplampuh

headphones de koptelefoon
koptelefohn

health food shop de
reformwinkel reformvinkel

healthy gezond KHezont

hear verstaan verstahn

DIALOGUE

can you hear me? kun je
me verstaan? koon yuh muh
verstahn

**I can't hear you, could you
repeat that?** ik kan je niet
verstaan, zou je dat kunnen
herhalen? neet verstahn zOw
yuh dat koonnuh hairhahluh

hearing aid het gehoorapparaat
кнehohr-apparaht

heart het hart

heart attack de hartaanval
hartahnval

heat de hitte hittuh

heater (in room) de kachel kaкнel
(in car) de verwarming

heating de verwarming

heavy zwaar zvahr

heel (of foot) de hiel heel
(of shoe) de hak

could you heel these?
zou u hier hakken onder
kunnen zetten? zow ∞ heer
hakkuh onder koonnuh

heelbar de hakkenbar

height (of person) de lengte
lengtuh
(of mountain) de hoogte hohкнtuh

helicopter de helikopter
haylikopter

hello hallo

helmet (for motorcycle) de valhelm
valhelm

help de hulp hoolp
(verb) helpen helpuh

help! help!

can you help me? kunt u me
helpen? koont ∞ muh
helpen? koont ∞ muh

**thank you very much for
your help** heel hartelijk dank
voor uw hulp hayl hartelik dank
vohr ∞

helpful behulpzaam behoolp-zahm

hepatitis de leverontsteking
layfver-ontstayking

her: I haven't seen her ik heb
haar niet gezien hep hahr neet
кнeseen

for her voor haar vohr

that's her dat is ze zuh

that's her bag dat is haar tas

herbal tea de kruidenthee
krowduhtay

herbs de kruiden krowduh

here hier heer

here is/are... hier is/zijn... zīn

here you are (offering: pol)
alstublieft alstoobleeft
(fam) alsjeblieft als-yuhbleeft

herring de haring hahring

hers: that's hers dat is van
haar hahr

hey! hé! hay

hi! (hello) hallo!

hide verbergen verberкнuh

high hoog hohкн

highchair de kinderstoel
kinderstool

highway de (auto)snelweg (owto)
snelvekн

hill de heuvel hurvel

him: I haven't seen him
ik heb hem niet gezien
hep uhm neet кнeseen

for him voor hem vohr hem

that's him dat is hem uhm

hip de heup hurp

hire huren hooruh

for hire te huur tuh hoor

where can I hire a bike?
waar kan ik een fiets huren?
vahr kan ik uhn feets

his: it's his car het is zijn auto
zīn

that's his dat is van hem

hit slaan slahn

hitchhike liften liftuh

hobby de hobby

hold vasthouden vast-howduh

hole het gat KHat

holiday de vakantie vakansee

on holiday op vakantie

Holland Nederland nayderlant

home het huis hows

at home (in my house etc) thuis
tows

(in England) bij ons in Engeland bī

we go home tomorrow
we gaan morgen terug naar
huis vuh KHahn morKHuh terooKH
nahr hows

honest eerlijk ayrlik

honey de honing hohning

honeymoon de huwelijksreis
hoo-liksrīs

hood (of a car) de motorkap

hope: I hope so ik hoop het hohp

I hope not ik hoop van niet neet

hopefully hopelijk hohpelik

horn (of car) de toeter tooter

horrible afschuwelijk
afsKHoo-uhlik

horse het paard pahrt

horse riding paardrijden
pahrt-rīduh

hospital het ziekenhuis
zeekenhows

hospitality de gastvrijheid
KHastvrīhit

**thank you for your
hospitality** dank u voor uw
gastvrijheid oo vohr oo

hot heet hayt

(spicy) pittig pittiKH

I'm hot ik heb het warm
hep het varm

it's hot today het is warm
vandaag

hotel het hotel

hotel room de hotelkamer
hotel-kahmer

hour het uur oor

house het huis hows

house wine de huiswijn howsvīn

hovercraft de hovercraft
hooverkraft

how hoe hoo

how many? hoeveel? hoovayl

how do you do? aangenaam
kennis te maken ahnKHenahm
kennis tuh mahkuh

how are you? hoe gaat het
met u? hoo KHaht uht met oo

fine, thanks, and you?
uitstekend, dank u, en met
u? owtstaykent

how much is it? wat kost
het? vat

5.25 (euros) vijf (euro)
vijfentwintig urroh vīf-
uhntvintikh

I'll take it dan neem ik het
naym

humid vochtig vo**KH**ti**KH**

hungry: I'm hungry ik heb
  honger hep

  are you hungry? heeft u trek?
  hayft ∞

hurry (zich) haasten (zi**KH**) h**ah**stuh

  I'm in a hurry ik heb haast
  hep hahst

  there's no hurry er is geen
  haast bij **KH**ayn hahst bi

  hurry up! schiet op! s**KH**eet

hurt (*verb*) pijn doen pin doon

  it really hurts het doet echt
  pijn doot e**KH**t

husband de echtgenoot
  e**KH**t-**KH**enoht

hyacinth de hyacint hee-ahsint

hydrofoil de vleugelboot
  vl**ow**KHelboht

I ik

ice het ijs is

  with ice met ijs

  no ice, thanks zonder ijs
  graag **KH**rah**KH**

ice cream het ijsje **i**shuh

ice-cream cone het horentje
  h**o**rent-yuh

ice lolly de ijslollie **i**slollee

ice rink de ijsbaan **i**sbahn

ice skates de schaatsen
  s**KH**ahtsuh

ice skating schaatsen s**KH**ahtsuh

idea het idee eed**ay**

idiot de idioot eedi-y**oh**t

if als

ignition de ontsteking ontst**ay**king

ill ziek zeek

  I feel ill ik voel me niet goed
  vool muh neet **KH**oot

illness de ziekte z**ee**ktuh

imitation (leather etc) kunst-
  k∞nst-

immediately onmiddelijk
  onm**i**ddelik

important belangrijk belangr**i**k

  it's very important het is erg
  belangrijk er**KH**

  it's not important het is niet
  belangrijk neet

impossible onmogelijk
  onm**oh**KHelik

impressive indrukwekkend
  indr∞k-v**e**kkent

improve verbeteren verb**ay**teruh

  **I want to improve my
  Dutch** ik wil mijn Nederlands
  verbeteren vil muhn n**ay**derlants

in: it's in the centre het is in het
  centrum s**e**ntr∞m

  in my car in mijn auto

  in two days from now over
  twee dagen over – d**ah**KHuh

  in five minutes over vijf
  min**u**ten

  in May in mei mi

  in English in het Engels

  in Dutch in het Nederlands
  n**ay**derlants

  is he in? is hij thuis? is-ee t**ow**s

inch de duim d**ow**m

include bevatten bev**a**ttuh

does that include meals?
zijn de maaltijden daarbij
inbegrepen? zīn duh m**ah**ltīduh
d**ah**rbī **ī**nbe**k**raypuh

is that included? is dat erbij
inbegrepen? erb**ī**

inconvenient ongelegen
on**k**He**lay**kHuh

incredible ongelooflijk
on**k**He**loh**felik

Indian Indiaas **ī**ndiahs

indicator de richtingaanwijzer
r**ī**kHting-ahnv**ī**zer

indigestion
spijsverteringsproblemen
sp**ī**sfert**ay**rings-pr**o**blaymuh

Indonesia Indonesië indon**ay**si-uh

Indonesian Indisch **ī**ndees,
Indonesisch indon**ay**sis

indoor pool het binnenbad
b**ī**nnuhbat

indoors binnen b**ī**nnuh

inexpensive goedkoop
kHootk**oh**p

infection de infectie inf**e**ksee

infectious besmettelijk
besm**e**ttelik

inflammation de ontsteking
ontst**ay**king

informal informeel inform**ay**l

information de informatie inform**ah**tsee

**do you have any
information about…?**
heeft u ook informatie over…?
hayft ○○ ohk – **o**ver

information desk
de informatiebalie
inform**ah**tsee-b**ah**lee

injection de injectie in-y**e**ksee

injured gewond **k**Hev**o**nt

she's been injured ze is
gewond zuh

in-laws de schoonouders
s**k**H**oh**n0wders

inner tube de binnenband
b**ī**nnuhbant

innocent onschuldig ons**k**H**oo**ldi**k**H

insect het ins**e**kt

insect bite de insektenbeet
ins**e**ktuhbayt

**do you have anything for
insect bites?** heeft u iets
tegen insektenbeten? ○○ eets
t**ay**kHuh ins**e**ktuh-baytuh

insect repellent het
insektenwerend middel
ins**e**ktuh-vayrent

inside binnen b**ī**nnuh

inside the hotel in het hotel

let's sit inside laten we
binnen zitten l**ah**tuh vuh

insist aandringen **ah**ndringuh

I insist ik sta er**o**p

insomnia de slapeloosheid
slahpel**ohs**-hīt

instant coffee de oploskoffie
oploskoffee

instead in plaats daarvan
plahts d**ah**rvan

give me that one instead
geef me die er maar voor in de
plaats кнayf muh dee er mahr vohr
in duh plahts

instead of... in plaats van...

insulin de insuline insool**ee**nuh

insurance de verzekering
verz**ay**kering

intelligent intelligent intelli**ke**nt

interested: I'm interested in...
ik ben geïnteresseerd in...
кneh-interres**ay**rt

interesting interess**a**nt

that's very interesting
dat is erg interessant er**к**н

international internationaal
internahshon**ah**l

interpret tolken t**o**lkuh

interpreter de tolk

intersection het kruispunt
kr**ow**spoont

interval (at theatre) de pauze
p**ow**zuh

into in

I'm not into...... interess**ee**rt
mij niet mī neet

introduce voorstellen
v**oh**rstelluh

may I introduce...? mag ik...
aan u voorstellen? ma**к**н – ahn oo

invitation de uitnodiging
owtnohdik**к**ning

invite uitnodigen **ow**tnohdik**к**nuh

Ireland Ierland **ee**rlant

Irish Iers eers

I'm Irish ik kom uit Ierland
owt **ee**rlant

iron (for ironing) het strijkijzer
str**ī**kizer

can you iron these for me?
kunt u deze voor me strijken?
koont oo d**ay**zuh vohr muh str**ī**kuh

is is

island het eiland **ī**lant

it het

it is... het is...

is it...? is het...?

where is it? waar is het? vahr

it's him hij is het hī

it was... het was... vas

Italian Italiaans eetal-y**ah**ns

Italy Italië it**ah**li-uh

itch: it itches het jeukt y**ow**kt

J

jack (for car) de krik

jacket het jack yak

(suit) het jasje y**a**s-yuh

jam de jam Jem

jammed: it's jammed het zit vast

January januari yanoo-**ah**ri

jar de pot

jaw de kaak kahk

jazz jazz

jealous jaloers yal**oo**rs

jeans de spijkerbroek
sp**ī**kerbrook

jellyfish de kwal kval

jersey de trui trOw

jetty de aanlegsteiger
ahnlekH-stĭkHer

jeweller's de juwelier yOO-uhleer

jewellery de juwelen yOO-ayluh

Jewish Joods yohts

job de baan bahn

jogging joggen joKHuh

  to go jogging gaan joggen
  KHahn

joke de grap KHrap

journey de reis rīs

  have a good journey!
  goeie reis! KHOO-yuh

jug de kan

  a jug of water een kan water
  uhn kan vahter

juice het (vruchten)sap
  (vrOOKHtuh)sap

July juli yOOli

jump springen sprInguh

jumper de trui trOw

jump leads de accukabels
  akkOOkabels

junction de kruising krOwsing

June juni yOOni

just (only) alleen allayn

  just two maar twee mahr

  just for me alleen voor mij
  vohr mī

  just here hier heer

  not just now nu even niet
  nOO ayvuh neet

  we've just arrived
  we zijn net aangekomen
  vuh zīn net ahnkHekomuh

K

keep houden hOwduh

  keep the change
  zo is het goed KHOot

  can I keep it?
  mag ik het houden? makH

  please keep it
  u kunt het houden OO koont

ketchup de ketchup

kettle de ketel kaytel

key de sleutel slOwtel

  **the key for room 201,
  please** de sleutel voor kamer
  201, alstublieft vohr kahmer
  tvay-hondert-ayn alstOObleeft

keyring de sleutelring
  slOwtelring

kidneys de nieren neeruh

kill doden dohduh

kilo de kilo

kilometre de kilometer
  keelomayter

  **how many kilometres is it
  to…?** hoeveel kilometer is het
  naar…? hoovayl – nahr

kind (generous) vriendelijk
  vreendelik

  that's very kind
  dat is erg vriendelijk erKH

king de koning

kiosk de kiosk

kiss de kus koos

  (*verb*) kussen koossuh

kitchen de keuken kowkuh

kitchenette de kleine keuken klīnuh

knee de knie k-nee

knickers het damesslipje dahmes-slip-yuh

knife het mes

knock kloppen kloppuh

knock down aanrijden ahnrīduh

  he's been knocked down hij is aangereden hī is ahnkHerayduh

knock over (object) omgooien omkHoyuh

  (pedestrian) omverrijden omverrīduh

know (somebody, place) kennen kennuh

  (something) weten vaytuh

I don't know ik weet het niet vayt het neet

I didn't know that dat wist ik niet vist

do you know where I can find...? weet u waar ik... kan vinden? vayt oo vahr – vinduh

L

label het etiket

  (for suitcase) de label

ladies' room, ladies' toilets het damestoilet dahmes-twa-let

ladies' wear de dameskleding dahmes-klayding

lady de dame dahmuh

lager het pils

  a glass of lager een pilsje uhn pilshuh

lake het meer

lamb (meat) het lamsvlees lamsvlays

lamp de lamp

lane (on motorway) de rijstrook rī-strohk

(small road) het weggetje veкнet-yuh

language de taal tahl

language course de taalcursus tahl-кoorsoos

laptop de laptop

large groot кнroht

last (*with nouns with het*) laatst lahtst

(*with nouns with de*) laatste lahtstuh

last week vorige week voнrikнuh vayk

last Friday afgelopen vrijdag afкнelopuh

last night gisteravond кнisterahvont

what time is the last train to Groningen? hoe laat gaat de laatste trein naar Groningen? hoo laht кнaht duh lahtstuh trīn nahr

late laat laht

sorry I'm late sorry dat ik zo laat ben

the train was late de trein was te laat vas tuh

we must go – we'll be late we moeten gaan – anders komen we te laat vuh mootuh кнahn

it's getting late het wordt laat vort

later later lahter

I'll come back later ik kom straks terug terooкн

see you later tot straks

later on later lahter

latest laatste lahtstuh

by Wednesday at the latest niet later dan woensdag neet lahter

laugh lachen lакнuh

launderette, laundromat de wasserette vasserettuh

laundry (clothes) het wasgoed vasкнoot

(place) de wasserij vasserī

lavatory de w.c. vay-say

law de wet vet

lawn het grasveld кнrasvelt

lawyer (*male/female*) de advocaat/advocate advokaht/advokahtuh

laxative het laxeermiddel laxayrmiddel

lazy lui low

lead (electrical) het (electrisch) snoer (aylektrees) snoor

(*verb*) leiden līduh

where does this road lead to? waar gaat deze weg naartoe? vahr кнaht dayzuh vekh nahrtoo

leaf het blad blat

leaflet de brochure brohshooruh

leak de lekkage lekkahsh-uh

(*verb*) lekken lekkuh

the roof leaks het dak lekt

learn leren layruh

least: not in the least helemaal niet helemahl neet

at least ten minste minstuh

leather het leer

leave vertrekken vertrekkuh

I am leaving tomorrow
ik vertrek morgen
vertrek morkнuh

he left yesterday
hij is gisteren vertrokken
hī is кнisteruh vertrokkuh

may I leave this here?
kan ik dit hier laten liggen?
heer lahtuh likнuh

I left my coat in the bar
ik heb mijn jas in de bar laten
liggen hep

**when does the bus for
Breda leave?** wanneer
vertrekt de bus naar Breda?
vannayr vertrekt duh bōos nahr

leeks de prei prī

left links

  on the left, to the left
  aan de linkerkant ahn duh

  turn left ga naar links кнa nahr

  there's none left er is er geen
  een over кнayn ayn ohver

left-handed linkshandig
links-handikн

left luggage (office) het
bagagedepot bakнahjuh-daypoh

leg het been bayn

lemon de citroen sitroon

lemonade de limonade
limonahduh

lemon tea de citroenthee
sitroontay

lend lenen laynuh

  will you lend me your... ?
  kunt u mij uw... lenen?
  koont ōō mī ōō

lens (of camera) de lens

lesbian lesbisch lesbees

less minder

  less than minder dan

  less expensive niet zo duur
  neet zo

lesson de les

let (allow) laten lahtuh

  will you let me know?
  laat u het me weten?
  laht ōō het muh vaytuh

  I'll let you know
  ik laat het u weten

  **let's go for something to
  eat** laten we wat gaan eten
  vuh vat кнahn aytuh

let off laten uitstappen
lahtuh owtstappuh

  will you let me off at...? wilt
  u mij uit laten stappen bij...?
  vilt ōō mī owt lahtuh stappuh bī

letter de brief breef

  **do you have any letters for
  me?** is er post voor me?
  posst vohr muh

letterbox de brievenbus
breevuhbōos

lettuce de sla

lever de hendel

library de bibliotheek bibliotayk

licence de vergunning
verкнōonning

lid het deksel

lie (tell untruth) liegen leeкнuh

lie down gaan liggen кнahn likнuh

life het leven layvuh

lifebelt de reddingsgordel
reddingsкнordel

lifeguard de strandwacht
strantvak**H**t

life jacket het reddingsvest
reddingsvest

lift (in building) de lift

could you give me a lift?
zou u mij een lift kunnen
geven? z**o**w **o**o m**ī** uhn lift k**oo**nnuh
KHayvuh

would you like a lift? wil je
een lift h**e**bben? vil yuh uhn

light het licht li**KH**t

(not heavy) licht

do you have a light? (for
cigarette) heeft u een vuurtje?
hayft **oo** uhn v**oo**rt-yuh

light green lichtgroen
li**KH**tk**KH**r**oo**n

light bulb de gloeilamp
KHl**oo**-eelamp

I need a new light bulb ik heb
een nieuwe gloeilamp nodig hep
uhn n**ew**-uh **KH**l**oo**-eelamp n**oh**di**KH**

lighter (cigarette) de aansteker
ahnsteker

lightning de bliksem

like houden van h**o**wduh van

I like it (food) ik vind het l**e**kker
vint

(situation, activity) ik vind het
leuk l**o**wk

(view, ornament etc) ik vind het
mooi m**o**y

I like going for walks
ik houd van wandelen
h**o**wt van v**a**ndeluh

I like you ik vind je aardig
yuh **ah**rdi**KH**

I don't like it (food) ik vind het
niet l**e**kker neet

(situation, activity) ik vind het
niet leuk l**o**wk

(view, ornament etc) ik vind het
niet mooi m**o**y

do you like…? hou je van…?
h**o**w yuh van

I'd like a beer ik wil graag een
biertje vil k**KH**rah**KH** uhn b**ee**rt-yuh

I'd like to go swimming
ik wil graag gaan zw**e**mmen
KHahn

would you like a drink?
wilt u iets drinken? vilt **oo** eets

**would you like to go
for a walk?** zullen we een
wandeling gaan maken? z**oo**lluh
vuh uhn v**a**ndeling **KH**ahn m**a**hkuh

what's it like? hoe is dat? h**oo**

I want one like this ik wil er
zo een vil er zo ayn

lily de lelie l**a**ylee

lime de limoen lim**oo**n

lime cordial de limoensiroop
lim**oo**nsirohp

line (on paper) de regel r**a**yk**KH**el

(phone) de lijn l**ī**n

**could you give me an
outside line?** kunt u mij een
buitenlijn geven? k**o**ont **oo** m**ī**
uhn b**o**wtuhl**ī**n **KH**ayvuh

lips de lippen l**i**ppuh

lip salve de lippenzalf

lipstick de lippenstift

liqueur de likeur lik**u**r

listen luisteren l**o**wsteruh

litre de liter

a litre of white wine een liter witte wijn

little klein klin

just a little, thanks een klein beetje graag bayt-yuh KHrahKH

a little milk een klein scheutje melk skhurt-yuh

a little bit more ietsjes meer eets-yuh mayr

live leven layvuh

we live together we wonen samen vuh vohnuh sahmuh

where do you live? waar woon je? vahr vohn yuh

I live in London ik woon in Londen

lively (town) druk drook
(person) levendig layvendikH

liver de lever layver

loaf het brood broht

lobby (in hotel) de lounge

lobster de kreeft krayft

local in de omgeving duh omkHayving

can you recommend a local restaurant? kunt u een restaurant hier in de omgeving aanbevelen? koont oo uhn restowrant heer in duh omkHayving ahnbevayluh

local call het lokale gesprek lokahluh KHesprek

lock het slot
(on canal) de sluis slows
(verb) op slot doen doon

it's locked het zit op slot

lock in insluiten inslowtuh

lock out buitensluiten bowtuhslowtuh

I've locked myself out ik heb mezelf buitengesloten hep muhzelf bowtuhKHeslohtuh

locker (for luggage etc) de bagagekluis bakHahJuh-klows

lollipop de lollie lollee

London Londen

long lang

how long will it take to fix it? hoe lang duurt het om het te maken? hoo lang doort het om het tuh mahkuh

how long does it take? hoe lang duurt het?

a long time een lange tijd uhn languh tit

one day/two days longer een/twee dagen langer

long-distance call het interlokaal gesprek interlokahl KHesprek

look: I'm just looking, thanks ik kijk alleen wat rond kik allayn vat ront

you don't look well je ziet er niet zo goed uit yuh zeet er neet zo KHoot owt

look out! kijk uit!

can I have a look? mag ik even kijken? makH ik ayvuh kikuh

look after zorgen voor zorKHuh vohr

look at kijken naar kikuh nahr

look for zoeken zookuh

I'm looking for... ik ben op zoek naar… zook nahr

look forward to ergens naar uitkijken erkHens nahr owtkikuh

I'm looking forward to it ik kijk ernaar uit kik ernahr owt

loose (handle etc) los

lorry de vrachtwagen vraKHt-vahKHuh

lose verliezen verleesuh

I've lost my way ik ben verdwaald verdvahlt

I'm lost, I want to get to... ik ben verdwaald, ik wil naar… vil nahr

I've lost my bag ik ben mijn tas verloren muhn tas verlohruh

lost property (office) (het bureau voor) gevonden voorwerpen (booroh vohr) KHevonduh vohrverpuh

lot: a lot, lots veel vayl

not a lot niet veel neet

a lot of people veel mensen

a lot bigger veel groter KHrohter

lotion de lotion lohshon

loud luid lowt

lounge de lounge

love de liefde leefduh

(verb) houden van howduh

I love Holland ik hou van Nederland how van nayderlant

lovely prachtig praKHtiKH

low laag lahKH

luck het geluk KHelook

good luck! veel succes! vayl sookses

luggage de bagage baKHahJuh

luggage trolley het bagagewagentje baKHahJuh-vahKHent-yuh

lump (on body) de bult boolt

lunch de lunch loonsh

lungs de longen long-uh

Luxembourg Luxemburg loOxemboOrkH

luxurious luxueus loOx-urs

luxury luxe loOxuh

M

machine de machine masheenuh

mackerel de makreel makrayl

mad (insane) gek KHek

(angry) boos bohs

magazine het tijdschrift titsKHrift

maid (in hotel) het kamermeisje kahmer-mishuh

maiden name de meisjesnaam mishuhs-nahm

mail de post posst

(verb) posten posstuh

is there any mail for me? is er post voor mij? vohr mi

mailbox de brievenbus breevuhboOs

main hoofd- hohft-

main course het hoofdgerecht hohft-KHereKHt

main post office het hoofdpostkantoor hohft-posstkantohr

main road de hoofdweg
hohft-veкн

mains switch
de elektriciteitsschakelaar
aylektrisiteets-sкнahkelahr

make (brand name) het merk
(*verb*) maken mahkuh

I make it 95 euros ik kom op
vijfennegentig euro urroh

what is it made of? waar is
het van gemaakt? vahr is het van
кнemahkt

make-up de make-up

man de man

manager (hotel, business)
de manager
(restaurant) de chef

can I see the manager?
mag ik de chef even
spreken? maкн ik duh shef ayvuh
spraykuh

manageress (hotel, business)
de manageress
(restaurant) de chef

many veel vayl

not many niet veel neet

map de kaart kahrt

network map de
transportkaart transportkahrt

March maart mahrt

margarine de margarine
marкнah-reenuh ·

marijuana de marihuana
maroowahna

market de markt

marmalade de marmelade
marmelahduh

married: I'm married ik ben
getrouwd кнetrowt

are you married? bent u
getrouwd? oo

mascara de mascara
maskahra

match (football etc) de wedstrijd
vedstrit

matches de lucifers loosifers

material (fabric) de stof

matter: it doesn't matter
het geeft niet кнayft neet

what's the matter? wat is er?
vat

mattress de matras

May mei mi

**may: may I have another
one?** mag ik er nog een?
maкн ik er noкн ayn

may I come in?
mag ik binnenkomen?

may I see it? mag ik het even
zien? ayvuh zeen

may I sit here? mag ik hier
gaan zitten? heer кнahn

maybe misschien missкнeen

mayonnaise de mayonaise
mah-yonaysuh

me me muh
(emphatic) mij mi

that's for me dat is voor mij
vohr

send it to me stuur het naar
mij stoor het nahr

me too ik ook ohk

meal de maaltijd mahltit

did you enjoy your meal?
heeft het gesmaakt? hayft uht
KHesma**h**kt

**it was excellent, thank
you** ja, het was heerlijk,
dank u wel ya het vas ha**y**rlik
dank ∞ vel

mean (*verb*) bedoelen
bed**oo**luh

what do you mean?
wat bedoelt u? vat bed**oo**lt ∞

**what does this word
mean?** wat betekent dit
woord? vat bet**ay**kent dit v**oh**rt

it means... in English
in het Engels betekent het...

measles de mazelen ma**h**zeluh

German measles
de rodehond rohdeh**o**nt

meat het vlees vlays

mechanic de monteur mont**u**r

medicine het medicijn maydees**i**n

medium (size) gemiddeld
KHem**i**ddelt

medium-dry medium-dry

medium-rare medium

medium-sized middelgroot
m**i**ddelKHroht

meet afspreken **a**fspraykuh

nice to meet you aangenaam
ahnKHenahm

where shall I meet you?
waar zullen we afspreken?
vahr z**oo**lluh vuh

meeting de vergadering
verKHa**h**dering

meeting place
de ontmoetingsplaats
ontm**oo**tings-plahts

melon de meloen mel**oo**n

memory stick de geheugenstick
KHeh**u**r-KHuh-stik

men de mannen m**a**nnuh

mend maken ma**h**kuh

**could you mend this for
me?** kunt u dit voor me
maken? koont ∞ dit vohr muh

men's room het herentoilet
h**a**yruh-twa-let

menswear de herenkleding
h**a**yruh-klayding

mention noemen n**oo**muh

don't mention it geen dank
KH**a**yn

menu het menu men**∞**, de kaart
kahrt

**may I see the menu,
please?** kan ik de kaart
krijgen? duh kahrt kr**i**KHuh
see Menu reader

message de boodschap b**oh**tsKHap

**are there any messages
for me?** heeft er iemand
een boodschap voor me
achtergelaten? hayft er **ee**mant
uhn b**oh**tsKHap vohr muh
a**KH**terKHelahtuh

**I want to leave a message
for...** ik wil graag een
boodschap achterlaten voor...
vil KHra**h**KH

metal het metaal mayt**ah**l

metre de meter m**ay**ter

microwave (oven) de magnetron
maк**н**naytron

midday middag m**i**ddaкн

   at midday tussen de middag
t**oo**ssuh duh

middle: in the middle
in het midden m**i**dduh

   in the middle of the night
m**i**ddenin de nacht duh naкнt

   the middle one de middelste
m**i**ddelstuh

midnight middernacht
middern**a**кнt

   at midnight om twaalf uur 's
nachts tvahlf **oo**r snaкнts

might: I might misschien
missк**нee**n

   I might not misschien niet neet

   **I might want to stay
another day** ik wil misschien
een dag langer blijven vil
missк**нee**n ayn daкн langer bl**ī**vuh

migraine de migraine
meegr**ay**nuh

mild zacht zaкнt

mile de mijl m**ī**l

milk de melk

milkshake de milkshake

mill de molen m**oh**luh

millimetre de millimeter
m**i**llimayter

minced meat het gehakt кнeh**a**kt

mind: never mind het geeft
niks кн**a**yft

   I've changed my mind
ik ben van gedachten
veranderd кнеda**кн**tuh ver**a**ndert

mine: it's mine het is van mij m**ī**

mineral water het spawater
sp**ah**-vahter

   fizzy mineral water spa rood
roht

   still mineral water spa blauw
blow

mints de mentholsnoepjes
mentol-snoop-yes

minute de minuut min**oo**t

   in a minute zo meteen
met**ay**n

   just a minute een ogenblikje
uhn ohкнenbl**i**k-yuh

mirror de spiegel sp**ee**кнel

Miss mevrouw mevr**ow**

miss: I missed the bus
ik hebt de bus gemist
duh b**oo**s кнеm**i**st

missing ontbrekend ontbr**ay**kent

   one of my... is missing
er ontbreekt een van mijn...
ontbr**ay**kt ayn van muhn

   there's a suitcase missing
er is een koffer zoek zook

mist de mist

mistake de fout f**ow**t

I think there's a mistake
ik geloof dat er een fout in zit
KHel**oh**f dat er uhn f**ow**t

sorry, I've made a mistake
sorry, ik heb een fout gemaakt
hep uhn f**ow**t KHem**ah**kt

misunderstanding
het misverstand m**i**sverstant

**mix-up: sorry, there's been
a mix-up** sorry, er is een
vergissing gemaakt uhn
verk**hi**ssing KHem**ah**kt

mobile phone de GSM KH**ay**-
ess-em, de mobiele telefoon
mob**ee**luh telef**oh**n

modern modern mohd**air**n

modern art gallery het museum
van moderne kunst m**oo**say-um
van mohd**air**nuh k**oo**nst

moisturizer de
vochtinbrengende crème v**o**KHt-
inbrengenduh krem

moment: I won't be a moment
ik ben zo terug ter**oo**KH

monastery het (mannen)
klooster (m**a**nnuh)kl**oh**ster

Monday maandag m**ah**ndaKH

money het geld KHelt

month de maand mahnt

monument het monument
mohn**oo**ment

moon de maan mahn

moped de bromfiets br**o**mfeets

more meer mayr

**can I have some more
water, please?** mag ik nog
wat water, alstublieft? maKH ik
noKH vat v**ah**ter alst**oo**bleeft

**more expensive/more
interesting** duurder/
interess**a**nter d**oo**rder

more than 50 meer dan
v**ij**ftig

more than that nog meer
noKH

a lot more veel meer vayl

DIALOGUE

**would you like some
more?** wilt u nog wat
(meer)? v**i**lt oo nokh vat (mayr)

**no, no more for me,
thanks** nee, voor mij niet,
dank u wel nay vohr m**ī** neet
dank **oo** vel

how about you? en u?

**I don't want any more,
thanks** ik wil ook niet
meer, dank u wel v**i**l ohk neet

morning de morgen m**o**rKHuh

this morning vanochtend
van**o**KHtent

in the morning 's morgens
sm**o**rKHens

mosquito de mug m**oo**KH

**most: I like this one most of
all** deze bevalt me het beste
d**ay**zuh bevalt muh het b**e**stuh

most of the time meestal
m**ay**stal

most tourists de meeste
toer**i**sten m**ay**stuh

mostly vooral v**oh**ral

mother de moeder m**oo**der

mother-in-law de
schoonmoeder sKH**ohn**-m**oo**der

motorbike de motorfiets
motorfeets

motorboat de motorboot
motorboht

motorway de (auto)snelweg
(**OW**to)snelveKH

mountain de berg berKH

mouse de muis mOWs

moustache de snor

mouth de mond

mouth ulcer de mondzweer
montzvayr

move bewegen bev**ay**KHuh

he's moved to another
room hij is naar een andere
kamer verhuisd hī is nahr uhn
anderuh kahmer verh**OW**st

could you move your
car? zou u uw auto kunnen
verzetten? zOW oo oo **OW**to
k**oo**nnuh verz**e**ttuh

could you move up a little?
zou u wat op kunnen schuiven?
zOW oo vat op k**oo**nnuh sKH**OW**vuh

where has it moved to?
waar is het heen verhuisd?
vahr is uht hayn verh**OW**st

where has it been moved
to? waar is het neergezet?
n**ay**rkHezet

movie de film

movie theater de bioscoop
biosk**oh**p

MP3 format het mp-drie-
formaat em-pay-dr**ee**-form**ah**t

Mr mijnheer muhn**ay**r

Mrs, Ms mevrouw mevr**OW**

much veel vayl

much better/worse veel
beter/slechter b**ay**ter/sl**e**KHter

much hotter veel heter

not much niet veel neet

not very much niet zo veel

I don't want very much
ik wil niet zo veel

mud de modder

mug (for drinking) de beker b**ay**ker

I've been mugged ik ben
beroofd ber**oh**ft

mum ma, mama

mumps de bof

museum het museum m**oo**s**ay**um

mushrooms de champignons
shampin-y**on**

music de muziek m**oo**z**ee**k

musician (male/female)
de musicus/musicienne
m**oo**sik**oo**s/m**oo**sish**e**nnuh

Muslim Mohammedaans mohammedahns

mussels de mosselen mossuhluh

must: I must ik moet moot

I mustn't drink alcohol ik moet geen alcohol drinken KHayn

mustard de mosterd mostert

my mijn mīn

myself: I'll do it myself ik doe het zelf doo

by myself alleen allayn

N

nail (finger) de nagel nahKHel
(metal) de spijker spīker

nailbrush het nagelborsteltje nahKHelborstelt-yuh

nail varnish de nagellak nahKHellak

name de naam nahm

my name's John ik heet John hayt

what's your name? wat is uw naam? vat is oo nahm

what is the name of this street? hoe heet deze straat? hoo hayt dayzuh straht

napkin het servet

nappy de luier low-yer

narcissus de narcis

narrow (street) nauw now

nasty (person, weather) akelig ahkeliKH
(accident) ernstig ernstiKH

national nationaal nashonahl

nationality de nationaliteit nashonalitīt

natural natuurlijk natoorlik

nausea de misselijkheid misselikhīt

navy (blue) donkerblauw donkerblow

near dichtbij diKHtbī, vlakbij vlakbī

is it near...? is het vlakbij...?

do you go near...? komt u in de buurt van...? oo in duh boort

where is the nearest...? waar is de dichtstbijzijnde...? vahr is duh diKHtst-bizīnduh

nearby dichtbij diKHtbī

nearly bijna bīna

necessary noodzakelijk nohtzahkelik

neck de nek

necklace de halsketting

necktie de stropdas

need: I need... ik moet... moot

do I need to pay? moet ik betalen? betahluh

needle de naald nahlt

negative (film) het negatief nayKHateef

neither: neither (one) **of them** geen van beiden KHayn van bīduh

neither... nor... noch... noch... noKH

nephew de neef nayf

net (in sport) het net

Netherlands Nederland nayderlant

never nooit noyt

have you ever been to Utrecht ? bent u wel eens in Utrecht geweest? oo vel ayns in ootrekHt kHevayst

no, never, I've never been there nee, daar ben ik nog nooit geweest nay dahr ben ik nokH noyt

new nieuw new

news (radio, TV etc) het nieuws news

newsagent's de tijdschriften-winkel tītskHriftuh-vinkel

newspaper de krant

newspaper kiosk de krantenkiosk

New Year Nieuwjaar new-yahr

Happy New Year! Gelukkig Nieuwjaar! kHelookkikH

New Year's Eve Oudejaarsavond owduh-yahrs-ahvont

New Zealand Nieuw-Zeeland new-zaylant

New Zealander: I'm a New Zealander ik kom uit Nieuw-Zeeland owt

next volgend volkHent

the next turning/street on the left de volgende bocht/straat links volkHenduh bokHt/straht

at the next stop bij de volgende halte bī duh

next week volgende week vayk

next to naast nahst

nice (food) lekker

(looks) leuk lOWk

(person) aardig ahrdikH

(view) mooi moy

niece de nicht nikHt

night de nacht nakHt

at night 's nachts snakHts

good night goedenacht kHooyuh-nakHt

do you have a single room for one night? heeft u een eenpersoonskamer voor een nacht? hayft oo uhn aynpersohns-kahmer vohr ayn nakHt

yes, madam ja, mevrouw ya mevrow

how much is it per night? wat kost het per nacht? vat

it's 125 euros for one night het is honderdvijfentwintig euro per nacht urroh

thank you, I'll take it dank u wel, dan neem ik hem oo vel dan naym

nightclub de nachtclub nakHtkloop

nightdress de nachtjapon nakHt-yahpon

night porter de nachtportier nakHtporteer

no nee nay

I've no change ik heb geen wisselgeld hep kHayn visselkHelt

there's no... left er is geen... meer mayr

no way! het is niet waar!
neet vahr

oh no! (upset) o nee toch!
nay toKH

nobody niemand ne**e**mant

there's nobody there
er is niemand

noise het lawaai lav**ī**

noisy: it's too noisy het is te
lawaaierig tuh lav**ah**-yuhrikH

non-alcoholic niet-alcoholisch
neet-alkoh**o**lees

none niets neets

noodles de noedels n**oo**dels

noon middag m**i**ddakH

at noon om twaalf uur
's middags tvahlf oor sm**i**ddakHs

no-one niemand ne**e**mant

nor: nor do I ik ook niet
ohk neet

normal normaal norm**ah**l

north het noorden n**oh**rduh

in the north in het noorden

to the north naar het noorden
nahr

north of Amsterdam
ten noorden van Amsterd**a**m

northeast het noordoosten
nohrt**oh**stuh

northern noordelijk n**oh**rdelik

Northern Ireland Noord-Ierland
nohrt-**ee**rlant

North Sea de Noordzee
n**oh**rtzay

northwest het noordwesten
nohrdv**e**stuh

Norway Noorwegen

n**oh**rvaykHuh

Norwegian Noors nohrs

nose de neus n**o**ws

nosebleed de neusbloeding
n**o**wsblooding

not niet neet

I don't want to ik wil niet

it's not necessary
het is niet nodig neet n**oh**dikH

I didn't know that
dat wist ik niet vist

no, I'm not hungry
nee, ik heb geen h**o**nger
nay ik hep KHayn

not that one – this one
niet die – maar deze
dee mahr d**a**yzuh

note (banknote) het bankbiljet
b**a**nkbil-yet

notebook (paper)
het notitieboekje
noht**ee**tsee-book-yuh

notepaper (for letters)
het schrijfpapier sKHr**ī**fpapeer

nothing niets neets

nothing for me, thanks
voor mij niet, dank u wel
vohr m**ī** neet dank **oo** vel

nothing else niets **a**nders

novel de roman rohm**a**n

November nov**e**mber

now nu noo

number het nummer n**oo**mmer
(figure) het cijfer s**ī**fer

I've got the wrong number
ik heb het verkeerde nummer
gedraaid hep het verk**a**yrduh
n**oo**mmer KHedr**ī**t

what is your phone number? wat is uw telefoonnummer? vat is OO telefohn-noommer?

number plate de nummerplaat noommer-plaht

nurse (*male/female*) de verpleger/ verpleegster verplayKHer/ verplayKHster

nursery (for plants) de kwekerij kwaykerÿ

nut (for bolt) de moer moor

nutmeg de nootmuskaat nohtmOOskaht

nuts de noten nohtuh

O

occupied (toilet, phone) bezet

o'clock uur OOr

October oktober

odd (strange) vreemd vraymt

of van

off (lights) uit OWt

  it's just off Leidseplein het is vlakbij het Leidseplein vlakbÿ

  we're off tomorrow we vertrekken morgen vuh vertrekkuh morKHuh

offensive (language, behaviour) beledigend belaydikHent

office (place of work) het kantoor kantohr

officer (said to policeman) agent ahKHent

often vaak vahk

not often niet vaak neet

  how often are the buses? hoe vaak gaan de bussen? hoo vahk KHahn duh bOOssuh

oil (for car) de olie ohlee

  (for salad) de slaolie slah-ohlee

ointment de zalf

OK oké

  are you OK? bent u in orde? OO in orduh

  is that OK with you? vindt u dat goed? vint OO dat KHoot

  is it OK to park here? mag ik hier parkeren? maKH ik heer parkayruh

  that's OK, thanks het geeft niet dank u KHayft neet dank OO

  I'm OK (nothing for me) ik heb genoeg gehad hep KHenooKH KHehat

  (I feel OK) met mij is het goed mÿ is het KHoot

  is this train OK for...? is dit de trein naar...? duh trÿn nahr

  I said I'm sorry, OK? ik zei toch dat het me spijt? zÿ toKH dat uht muh spÿt

old oud OWt

  how old are you? hoe oud ben je? hoo OWt ben yuh
  I'm 25 ik ben vijfentwintig
  and you? en jij? yÿ

old-fashioned ouderwets OWdervets

old town (old part of town) het oude stadsdeel OWduh statsdayl

in the old town in het oude stadsdeel

olives de olijven ohl*ee*vuh

omelette de omelet

on op

on the street/beach op straat/het strand

is it on this road? ligt het aan deze weg? li*kh*t uht ahn d*ay*zuh ve*kh*

on the plane in het vliegtuig

on Saturday op zaterdag

on television op de televisie telev*ee*see

I haven't got it on me ik heb het niet bij me hep het neet b*ī* muh

this one's on me (drink) deze betaal ik d*ay*zuh bet*ah*l

the light wasn't on het licht was niet aan li*kh*t vas neet ahn

what's on (TV) tonight? wat is er vanavond op TV? van*ah*vont op tayv*ay*

once (one time) een keer ayn keer

at once (immediately) meteen met*ay*n

one een ayn

the white one de witte duh v*i*ttuh

one-way ticket: a one-way ticket to... een enkele reis naar... uhn *e*nkeluh ris nahr, een enkeltje naar... *e*nkelt-yuh

onion de ui *OW*

online (book, check) online

only maar mahr

only one maar een ayn

it's only 6 o'clock het is pas zes uur OOr

I've only just got here ik ben hier nog maar net aangekomen heer no*KH* mahr net *ah*n*KH*ekohmuh

on/off switch de aan/uit-schakelaar ahn/OWt-s*KH*ah*kelahr

open (adjective) geopend *KH*uh-*oh*pent

(verb: door) open doen doon

(of shop) openen *oh*penuh

when do you open? wanneer gaat u open? vann*ayr* *KH*aht OO

I can't get it open ik kan het niet open krijgen neet *oh*puh kr*ī*KHuh

in the open air in de buitenlucht duh b*OW*tuhloo*KH*t

opening times de openingstijden *oh*penings-t*ī*duh

open ticket het ticket geldig voor onbepaalde duur *KH*el*di*KH vohr onbep*ah*lduh door

opera de opera

operation (medical) de operatie operh*ah*tsee

operator (telephone: male/female) de telefonist/telefoniste telefon*i*stuh

opposite: the opposite direction de tegenovergestelde richting tay*KH*en*oh*ver-*KH*estelduh r*i*KHting

the bar opposite de bar hier tegenover heer tay*KH*en*oh*ver

opposite my hotel tegenover mijn hotel

optician de opticien opteeshen

or of

orange (fruit) de sinaasappel
seenahsappel

(colour) oranje oran-yuh

orange cordial
de sinaasappellimonade
seenahs-appel-limonahduh

orange juice het sinaasappelsap
seenahs-appelsap

orchestra het orkest

order: can we order now?
(in restaurant) kunnen we nu
bestellen? koonnuh vuh noo

**I've already ordered,
thanks** ik heb al besteld, dank
u hep al bestelt dank oo

I didn't order this ik heb dit
niet besteld neet

out of order defect

ordinary gewoon кнеvohn

other andere anderuh

the other one de andere

the other day pas

I'm waiting for the others
ik wacht op de anderen vaкнt
op duh

do you have any others?
heeft u ook andere? hayft oo ohk

otherwise anders

our (with nouns with de) onze onzuh

(with nouns with het) ons

our flat onze flat

our house ons huis

ours van ons

out: he's out hij is er niet
hī is er neet

**three kilometres out of
town** drie kilometer buiten de
stad kilomayter bowtuh duh stat

outdoors buiten bowtuh

outside buiten bowtuh

can we sit outside? kunnen
we buiten zitten? koonnuh vuh

oven de oven ohvuh

over: over here hier heer

over there daar dahr

over 500 meer dan
vijfhonderd mayr

it's over het is voorbij vohrbī

**overcharge: you've
overcharged me** u heeft
teveel in rekening gebracht
oo hayft tevayl in raykening
кнebraкнt

overcoat de overjas over-yas

**overlooking: I'd like a room
overlooking the courtyard**
ik wil graag een kamer met
uitzicht op de binnenplaats vil
кнrahкн uhn kahmer met owtziкнt
op duh binnuhplahts

overnight (travel) 's nachts
snaкнts

overnight train de nachttrein
naкнt-trīn

overtake inhalen inhahluh

**owe: how much do I owe
you?** hoeveel krijgt u van me?
hoovayl krīкнt oo van muh

own: my own... mijn eigen...
mīn īкнuh

are you on your own?
bent u alleen? oo allayn

I'm on my own ik ben alleen

owner (*male/female*)
de eigenaar/eigenaresse
īkнenahr/īкнenar**e**ssuh

P

pack pakken pakkuh

 a pack of... een pakje...
uhn pak-yuh

package (parcel) het pakje

package holiday de volledig
verzorgde vakantie voll**ay**diкн
verz**o**rкнduh vah**ka**nsee

packed lunch het lunchpakket
l**oo**nshpakket

packet: a packet of cigarettes
het pakje sigaretten pak-yuh
seeкнar**e**ttuh

padlock het hangslot

page (of book) de bladzijde blatz**ī**duh

 could you page Mr...?
kunt u de heer... oppiepen?
koont oo duh hayr... **o**ppeepuh

pain de pijn pīn

 I have a pain here het doet
hier pijn doot heer

painful pijnlijk p**ī**nlik

painkillers de pijnstillers p**ī**nstillers

paint de verf vairf

painting het schilderij sкн**i**lderī

pair: a pair of... een paar...
uhn pahr

Pakistani Pakistaans pakist**ah**ns

palace het paleis pal**ī**s

pale bleek blayk

 pale blue lichtblauw liкнtbl**ow**

pan de pan

panties het damesslipje
d**ah**muhs-slip-yuh

pants (underwear: men's)
de onderbroek **o**nderbrook

 (women's) het damesslipje
d**ah**muhs-slip-yuh

 (trousers) de broek brook

pantyhose de panty p**e**nti

paper het papier pap**ee**r

 (newspaper) de krant

 a piece of paper een
papiertje uhn pap**ee**rt-yuh

paper handkerchiefs papieren
zakdoekjes pap**ee**ruh zakd**oo**k-
yuhs

parcel het pakket

pardon (me)? (didn't understand/
hear) pardon (wat zei u)? vat zī oo

parents de ouders **ow**ders

parents-in-law de
schoonouders sкн**ohn**-owders

park het park

 (*verb*) parkeren park**ay**ruh

 can I park here? mag ik hier
parkeren? maкн ik heer

parking lot het parkeerterrein
park**ayr**-terrīn

part het deel dayl

partner (boyfriend, girlfriend etc)
de partner

party (group) het gezelschap
кнez**e**lsкнap

 (celebration) het feest fayst

pass (in mountains) de bergpas
b**e**rкнpas

passenger de passagier
passaJ**ee**r

passport het paspoort paspohrt

password het wachtwoord vaKHt-vohrt

past: in the past in het verleden verlayduh

just past the information office net voorbij het informatiekantoor vohrbī het informahtsee-kantohr

path het pad pat

pattern het patroon pahtrohn

pavement de stoep stoop

on the pavement op de stoep

pay betalen betahluh

can I pay, please? kan ik afrekenen, alstublieft? afraykenuh alstOObleeft

it's already paid for het is al betaald betahlt

who's paying? wie betaalt er? vee

I'll pay ik betaal betahl

no, you paid last time, I'll pay nee, jij hebt de afgelopen keer betaald, ik betaal nay yī hebt duh afKHelohpuh kayr betahlt

payphone (coin-operated) de munttelefoon mOOnt-telefohn

(cardphone) de kaarttelefoon kahrt-telefohn

peaceful vredig vraydiKH

peach de perzik pairzik

peanuts de pinda's pindas

pear de peer payr

peas de doperwten dopertuh

peculiar (taste, custom) merkwaardig merkvahrdiKH

pedalboat de waterfiets vahterfeets

pedestrian crossing de voetgangersoversteekplaats vOOtKHangers-ohverstayk-plahts

pedestrian precinct het voetgangersgebied vOOtKHangers-KHebeet

peg (for washing) de wasknijper vask-nīper

(for tent) de haring hahring

pen de pen

pencil het potlood potloht

penfriend (male/female) de penvriend/penvriendin penvreend/penvreendin

penicillin de penicilline payneeseeleenuh

penknife het zakmes

pensioner de gepensioneerde KHepenshonayr-duh

people mensen mensuh

the other people in the hotel de andere mensen in het hotel anderuh

too many people te veel mensen tuh vayl

pepper (spice) de peper payper

(vegetable) de paprika pahprika

peppermint (sweet) de pepermunt paypermOOnt

per: per night per nacht naKHt

how much per day? hoeveel per dag? hoovayl per daKH

per cent procent

perfect perfect

perfume de parfum parf**oo**m

perhaps misschien miss**KH**een

  perhaps not misschien niet neet

period (of time) de periode payri-**oh**duh

  (menstruation) de menstruatie menstroo-**ah**tsee

perm het perman**e**nt

permit de vergunning ver**KHoo**nning

person de persoon pers**oh**n

petrol de benzine benz**ee**nuh

petrol can het benzineblik benz**ee**nuh-blik

petrol station het benzinestation benz**ee**nuh-stash**o**n

pharmacy de apotheek apot**ayk**

phone de telefoon telef**oh**n

  (*verb*) telefoneren telefon**ay**ruh

phone book het telefoonboek telef**oh**nbook

phone box de telefooncel telef**oh**n-sel

phonecard de telefoonkaart telef**oh**nkahrt

phone charger de telefoonoplader telef**oh**n-oplahder

phone number het telefoonnummer telef**oh**n-noommer

photo de foto

  excuse me, could you take a photo of us? pardon, wilt u misschien een foto van ons maken? vilt **oo** miss**KH**een uhn foto van ons m**ah**kuh

phrasebook de taalgids t**ah**l**KH**its

piano de piano pi**a**no

pickpocket de zakkenroller

pick up: will you be there to pick me up? komt u me afhalen? koh muh **af**hahluh

picnic de picknick

picture (painting) het schilderij s**KH**ilder**ī**

  (photo) de foto

  (drawing) de tekening t**ay**kening

pie (meat) de pastei past**ī**

  (fruit) de vlaai vl**ī**

piece het stuk st**oo**k

  a piece of... een stuk...

pill de pil

  I'm on the pill ik gebruik de pil **KH**ebr**ow**k duh

pillow het kussen k**oo**ssuh

pillow case het kussensloop k**oo**ssuh-slohp

pin de speld spelt

pineapple de ananas

pineapple juice het ananas-sap

pink roze r**o**zuh

pipe (for smoking) de pijp pīp

  (for water) de leiding l**ī**ding

pity: it's a pity het is jammer y**a**mmer

pizza de pizza p**ee**tsah

place de plaats plahts

  at your place bij jou thuis bī yow tows

  at his place bij hem thuis

plain (not patterned) effen

  (food) eenvoudig aynv**ow**di**KH**

plane het vliegtuig vleeKHtowKH

   by plane met het vliegtuig

plant de plant

plaster cast het gipsverband
KHipsverbant

plasters de pleisters plīsters

plastic het plastic plestik

   (credit cards) het plastic (geld)
KHelt

plastic bag de plastic tas

plate het bord

platform het perron

   **which platform is it for
Gouda?** vanaf welk perron
gaat de trein naar Gouda? vanaf
velk perron KHaht duh trīn nahr
KHOWdah

play (*verb*) spelen spayluh

   (*noun*: in theatre) het toneelstuk
tonaylstook

playground de speelplaats
spaylplahts

pleasant aangenaam ahnKHenahm

please alstublieft alstoobleeft

   yes, please ja, graag
ya KHrahKH

   could you please…?
kunt u…, alstublieft? koont OO

   please don't niet doen,
alstublieft neet doon

pleased: pleased to meet you
aangenaam (kennis te maken)
ahnKHenahm (kennis tuh mahkuh)

pleasure: my pleasure graag
gedaan KHrahKH KHedahn

plenty: plenty of… volop…

   there's plenty of time
er is nog genoeg tijd
noKH KHenooKH tīt

   that's plenty, thanks
dat is meer dan genoeg, dank u
mayr dan KHenooKH dank OO

pliers de buigtang bowKHtang

plug (electrical) de stekker

(for car) de bougie boo**jee**

(in sink) de stop

plumber de loodgieter
loht KHeeter

pm: 2pm twee uur 's middags
00r smidda**kH**s

5pm vijf uur 's middags

8pm acht uur 's avonds
sah**v**onts

poached egg het gepocheerde
ei KHepohsh**ay**rduh ī

pocket de zak

point: two point five
twee k**o**mma vijf

there's no point het heeft
geen zin hayft KH**ay**n

points (in car) de contactpunten
kontak**t**-p00ntuh

poisonous giftig KH**i**ftikH

police de politie pol**ee**tsee

call the police! bel de politie!
duh

policeman de politieagent
pol**ee**tsee-ahkHent

police station het politiebureau
pol**ee**tsee-b00roh

policewoman de politieagente
pol**ee**tsee-ahkHentuh

polish de schoensmeer
skH**oo**nsmayr

polite beleefd bel**ay**ft

polluted verontreinigd
veront-r**ī**nikHt

pond de vijver v**ī**ver

pony de pony p**o**nnee

pool (for swimming) het zwembad
zv**e**mbat

poor (not rich) arm

(quality) slecht sle**kH**t

pop music de popmuziek
popm00zeek

pop singer (male/female)
de p**o**pzanger/p**o**pzangeres

popular populair pop00**lay**r

pork het varkensvlees
v**a**rkensvlays

port (for boats) de haven hah**v**uh

(drink) de port

porter (in hotel) de portier port**eer**

portrait het portret

posh (restaurant, people) chic

possible mogelijk m**o**hkHelik

is it possible to…?
is het mogelijk om te…? tuh

as… as possible
zo… mogelijk

post (mail) de post posst

(verb) posten p**o**sstuh

could you post this for me?
zou u dit voor mij kunnen
posten? z**o**w 00 dit vohr mī k**oo**nnuh

postbox de brievenbus
br**ee**vuhb00s

postcard de briefkaart br**ee**fkahrt

postcode de postcode
p**o**sstkohduh

poster de poster

poste restante poste-restante
posst-r**e**sstant

post office het postkantoor
p**o**sstkantohr

potato de aardappel **ah**rdappel

pots and pans de p**o**tten en
p**a**nnen

pottery (objects) het aardewerk
ahrdeverk

pound (money, weight) het pond
pont

power cut de elektriciteitsstoring
aylektrisit**ī**ts–

power point het st**o**pcontact

**practise: I want to practise
my Dutch** ik wil mijn
Nederlands oefenen vil muhn
n**ay**derlants **oo**fenuh

prawns de garnalen KHarn**ah**luh

prefer: I prefer… ik heb liever…
hep l**ee**ver

pregnant zwanger zv**a**nger

prescription (for medicine)
het recept res**e**pt

present (gift) het cadeau kahd**oh**

president (of country)
de presid**e**nt
(of company) de directeur
deerekt**u**r

pretty mooi moy

it's pretty expensive
het is vrij duur vr**ī** d**oo**r

price de prijs pr**ī**s

priest de priester pr**ee**ster

prime minister de min**i**ster-
presid**e**nt

printed matter drukwerk
dr**oo**kverk

priority (in driving) voorrang
v**oh**r-rang

prison de gevangenis KHev**a**ngenis

private particulier partik**oo**l**ee**r

private bathroom de eigen
b**a**dkamer **ī**KHuh

probably waarschijnlijk
vahrsKH**ī**nlik

problem het probleem probl**ay**m

no problem! geen probleem!
KH**ay**n

program(me) het programma
proKHr**a**mma

promise: I promise ik beloof
het bel**oh**f het

**pronounce: how is this
pronounced?** hoe spreek je
dit uit? hoo spr**ay**k yuh dit **o**wt

properly (repaired, locked etc)
goed KH**oo**t

protection factor
de beschermingsfactor
besKH**er**mings-faktor

Protestant prot**e**stant

public holiday de feestdag
f**ay**stdaKH

Travel tip One of the most
popular dates in the Dutch
calendar is Queen's Day, April
30. Held in honour of Queen
Beatrix, this street event
par excellence is celebrated
throughout the Netherlands,
but festivities tend to be
wildest in Amsterdam, with
the city's streets and canals
lined with people in ridiculous
costumes. Anything goes,
especially if it's orange – the
Dutch national colour.

public toilets de openbare
toiletten openb**ah**ruh
twa-l**e**ttuh

public transport het openbaar
vervoer openb**ah**r verv**oo**r

pudding (dessert) het toetje
toot-yuh

pull trekken trekkuh

pullover de pullover poolohver

puncture de lekke band
lekkuh bant

purple violet vee-ohlet

purse (for money)
de portemonnee portuhmonnay
(handbag) de handtas hant-tas

push duwen doowuh

pushchair de wandelwagen
vandelvahkHuh

put zetten zettuh

where can I put…?
waar kan ik… zetten? vahr

could you put us up for the night? kunt u ons onderdak
verlenen voor vannacht?
koont oo ons onderdak verlaynuh
vohr vannakHt

pyjamas de pyjama
pee-yahmah

Q

quality de kwaliteit kvalitīt

quarantine de quarantaine
kahrantaynuh

quarter het kwart kvart

quayside: on the quayside
op de kade duh kahduh

question de vraag vrahkH

queue de rij rī

quick snel

that was quick dat was snel
vas

what's the quickest way there? wat is de snelste weg
daar naartoe? vat is duh snelstuh
vekH dahr nahrtoo

fancy a quick drink? heb je
zin om even wat te drinken?
hep yuh zin om ayvuh vat tuh

quickly snel

quiet (place, hotel) rustig roostikH

quiet! stilte! stiltuh

quite (fairly) tamelijk tahmelik
(very) heel hayl

that's quite right dat is zo

quite a lot heel wat hayl vat

R

rabbit het konijn konīn

race (for runners, cars) de race

racket (tennis, squash) het racket

radiator (in room) de radiator
rah-di-ahtor
(of car) de radiateur rah-diatoor

radio de radio rah-dio

on the radio op de radio

rail: by rail per spoor spohr

railway de spoorweg spohrvekH

rain de regen raykHuh

in the rain in de regen

it's raining het regent
raykHent

raincoat de regenjas raykHen-yas

rape de verkrachting verkrakHting

rare (uncommon) zeldzaam
zeltzahm
(steak) rood roht

rash (on skin) de huiduitslag
h**ow**t-**ow**tslakH

raspberry de framboos framb**oh**s

rat de rat

rate (for changing money) de koers
koors

rather: it's rather good het is
tamelijk goed t**ah**melik KH**oo**t

I'd rather... ik heb liever...
hep l**ee**ver

razor het scheerapparaat
sKH**ay**r-apparaht

razor blades de scheermesjes
sKH**ay**r-meshus

read lezen l**ay**zuh

ready klaar klahr

are you ready? ben je klaar?
yuh

I'm not ready yet ik ben nog
niet klaar noKH neet

when will it be ready?
wanneer is het klaar?
vann**ee**r

**it should be ready in a
couple of days** als het
goed is, is het over een paar
dagen klaar KH**oo**t – **oh**ver
uhn pahr dah**KH**uh

real echt eKHt

really echt

I'm really sorry het spijt me
echt sp**i**t muh

that's really great dat is echt
geweldig KHev**e**ldiKH

really? (doubt) echtwaar?
eKHtv**ah**r

(polite interest) o ja? ya

rear lights de achterlichten
aKHter-l**i**KHtuh

rearview mirror
de achteruitkijkspiegel
aKHter**ow**tkik-sp**ee**KHel

reasonable (prices etc) redelijk
r**ay**delik

receipt het ontvangstbewijs
ontv**a**ngst-bev**i**s

(at cash desk) de kassabon

recently onlangs

reception de receptie res**e**psee

at reception bij de receptie b**i**

reception desk de receptie

receptionist de receptioniste
resepshon**i**stuh

recognize herkennen hairk**e**nnuh

**recommend: could you
recommend...?** zou u... aan
kunnen bevelen? z**ow** ∞... ahn
k**oo**nnuh bev**ay**luh

record (music) de plaat plaht

red rood roht

red wine de rode wijn r**oh**duh v**i**n

refund de vergoeding verKH**oo**ding

can I have a refund?
kan ik het vergoed krijgen?
verKH**oo**t kr**i**KHuh

region de streek strayk

**registered: by registered
mail** per aangetekende post
ahnKHetaykenduh posst

registration number
het kentekennummer
k**e**ntaykuh-noommer

relative het familielid fam**ee**leelit

religion de godsdienst
KHotsdeenst

remember: I don't remember
ik kan het me niet herinneren
muh neet

I remember ik weet het nog
vayt het noKH

do you remember? weet jij
het nog? yī

rent (*for apartment etc*) de huur hoor
(*verb:* car etc) huren hooruh

for rent te huur tuh

rented car de huurauto hrowto

repair repareren rayparayruh

can you repair it? kunt u het
maken? koont oo het mahkuh

repeat herhalen herhahluh

could you repeat that?
zou u dat kunnen herhalen?
zow oo dat koonnuh

reservation de reservering
raysairvayring

**I'd like to make a
reservation** ik wil graag iets
reserveren vil KHrahKH eets
raysairvayruh

DIALOGUE

I have a room reservation
ik heb een kamer
gereserveerd hep uhn kahmer
KHeraysairvayrt

**yes sir, what name
please?** goed meneer, wat
is de naam? KHoot muhnayr
vat is duh nahm

reserve (*verb*) reserveren
raysairvayruh

DIALOGUE

**can I reserve a table
for tonight?** kan ik
voor vanavond een tafel
reserveren? vohr vanahvont
uhn tahfel

**yes madam, for how many
people?** ja mevrouw,
voor hoeveel personen?
ya mevrow vohr hoovayl
persohnuh

for two voor twee

and for what time? en voor
hoe laat? vohr hoo laht

for eight o'clock voor acht
uur oor

**and could I have your
name please?** en mag ik
uw naam even? maKH ik oo
nahm ayvuh
see **alphabet** *for spelling*

rest: I need a rest ik wil graag
even uitrusten vil KHrahKH ayvuh
owtroostuh

the rest of the group de rest
van de groep duh KHroop

restaurant het restaurant
restowrant

restaurant car
de restauratiewagen
restowrahtsee-vahKHuh

rest room het toilet twa-let

retired: I'm retired
ik ben gepensioneerd
KHepenshonayrt

return: a return to... een retour
naar... uhn retoor nahr

return ticket het retourtje
retoort-yuh

reverse charge call het collect
gesprek кнesprek

reverse gear
de achteruitversnelling
aкнterowt-versnelling

revolting walgelijk valкнelik

rib de rib

rice de rijst rīst

rich (person) rijk rīk

(food) machtig maкнtiкн

ridiculous belachelijk
belaкнelik

right (correct) juist yowst

(not left) rechts reкнts

you were right je had gelijk
yuh hat кнelīk

that's right dat klopt

this can't be right dit kan
nooit goed zijn noyt кноot zīn

right! oké! okay

is this the right road for…?
is dit de weg naar…?
duh veкн nahr

on the right, to the right
rechts

turn right ga naar rechts
кна nahr

right-hand drive met het stuur
aan de rechterkant stoor ahn duh
reкнterkant

ring (on finger) de ring

I'll ring you ik bel je yuh

ring back terugbellen
terooкн-belluh

ripe (fruit) rijp rīp

rip-off: it's a rip-off het is
afzetterij afzetterī

rip-off prices nepprijzen
nepprīzuh

risky riskant

river de rivier riveer

road de weg veкн

is this the road for…?
is dit de weg naar…?
duh veкн nahr

down the road verderop
verderop

road accident het wegongeluk
veкн-onкнelook

road map de wegenkaart
vayкнenkahrt

roadsign het verkeersbord
verkayrsbort

rob: I've been robbed ik ben
bestolen bestohluh

rock de rots

(music) rock(muziek)
rok(moozeek)

on the rocks (with ice)
met ijs īs

roll (bread) het broodje broht-yuh

roof het dak

roof rack de imperiaal
impayriahl

room de kamer kahmer

in my room in mijn kamer
mīn

room service de kamerservice
kahmer-service

rope het touw tow

rose de roos rohs

rosé rosé rosay**

roughly (approximately) ongeveer onkHev**ay**r

round: it's my round ik betaal dit rondje bet**ah**l dit r**o**nt-yuh

roundabout (for traffic) de rotonde roht**o**nduh

round-trip ticket het retourtje… ret**oo**rt-yuh

 a round-trip ticket to… een retour naar… uhn ret**oo**r nahr

route de route r**oo**tuh

 what's the best route? wat is de beste route? vat is duh b**e**stuh

rubber (material) rubber r**oo**bber

 (eraser) het gummetje KH**oo**mmet-yuh

rubber band het elastiekje aylast**ee**k-yuh

rubbish (waste) het afval **a**f-val

 (poor quality goods) de rotzooi r**o**tzoy

 rubbish! (nonsense) **o**nzin!

rucksack de rugzak r**oo**KHzak

rude onbeleefd onbel**ay**ft

ruins de ruïne r**oo**-eenuh

rum de rum r**oo**m

 rum and Coke de rum-c**o**la

run (person) rennen r**e**nnuh

 how often do the buses run? hoe vaak rijden de bussen? hoo vahk r**i**duh duh b**oo**ssuh

 I've run out of money ik heb geen geld meer hep KH**ay**n KH**e**lt mayr

rush hour het spitsuur sp**i**ts**oo**r

sad bedroefd bedr**oo**ft

saddle het zadel z**ah**del

safe veilig v**i**liKH

safety pin de veiligheidsspeld v**i**likHhids-spelt

sail het zeil z**i**l

sailboard de (wind)surfplank (vint)s**oo**rfplank

sailboarding het windsurfen v**i**nts**oo**rfuh

salad de salade sal**ah**duh

salad dressing de dr**e**ssing

sale: for sale te koop tuh kohp

salmon de zalm

salt het zout z**o**wt

same: the same hetzelfde uhtz**e**lfduh

 the same as this hetzelfde als dit

 the same again, please graag nog een keer hetzelfde KHrahkH noKH uhn kayr

 it's all the same to me het maakt mij niets uit mahkt m**i** neets **o**wt

sand het zand zant

sandals de sandalen sand**ah**luh

sandwich de sandwich, de dubbele boterham d**oo**bbeluh b**oh**terham

sanitary towels/napkins het maandverband m**ah**ntverbant

sardines de sardientjes sard**ee**nt-yuhs

Saturday zaterdag z**ah**terdaKH

sauce de saus sows

saucepan de steelpan st**ay**lpan

saucer het schoteltje
skH**oh**telt-yuh

sauna de sauna s**ow**na

sausage de worst vorst

say zeggen ze**kH**uh

**how do you say... in
Dutch?** hoe zeg je... in het
Nederlands? hoo ze**kH** yuh... in
uht n**ay**derlants

what did he say? wat zei hij?
vat z**i** h**i**

she said... ze zei... zuh

could you say that again?
zou u dat kunnen herhalen?
z**ow** oo dat k**oo**nnuh herh**ah**luh

scarf (for neck) de sjaal shahl

(for head) de hoofddoek
h**oh**ftdook

scenery het landschap lantsk**Ha**p

schedule de dienstregeling
d**ee**nst-rayk**He**ling

scheduled flight de lijnvlucht
l**i**nvl**oo**kHt

school de school skH**oh**l

scissors de schaar skH**ah**r

scooter de scooter

scotch de whisky

Scotland Schotland skH**o**tlant

Scottish Schots skH**o**ts

I'm Scottish ik kom uit
Schotland **ow**t skH**o**tlant

scrambled eggs het roerei
r**oo**r**i**

scratch de schram skH**ra**m

screw de schroef skH**roo**f

screwdriver de schroevendraaier
skH**roo**vuhdr**i**-er

sea de zee zay

by the sea aan zee ahn

seafood het zeebanket z**ay**banket

seafood restaurant
het visrestaurant v**i**srest**ow**rant

seafront de boulevard boolevar

on the seafront op de
boulevard

search zoeken z**oo**kuh

seasick: I feel seasick ik voel
me zeeziek vool muh z**ay**zeek

I get seasick ik heb last van
zeeziekte hep last van z**ay**zeektuh

seaside: by the seaside
aan zee ahn zay

seat de zitplaats z**i**tplahts

is this seat taken? is deze
plaats bezet? d**ay**zuh plahts

seat belt de veiligheidsgordel
v**i**lik**Hi**ts-kH**o**rdel

secluded afgezonderd
afkHezondert

second (adj) tweede tv**ay**duh

(of time) de seconde sek**o**nduh

just a second! een ogenblik,
alstublieft! uhn **oh**kHenblik
alst**oo**bleeft

second class (travel etc)
tweede klas tv**ay**duh

second floor de tweede
verdieping verd**ee**ping
(US) de eerste verdieping **ay**rstuh

second-hand tweedehands
tv**ay**duh-hants

see zien zeen

can I see? mag ik even
kijken? maKH ik **ay**vuh k**ī**kuh

have you seen…? heeft u…
gezien? hayft oo… KHez**ee**n

I saw him this morning ik
heb hem vanochtend gezien
hep uhm van**o**KHtent

see you! tot ziens! z**ee**ns

I see (I understand) ik begrijp
het beKH**rī**p

self-catering apartment de
flat met eigen kookgelegenheid
īKHuh k**oh**k-KHel**ay**KHenh**ī**t

self-service de zelfbediening
zelfbed**ee**ning

sell verkopen verk**oh**puh

do you sell…? verkoopt u…?
verk**oh**pt oo

send versturen verst**oo**ruh

**I want to send this to
England** ik wil dit naar
Engeland versturen vil dit nahr
engelant

senior citizen de bejaarde
buh-y**ah**rduh

separate apart

separated: I'm separated
ik ben gescheiden KHesKH**ī**duh

separately (pay, travel)
afzonderlijk afz**o**nderlik

September september
sept**e**mber

septic septisch s**e**ptees

serious (situation, illness) ernstig
airnstikH

(person) serieus sayri-**ur**s

service charge het
bedieningsgeld
bed**ee**nings-KH**e**lt

service station het
servicestation service-stashon

serviette het servet serv**e**t

set menu het vaste menu
v**a**stuh men**oo**

several verscheidene
versKH**ī**denuh

sew naaien n**ah**-yuh

**could you sew this back
on?** zou u dit er weer aan
kunnen naaien? z**ow** oo dit er
vayr ahn k**oo**nnuh

sex sex

sexy sexy

shade: in the shade in de
schaduw duh sKH**ah**doo

shallow (water) ondiep ond**ee**p

shame: what a shame!
wat jammer! vat y**a**mmer

shampoo de shampoo sh**a**mpoh

shampoo and set
wassen en watergolven
v**a**ssuh en v**ah**terKH**o**lvuh

share (room, table etc) delen
d**ay**luh

sharp (knife, taste) scherp sKH**ai**rp

(pain) stekend st**ay**kuht

shattered (very tired) doodop
d**oh**top

shaver het scheerapparaat
sKH**ay**r-apparaht

shaving foam het scheerschuim
sKH**ay**r-sKH**ow**m

shaving point het stopcontact
voor scheerapparaten vohr
sKH**ay**r-apparahtuh

she ze zuh

(emphatic) zij z**ī**

is she here? is ze hier?
zuh heer

sheet (for bed) het laken l**ah**kuh

shelf de plank

shellfish de schelpdieren
SKH**e**lpdeeruh

sherry de sherry

ship het schip SKH**i**p

  by ship per schip

shirt het overhemd **o**hverhemt

shit! verdomme! verd**o**mmuh

shock de schok SKH**o**k

  **I got an electric shock from
  the...** ik kreeg een elektrische
  schok van de... krayKH uhn
  ayl**e**ktreesuh SKH**o**k van duh

shock-absorber de schokbreker
SKH**o**kbrayker

shocking schokkend SKH**o**kkent

shoe de schoen SKH**oo**n

  a pair of shoes een paar
  schoenen uhn pahr SKH**oo**nuh

shoelaces de schoenveters
SKH**oo**nvayters

shoe polish de schoensmeer
SKH**oo**nsmayr

shoe repairer de schoenmaker
SKH**oo**nmahker

shop de winkel v**i**nkel

shopping: I'm going shopping
ik ga winkelen KHah v**i**nkeluh

shopping centre het
winkelcentrum v**i**nkel-sentr**oo**m

shop window de etalage
aytal**ah**Juh

shore de oever **oo**ver

short (person) klein kl**i**n

(time, journey) kort

shortcut de kortere weg
k**o**rteruh veKH

shorts de korte broek k**o**rtuh brook

should: what should I do? wat
moet ik doen? vat moot ik doon

  you should... je moet... yuh

  you shouldn't... je moet
  niet... neet

  he should be back soon
  als het goed is, is hij zo terug
  KHoot – hï zo ter**oo**KH

shoulder de schouder SKH**OW**der

shout schreeuwen SKHr**ay**oo-wuh

show (in theatre) de voorstelling
v**oh**rstelling

  could you show me? kunt u
  mij dat laten zien? koont oo mï
  dat l**ah**tuh zeen

shower (in bathroom) de douche
doosh

(of rain) de regenbui ray<small>KH</small>en**bow**

with shower met douche

shower gel de douchegel
dooshJel

shut (*verb*) sluiten s**low**tuh

   when do you shut?
   hoe laat sluit u? hoo laht s**low**t ∞

   when does it shut?
   hoe laat sluit het?

   they're shut ze zijn gesloten
   zuh zin <small>KH</small>es**loh**tuh

   shut up! houd je kop! h**ow**t yuh

shutter (on camera) de sluiter
s**low**ter

   (on window) het luik l**ow**k

shy verlegen verl**ay**<small>KH</small>uh

sick (ill) ziek zeek

   I'm going to be sick (vomit)
   ik moet overgeven moot
   ohver<small>KH</small>ayvuh

side de kant

   the other side of the street
   de andere kant van de straat
   anderuh kant van duh straht

side lights de stadslichten
stats-li<small>KH</small>tuh

side salad het schaaltje salade
s<small>KH</small>**ah**lt-yuh sal**ah**duh

side street de zijstraat z**ī**straht

sidewalk de stoep stoop

   on the sidewalk op de stoep

sight: the sights of... de
bezienswaardigheden van...
bezeens-**vah**rdi<small>KH</small>-hayduh

**sightseeing: we're going
sightseeing** we gaan de
bezienswaardigheden bekijken
vuh <small>KH</small>**ah**n duh – bek**ī**kuh

sightseeing tour (by bus)
de toeristische rondrit
too**ri**steesuh **ro**ntrit

   (by boat) de toeristische
   rondvaart **ro**ntvahrt

sign (road sign etc) het
verkeersbord verk**ay**rsbort

signal: he didn't give a signal
hij gaf geen signaal
h**ī** <small>KH</small>af <small>KH</small>ayn sin-y**ah**l

signature de handtekening
hant-**tay**kening

signpost de wegwijzer ve<small>KH</small>v**ī**zer

silence de stilte st**i**ltuh

silk de zijde z**ī**duh

silly dwaas dvahs

silver het zilver

similar soortgelijk sohrt<small>KH</small>el**ī**k

   a similar dress een
   soortgelijke jurk ayn
   sohrt<small>KH</small>el**ī**kuh y**oo**rk

   they look similar ze lijken op
   elkaar zuh l**ī**kuh op elk**ah**r

simple (easy) eenvoudig
aynv**ow**di<small>KH</small>

since: since last week sinds
vorige week v**oh**ri<small>KH</small>uh vayk

   since I got here sinds ik
   hier aangekomen ben heer
   ahn<small>KH</small>ekohmuh

sing zingen z**i**ng-uh

singer (male/female) de zanger/
zanger**es**

single: a single to... een enkele
reis naar... uhn **e**nkeluh ris nahr,
een enkeltje naar... **e**nkelt-yuh

   I'm single ik ben niet
   getrouwd neet <small>KH</small>etr**ow**t

single bed het eenpersoonsbed
aynpersohns-bet

single room
de eenpersoonskamer
aynpersohns-kahmer

single ticket de enkele reis
enkeluh ris, het enkeltje
enkelt-yuh

sink (in kitchen) de gootsteen
KH**oh**tstayn

(in bathroom) de wasbak **va**sbak

sister de zus z**oo**s

sister-in-law de schoonzus
sKH**ohn**nz**oo**s

sit: can I sit here?
kan ik hier z**i**tten? heer

is anyone sitting here?
zit hier iemand? **ee**mant

sit down gaan z**i**tten KHahn

sit down! ga z**i**tten! KHah

size de maat maht

skinny mager m**ah**KHer

skirt de rok

sky de hemel h**ay**mel

sleep slapen sl**ah**puh

did you sleep well? heb je
goed geslapen? hep yuh KHoot
KHesl**ah**puh

sleeper (on train) de couchette

sleeping bag de slaapzak
sl**ah**pzak

sleeping car de slaapwagen
sl**ah**pvahKHuh

sleeping pill de slaappil
sl**ah**p-pil

sleepy: I'm feeling sleepy
ik voel me slaperig vool muh
sl**ah**periKH

sleeve de mouw mow

slice de plak

(of bread) de snee snay

slide (photographic) de dia **dee**-ah

slip (garment) de onderjurk
onder-y**oo**rk

slippery glad KHlat

slow langzaam l**a**ngzahm

slow down! l**a**ngzamer!

slowly langzaam l**a**ngzahm

very slowly heel langzaam hayl

**could you speak more
slowly?** kunt u wat langzamer
spreken? koont oo vat l**a**ngzahmer
spr**ay**kuh

small klein klin

smell: it smells (smells bad)
het stinkt

smile glimlachen KHl**i**mlaKHuh

smoke de rook rohk

do you mind if I smoke?
heeft u er bezwaar tegen als ik
rook? hayft oo er bezv**ah**r tayKHuh
als ik rohk

I don't smoke ik rook niet neet

do you smoke? rookt u? oo

snack: just a snack alleen een
snack all**ay**n uhn

sneeze niezen n**ee**zuh

snow de sneeuw snay-oo

it's snowing het sneeuwt
snay-oot

so: it's so expensive het is zo
duur

not so much niet zo veel
neet zo vayl

not so bad niet zo slecht sleKHt

so am I, so do I ik ook ohk

so-so zo-zo

soaking solution (for contact lenses) de lensvloeistof lensvloo-eestof

soap de zeep zayp

soap powder het waspoeder vaspooder

sober nuchter nooKHter

sock de sok

socket (electrical) het stopcontact

soda (water) het sodawater sohda-vahter

sofa de sofa

soft (material etc) zacht zaKHt

soft-boiled egg het zachtgekookt ei zaKHt-KHekohkt ī

soft drink het glas fris KHlas

soft lenses de zachte lenzen zaKHtuh

sole (of shoe) de zool zohl
    (of foot) de voetzool vootzohl
    could you put new soles on these? kunt u hier nieuwe zolen onder zetten? koont oo heer new-uh

some: can I have some water/rolls? kan ik wat water/broodjes krijgen? vat – krīKHuh
    can I have some? kan ik er een paar krijgen? uhn pahr

somebody, someone iemand eemant

something iets eets
    something to eat iets te eten tuh aytuh

sometimes soms

somewhere ergens erKHens

son de zoon zohn

song het lied leet

son-in-law de schoonzoon sKHohnzohn

soon gauw KHOW
    I'll be back soon ik blijf niet lang weg blīf neet lang veKH
    as soon as possible zo snel mogelijk mohKHHelik

sore: it's sore het doet zeer doot zayr

sore throat de zere keel zayruh kayl

sorry: (I'm) sorry sorry
    sorry? (didn't understand) pardon, wat zei u? vat zī oo

sort: what sort of…? wat voor soort…? vohr

soup de soep soop

sour (taste) zuur zoor

south het zuiden zowduh
    in the south in het zuiden

South Africa Zuid-Afrika zowt-ahfrika

South African Zuid-Afrikaans zowt-afrikahns
    I'm South African ik kom uit Zuid-Afrika owt zowt-ahfrika

southeast het zuidoosten zowt-ohstuh

southern zuidelijk zowdelik

southwest het zuidwesten zowt-vestuh

souvenir het souvenir

Spain Spanje span-yuh

Spanish Spaans spahns

spanner de moersleutel
moorslurtel

spare part het reserveonderdeel
resairvuh-onderdayl

spare tyre de reserveband
resairvuh-bant

spark plug de bougie booJee

speak: do you speak English?
spreekt u Engels? spraykt oo

I don't speak... ik spreek
geen... sprayk khayn

can I speak to...? kan ik...
spreken? spraykuh

can I speak to Jan? kan ik
Jan even spreken? ayvuh

who's calling? met wie
spreek ik? vee

it's Patricia met Patricia

**I'm sorry, he's not in, can
I take a message?** sorry,
hij is niet thuis, kan ik een
boodschap aannemen? hi
is neet tows – uhn bohtskhap
ahnnaymuh

**no thanks, I'll call back
later** nee bedankt, ik bel
straks wel terug nay bedankt
ik bel straks vel trookh

please tell him I called zou
u hem willen vertellen dat ik
gebeld heb? zow oo hem villuh
vertelluh dat ik khebelt hep

spectacles de bril

speed de snelheid snelhīt

speed limit de maximum
snelheid maximoom

speedometer de snelheidsmeter
snelhīts-mayter

spell: how do you spell it?
hoe spel je het? hoo spel yuh
see **alphabet**

spend uitgeven owtkHayfvuh

spices de specerijen spayserī-uh

spider de spin

spin-dryer de droogtrommel
drohkHtrommel

splinter de splinter

spoke (in wheel) de spaak spahk

spoon de lepel laypel

sport de sport

sprain: I've sprained my...
ik heb mijn... verstuikt hep
muhn... verstowkt

spring (season) de lente lentuh
(of car, seat) de springveer
springvayr

in the spring in de lente

square (in town) het plein plīn

stairs de trap

stale oud owt

**stall: the engine keeps
stalling** de motor slaat steeds
af duh mohtor slaht stayts

stamp de postzegel
posstzaykhel

**a stamp for England,
please** een postzegel voor
Engeland, alstublieft uhn
posstzaykhel vohr engelant
alstoobleeft

standby standby

star de ster

start het begin beKHin

(*verb*) beginnen beKHinnuh

when does it start? hoe laat
begint het? hoo laht beKHint

the car won't start
de auto wil niet starten
duh **ow**to vil neet

starter (of car) de startmotor
startmohtor

(food) het voorgerecht
v**oh**rKHereKHt

starving: I'm starving
ik heb ontzettende honger
hep ontz**e**ttenduh

state (country) de staat staht

the States (USA) de Verenigde
Staten ver**ay**niKHduh st**ah**tuh

station het station stash**on**

statue het standbeeld st**a**ntbaylt

stay: where are you staying?
waar logeert u? vahr loJ**ay**rt OO

I'm staying at... ik logeer
in... l**oh**-jayr

**I'd like to stay another two
nights** ik wil graag nog twee
nachten blijven vil KHrahKH noKH
tvay n**a**KHtuh bl**ī**vuh

steak de biefstuk beefst**oo**k

steal stelen st**ay**luh

my bag has been stolen
mijn tas is gestolen mīn tas is
KHest**o**luh

steep (hill) steil stīl

steering de stuurinrichting
st**OO**r-inriKHting

step: on the steps (of building)
op de trap duh

stereo de stereo st**ay**ree-o

sterling sterling

steward (on plane) de steward

stewardess de steward**e**ss

still: I'm still here ik ben er
nog noKH

is he still there? is hij er nog?
is ee air

keep still! niet bewegen!
neet bev**ay**KHuh

sting: I've been stung ik ben
gestoken KHest**oh**kuh

stockings de kousen k**ow**suh

stomach de maag mahKH

I have a stomach upset
ik heb last van mijn maag
hep last van muhn

stomachache de maagpijn
m**a**hKHpīn

stone (rock) de steen stayn

stop stoppen st**o**ppuh

please, stop here (to taxi
driver etc) kunt u hier stoppen,
alstublieft? koont OO heer st**o**ppuh
alstOObleeft

do you stop near...?
stopt u in de buurt van...?
OO in duh bOOrt

stop it! houd op! h**ow**t

stopover de reisonderbreking rīs-onderbrayking

storm de storm

straight (whisky etc) puur pOOr

it's straight ahead het is recht door reкнt dohr

straightaway onmiddellijk onmiddelik

strange (odd) vreemd vraymt

stranger de vreemdeling vraymdeling

I'm a stranger here ik ben hier vreemd heer vraymt

strap (on watch) het horlogebandje horl**oh**Juh-bant-yuh

(on suitcase) de riem reem

(on dress) het bandje bant-yuh

strawberry de aardbei **ah**rtbī

stream de stroom strohm

street de straat straht

on the street op straat

streetmap het stratenplan stra**h**tuhplan

string het touw tOW

strong sterk

stuck klem

it's stuck het zit klem

student de student stOOdent

stupid stom

suburb de buitenwijk bOWtuhvīk

subway (underground railway) de metro m**ay**tro

suddenly pl**o**tseling

suede suede

sugar de suiker s**OW**ker

suit het pak

it doesn't suit me (jacket etc) het staat me niet staht muh neet

it suits you het staat je staht yuh

suitcase de koffer

summer de zomer z**oh**mer

in the summer 's zomers s**oh**mers

sun de zon

in the sun in de zon

out of the sun uit de zon OWt duh

sunbathe zonnen z**o**nnuh

sunblock (cream) het sun block sOOn

sunburn de zonnebrand z**o**nnuh-brant

sunburnt door de zon verbrand dohr duh zon verbr**a**nt

Sunday zondag z**o**ndaкн

sunglasses de zonnebril z**o**nnebril

sun lounger de ligstoel l**i**кн-stool

sunny: it's sunny het is zonnig z**o**nniкн

sunroof het schuifdak sкн**OW**fdak

sunset de zonsondergang zons-**o**nderкнang

sunshine de zonneschijn z**o**nnuh-sкн**i**n

sunstroke de zonnesteek z**o**nnuh-stayk

suntan de bruine kleur br**OW**nuh klur

suntan lotion de zonnebrandcrème z**o**nnuh-brant-krem

suntanned bruingebrand
br**ow**n-KHebrant

suntan oil de zonnebrandolie
z**o**nnuh-brantohlee

super geweldig KHev**e**ldiKH

supermarket de supermarkt
s**oo**permarkt

supper het avondmaal
ahvontmahl

supplement (extra charge)
de toeslag t**oo**slaKH

sure: are you sure? weet je het
zeker? vayt yuh uht z**ay**ker

sure! zeker!

surname de achternaam
aKHternahm

sweater de sweater

sweatshirt het sweatshirt

Sweden Zweden zv**ay**duh

Swedish Zweeds zvayts

sweet (taste) zoet zoot

(dessert) het toetje t**oo**t-yuh

sweets het snoepgoed
sn**oo**pKH**oo**t

swelling de zwelling zv**e**lling

swim zwemmen zv**e**mmuh

I'm going for a swim
ik ga zwemmen KHa

let's go for a swim
laten we gaan zwemmen
l**ah**tuh vuh KHahn

swimming costume
het zwempak zv**e**mpak

swimming pool het zwembad
zv**e**mbat

swimming trunks
de zwembroek zv**e**mbrook

Swiss Zwitsers zv**i**tsers

switch de schakelaar sKH**ah**kelahr

switch off uitschakelen
owtsKH**a**hkeluh

switch on (TV, lights) aan doen
ahn doen

(engine) aanzetten **ah**nzettuh

Switzerland Zwitserland
zv**i**tserlant

swollen opgezet **o**pKHezet

T

table de tafel t**ah**fel

a table for two een tafel voor
twee vohr

tablecloth het tafel-laken

table tennis het tafeltennis

table wine de tafelwijn t**ah**felv**i**n

tailback (of traffic) de file f**ee**luh

tailor de kleermaker kl**ay**rmahker

take (lead) nemen n**ay**muh

(accept) accepteren aksept**ay**ruh

can you take me to the...?
wilt u me naar het... br**e**ngen?
vilt **oo** muh nahr

do you take credit cards?
accepteert u creditcards?
aksept**ay**rt **oo**

fine, I'll take it goed, ik neem
het KH**oo**t ik naym

can I take this? (leaflet etc)
mag ik dit zo meenemen?
maKH ik dit zo m**ay**naymuh

how long does it take? hoe
lang duurt het? hoo lang d**oo**rt

it takes three hours
het duurt drie uur oor

is this seat taken? is deze
plaats bezet? dayzuh plahts

hamburger to take away
een hamburger om mee te
nemen uhn hamboorkHer om may
tuh naymuh

**can you take a little off
here?** (to hairdresser) kunt u er
hier een stukje afhalen?
koont oo er heer uhn stook-yuh
afhahluh

talcum powder de talkpoeder
ta-lkpooder

talk praten prahtuh

tall (person) lang

(building) hoog hohKH

tampons de tampons

tan de bruine kleur brownuh klur

to get a tan bruin worden
brown vorduh

tank (of car) de tank

tap de kraan krahn

tap water het kraanwater
krahnvahter

tape (for cassette)
het cassettebandje
kassettuh-bant-yuh

tape measure de centimeter
sentimayter

tape recorder
de cassetterecorder
kassettuh-reekorder

taste de smaak smahk

can I taste it? kan ik het
proeven? proovuh

taxi de taxi

will you get me a taxi?
kunt u voor mij een taxi
regelen? koont oo vohr mī uhn taxi
rayKHeluh

where can I find a taxi?
waar kan ik een taxi vinden?
vahr – vinduh

**to the airport/to the
Krasnapolsky Hotel,
please** naar het vliegveld/
naar Hotel Krasnapolsky
graag nahr uht vleeKHvelt –
KHrahbKH

how much will it be?
hoeveel gaat het kosten?
hoovayl KHaht

30 euros dertig euro urroh

**that's fine right here,
thanks** hier is het goed,
bedankt heer is uht KHoot

taxi-driver de taxi-chauffeur

taxi rank de taxi-standplaats
-stantplahts

tea (drink) de thee tay

tea for one/two, please
een/twee thee, alstublieft
ayn/tvay tay alstoobleeft

teabags de theezakjes tayzak-yuhs

teach: could you teach me?
kunt u het me leren? koont oo
uht muh layruh

teacher (male/female: junior)
de onderwijzer/onderwijzeres
ondervīzer/ondervīzeres

(secondary) de leraar/lerares
layrahr/layrahres

team de ploeg plooKH

teaspoon de theelepel taylaypel

tea towel de theedoek taydook

teenager de tiener teener

telephone de telefoon telefohn

television de televisie televeesee

tell: could you tell him…?
zou u hem willen vertellen…?
zow oo hem villuh vertelluh

temperature (weather)
de temperatuur temperatoor
(fever) de verhoging verhoh-KHing

tennis het tennis

tennis ball de tennisbal

tennis court de tennisbaan
tennisbahn

tennis racket het tennisracket

tent de tent

terminus (rail) het eindstation
īnt-stashon

terrible verschrikkelijk
versKHrikkelik

terrific fantastisch fantastees

text (verb) een sms'je sturen
uhn es-em-es-yuh stooruh

text (message) de tekst
(mededeling) mayduhdayling,
de sms' je es-em-es-yuh

than dan

smaller than kleiner dan
klīner

thank: thank you (pol)
dank u wel oo vel
(fam) dankjewel dank-yevel

thanks bedankt

thank you very much (pol)
dank u vriendelijk oo vreendelik

(fam) dank je vriendelijk yuh

thanks for the lift bedankt
voor de lift vohr duh

no, thanks nee, bedankt nay

---

that: that boy die jongen
dee yonghun

that girl dat meisje mīshuh

that one die dee

I hope that… ik hoop dat…
hohp

that's… dat is…

is that…? is dat…?

that's it (that's right) juist
yowst

the (sing) de duh; het
(pl) de

theatre de schouwburg
sKHOW-boorKH

their hun hoon

theirs van hen

them hen

for them voor hen vohr

who? – them wie? – zij
vee – zī

then (at that time) toen toon
(after that) dan

there daar dahr

over there daarginds
dahrKHins

up there daarboven
dahrbohvuh

is there...? is er...?

are there...? zijn er...? zīn

there is... er is...

there are... er zijn... zīn

there you are (giving
something: *pol*) alstublieft
alstoobleeft

(*fam*) alsjeblieft als-yebleeft

thermometer de thermometer
termomayter

Thermos flask de thermosfles
termosfles

these: these men/women
deze mannen/vrouwen dayzuh

I'd like these ik wil deze
graag hebben vil dayzuh KHrahKH

they ze zuh

(*emphatic*) zij zī

thick dik

(*stupid*) dom

thief de dief deef

thigh de dij dī

thin (material) dun doon

(person) mager mahKHer

thing het ding

my things mijn spullen
mīn spoolluh

think denken denkuh

I think so ik denk van wel vel

I don't think so ik denk van
niet neet

I'll think about it ik zal erover
nadenken erohver

third party insurance de
aansprakelijkheidsverzekering
ahnsprahkelik-hīts-verzaykering

thirsty: I'm thirsty ik heb dorst
hep

this: this boy deze jongen
dayzuh yonguh

this girl dit meisje mīshuh

this one deze

this is my wife dit is mijn vrouw mīn vrOW

is this...? is dit...?

those: those men/women die mannen/vrouwen dee

which ones? – those welke? – die velkuh

thread de draad draht

throat de keel kayl

throat pastilles de keelpastilles kaylpastee-yuhs

through door dohr

does it go through...? (train, bus) gaat de trein/bus via...? KHaht duh trīn/boos via

throw gooien KHohyuh

throw away weggooien veKH-KHohyuh

thumb de duim dowm

thunderstorm de onweersbui onvayrsbOW

Thursday donderdag donderdaKH

ticket het kaartje kahrt-yuh

(for plane) de ticket

DIALOGUE

a return to Rotterdam een retourtje Rotterdam uhn retoort-yuh

coming back when? wanneer reist u terug? vannayr rīst oo teroOKH

today/next Tuesday vandaag/volgende week dinsdag vandahKH/volKHenduh vayk

that will be 15.50 dat is dan vijftien vijftig vīfteen vīftiKH

ticket office (bus, rail) het loket

tide het getij KHetī

tie de stropdas

tight (clothes etc) strak

it's too tight het zit te strak tuh

tights de panty penti

till de kassa

time de tijd tīt

what's the time? hoe laat is het? hoo laht

this time deze keer dayzuh

last time de vorige keer vohrikHuh

next time de volgende keer volKHenduh

three times drie keer

timetable de dienstregeling deenst-rayKHeling

tin (can) het blik

tinfoil het aluminiumfolie aloominium-fohlee

tin-opener de blikopener

tiny heel klein hayl klīn

tip (to waiter etc) de fooi foy

Travel tip Tipping isn't as routine as it is in the US or UK, but you are expected to leave something if you have enjoyed good service – up to around ten percent of the bill should suffice in most restaurants, while hotel porters and taxi drivers may expect a euro or two on top of the fare.

tired moe moo

  I'm tired ik ben moe

tissues de papieren zakdoekjes
papeeruh zakdook-yuhs, de
Kleenex

to: to London naar Londen nahr

  to Holland/England
naar Nederland/Engeland
nayderlant/engelant

  to the post office naar het
postkantoor

toast (bread) het geroosterd
brood кнerohstert broht

tobacco de tabak tahbak

today vandaag vandahкн

toe de teen tayn

together samen sahmuh

  we're together (in shop etc)
wij zijn samen vī zīn

toilet het toilet twa-let

  where is the toilet? waar is
het toilet? vahr

  I have to go to the toilet ik
moet naar het toilet moot nahr

toilet paper het toiletpapier
twa-let-papeer

tomato de tomaat tomaht

tomato juice het tomatensap

tomato ketchup
de tomatenketchup
tomatuh-ketchup

tomorrow morgen morкнuh

  tomorrow morning
morgenochtend morкнenокнtent

  the day after tomorrow
overmorgen ohvermorкнuh

toner (cosmetic) de toner

tongue de tong

tonic (water) de tonic

tonight vanavond vanahvont

tonsillitis de amandelontsteking
ahmandelontstayking

too (excessively) te tuh

  (also) ook ohk

  too hot te heet

  too much te veel vayl

  me too ik ook ohk

tooth de tand tant

toothache de kiespijn keespīn

toothbrush de tandenborstel

toothpaste de tandpasta

top: on top of... bovenop...
bovenop

  at the top bovenaan bovenahn

top floor de bovenste verdieping
bovuhstuh verdeeping

topless topless

torch de zaklantaarn zaklantahrn

total het totaal totahl

tour de rondreis rontrīs

  is there a tour of...?
is er een excursie naar...?
uhn exkoorsee nahr

tour guide de gids кнits

tourist de toerist toorist

tourist information office het
toeristenbureau tooristuh-booroh

tour operator de reisorganisatie
rīs-orкнanisatsee

towards in de richting van
duh rīкнting

towel de handdoek handook

town de stad stat

in town in de stad

just out of town even buiten de stad *ayvuh bowtuh duh*

town centre het stadscentrum *stats-sentroom*

town hall het stadhuis *stathows*

toy het stuk speelgoed *stook spaylkhoot*

toys het speelgoed

track (platform) het perron

which track is it for Zwolle? vanaf welk perron gaat de trein naar Zwolle? *vanaf velk perron khaht duh trin nahr*

tracksuit het trainingspak *trayningspak*

traditional traditioneel *tradishonayl*

traffic het verkeer *verkayr*

traffic jam de verkeersopstopping *verkayrs-opstopping*

traffic lights de verkeerslichten *verkayrs-likHtuh*

trailer (for carrying tent etc) de aanhangwagen *ahnhang-vakHuh* (US) de caravan

trailer park de camping *kemping*

train de trein *trin*

by train met de trein *duh*

trainers (shoes) de gymschoenen *KHim-skHoonuh*

train station het station *stahshon*

tram de tram

tram stop de tramhalte *tremhaltuh*

translate vertalen *vertahluh*

could you translate that? zou u dat kunnen vertalen? *zow oo dat koonnuh vertahluh*

translation de vertaling *vertahling*

translator (*male/female*) de vertaler/vertaalster *vertahler/vertahlster*

trash het afval *af-val*

trashcan de vuilnisbak *vowlnisbak*

travel reizen *rīzuh*

we're travelling around we trekken rond *vuh trekkuh ront*

travel agent's het reisbureau *rīsbooroh*

traveller's cheque de reischeque *rīs-shek*

tray het dienblad *deenblat*

tree de boom *bohm*

tremendous fantastisch *fantastees*

trendy modern *mohdairn*

it is trendy het is in

trim: just a trim, please (to hairdresser) alleen bijknippen, alstublieft *allayn bī-k-nippuh alstoobleeft*

trip (excursion) de reis *rīs*

I'd like to go on a trip to... ik

trolley (in shop)
het winkelwagentje
v**i**nkel-vah**K**H**uh**t-yuh

(at airport) het bagagewagentje
bak**Ha**juh-vak**K**H**uh**t-yuh

trouble de moeilijkheid
m**oo**-eelik-h**ī**t

I'm having trouble with…
ik heb moeilijkheden met…
hep m**oo**-eelik-h**ay**duh

trousers de broek br**oo**k

true waar vahr

that's not true dat is niet waar
neet

trunk (of a car) de kofferbak

trunks (swimming) de zwembroek
zv**e**mbrook

try proberen prob**ay**ruh

can I try it? kan ik het eens
proberen? uht uhs

try on aanpassen **ah**npassuh

can I try it on? kan ik het
p**a**ssen?

T-shirt het T-shirt

Tuesday dinsdag d**i**nsda**KH**

tulip de tulp t**oo**lp

tuna de tonijn ton**ī**n

tunnel de tunnel t**oo**nnel

turn: turn left/right ga naar
links/rechts **KH**a nahr links/
re**KH**ts

turn off: where do I turn off?
waar moet ik afslaan?
vahr moot ik **a**fslahn

**can you turn the heating
off?** kunt u de verwarming

uitdoen? koont **oo** duh
vervarming **ow**tdoon

**turn on: can you turn the
heating on?** kunt u de
verw**a**rming aandoen?
ahndoon

turning (in road) de bocht bo**KH**t

TV de TV tay-v**ay**

tweezers het pincet pins**e**t

twice twee keer tvay kayr

twice as much twee keer
zoveel zov**ay**l

twin beds twee
eenpersoonsbedden tvay
aynpersohns-beddduh

twin room de kamer met
twee eenpersoonsbedden
k**ah**mer met tvay **ay**npersohns-
beddduh

twist: I've twisted my ankle
ik heb mijn enkel verzwikt
hep muhn **e**nkel verzv**i**kt

type het soort sohrt

another type of…
een **a**nder soort…

typical typisch t**ī**pees

tyre de band bant

U

ugly lelijk l**ay**lik

UK het Verenigd Koninkrijk
ver**ay**nik**H**t k**oh**ninkr**ī**k

ulcer (stomach) de maagzweer
m**ah**KH-zvayr

umbrella de paraplu parapl**oo**

uncle de oom ohm

unconscious bewusteloos bev**oo**stelohs

under (in position) **o**nder

(less than) m**i**nder dan

underdone (meat) niet gaar neet кнahr

underground (railway) de metro m**ay**tro

underpants de onderbroek **o**nderbrook

understand: I understand ik begrijp het beкн**ri**p

I don't understand ik begrijp het niet neet

do you understand? begrijpt u het? ∞

unemployed werkeloos v**e**rkelohs

unfashionable niet modieus neet modi-**ur**s

United States de Verenigde Staten ver**ay**niкнduh st**a**htuh

university de universiteit ∞niversit**i**t

unleaded petrol de loodvrije benzine l**oh**tvri-uh benz**ee**nuh

unlimited mileage het onbep**e**rkt aantal kilometers **ah**ntal k**i**lomayters

unlock openmaken **o**penmahkuh

unpack uitpakken **ow**tpakkuh

until tot

unusual ongewoon onкн**e**v**oh**n

up omhoog omh**oh**кн

up there daarboven dahrb**oh**vuh

he's not up yet (not out of bed) hij is nog niet op hi is noкн neet op

what's up? (what's wrong?) wat is er aan de hand? vat is er ahn duh hant

upmarket (restaurant, hotel etc) chic

upset stomach de maagstoornis m**a**hкн-stohrnis

upside down ondersteboven ondersteb**oh**vuh

upstairs boven b**oh**vuh

upstream stroomopwaarts str**oh**mopvahrts

urgent dringend dr**i**ngent

us ons

with us met ons

for us voor ons vohr

USA de V.S. v**ay**-ess

use gebruiken кнebr**ow**kuh

may I use...? kan ik... gebruiken?

useful nuttig n**oo**ttiкн

usual gebruikelijk кнebr**ow**kelik

the usual (drink) het drankje wat ik altijd drink dr**a**nk-yuh vat ik alt**i**t

V

vacancy: do you have any vacancies? (hotel) heeft u nog kamers vrij? hayft ∞ noкн k**a**hmers vri

vacation de vakantie vak**a**nsee

on vacation op vak**a**ntie

vaccination de vaccinatie vaksin**ah**tsee

vacuum cleaner de stofzuiger st**o**fz**ow**кнer

valid (ticket etc) geldig KHeldiKH

how long is it valid for?
hoe lang is het geldig? hoo –
KHeldiKH

valley het dal

valuable waardevol va**h**rdevol

**can I leave my valuables
here?** kan ik mijn waardevolle
spullen hier achterlaten?
mīn va**h**rdevolluh sp**oo**lluh heer
aKHterlahtuh

value de waarde va**h**rduh

van de bestelwagen best**e**lvahKHuh

vanilla de vanille van**ee**-yuh

a vanilla ice cream het
vanille-ijsje van**ee**-yuh–**ī**shuh

vary: it varies het verschilt uht
versKH**ī**lt

vase de vaas vahs

veal het kalfsvlees k**a**lfsvlays

vegetables de groenten
KHr**oo**ntuh

vegetarian de vegetariër
vayKHet**a**hri-er

(adj: food) vegetarisch
vayKHet**a**hrees

vending machine de automaat
owtom**a**ht

very erg airKH

very little for me voor mij
maar een heel klein beetje vohr
mī mahr uhn hayl klīn b**ay**t-yuh

I like it very much (food) ik
vind het heel l**e**kker vint uht hayl

(situation, activity) ik vind het
heel leuk lurk

(view, ornaments) ik vind het
heel mooi moy

vest (under shirt) het hemd hemt

via via v**ee**-a

video (film) de video

(recorder) de video-recorder

view het uitzicht **ow**tzikHt

village het dorp

vinegar de azijn az**ī**n

visa het visum v**ee**s00m

visit bezoeken bez**oo**kuh

I'd like to visit... ik zou
graag... bezoeken zow KHrah**KH**

vital: it's vital that... het is
van essentieel belang dat...
essensh**ay**l

vodka de wodka v**o**dka

voice de stem

voltage het voltage v**o**lta**J**uh

vomit overgeven **o**verKHayvuh

W

waist de taille t**a**yuh

waistcoat het vest

wait wachten va**KH**tuh

wait for me wacht op mij
va**KH**t op mī

don't wait for me wacht niet
op mij neet

**can I wait until my wife/
partner gets here?** kan ik
even wachten tot mijn vrouw/
partner hier is? **a**yvuh va**KH**tuh
tot muhn vr**ow**/partner heer

can you do it while I wait?
kunt u het doen terwijl ik
wacht? koont 00 uht doen terv**ī**l ik
va**KH**t

could you wait here for me? kunt u hier even op me wachten? heer **a**yvuh op muh

waiter de k**e**lner

waiter! **o**ber!

waitress de serve**er**ster serv**ay**rster

waitress! juffrouw! y**oo**ffrow

wake: can you wake me up at 5.30? kunt u me om half zes wekken? koont oo muh – v**e**kkuh

wake-up call het telefoontje om u te wekken telef**oh**nt-yuh om oo tuh

Wales Wales

walk: is it a long walk? is het een lange wandeling? uhn l**a**nguh v**a**ndeling

it's not far to walk het is niet ver l**o**pen neet vair

I'll walk ik ga lopen кнa

I'm going for a walk ik ga een eindje wandelen кнa uhn **ī**nt-yuh v**a**ndeluh

wall de muur moor

wallet de portefeuille portuh-f**ur**-yuh

wander: I like just wandering around ik hou ervan om gewoon wat rond te zwerven how **a**irvan om кнev**oh**n vat ront tuh zv**a**irvuh

want: I want a... ik wil graag een... vil кнr**a**hкн uhn

I don't want any... ik wil geen... кн**ay**n

I want to go home ik wil naar huis nahr hows

I don't want to ik wil niet neet

he wants to... hij wil... hī

what do you want? wat wil je? vat vil yuh

ward (in hospital) de afdeling **a**fdayling

warm warm varm

I'm so warm ik heb het warm hep

was: I was ik was vas

he/she/it was hij/zij/het was hī/zī

wash wassen v**a**ssuh

can you wash these? kunt u deze wassen? koont oo d**ay**zuh

washhand basin de wasbak v**a**sbak

washing (clothes) de was vas, het wasgoed v**a**sкноot

washing machine de wasmachine v**a**smasheenuh

washing powder het waspoeder v**a**spooder

washing-up: to do the washing-up de afwas doen **a**fvas doon

washing-up liquid het afwasmiddel **a**fvasmiddel

wasp de wesp vesp

watch (wristwatch) het horloge horl**oh**Juh

will you watch my things for me? wilt u even op mijn spullen letten? vilt oo **a**yvuh op muhn sp**oo**lluh

watch strap het horlogebandje horl**oh**Juh-bant-yuh

water het water va**h**ter

may I have some water?
kan ik wat water krijgen?
vat va**h**ter kri**kh**uh

waterproof waterdicht
va**h**terdik**h**t

waterskiing het waterskiën
va**h**terski-uh

wave (in sea) de golf **kh**olf

way: it's this/that way
het is deze/die kant uit
da**y**zuh/dee kant owt

is it a long way to…?
is het ver naar…? vair nahr

no way! vergeet het maar!
verk**h**a**y**t uht mahr

DIALOGUE

could you tell me the way to…? kunt u mij de weg naar… vertellen? koont oo muh duh ve**kh** nahr… vert**e**lluh

go straight on until you reach the traffic lights
ga rechtuit totdat u bij de stoplichten komt **kh**a re**kh**towt t**o**tdat oo bi duh stoplik**h**tuh komt

turn left ga naar links
kha nahr

take the first on the right
neem de eerste straat rechts
naym duh **ay**rstuh straht re**kh**ts

see **where**

we we vuh
(emphatic) wij vi

weak zwak zvak

weather het weer vayr

DIALOGUE

what's the weather forecast? wat is de weersvoorspelling? vat is duh v**ay**rsvohr-spelling

it's going to be fine
het wordt mooi weer
vort moy vayr

it's going to rain het gaat regenen **kh**aht ra**y**k**h**enuh

it'll brighten up later
het zal later opklaren
l**ah**ter **o**pklahruh

website de website

wedding de trouwerij trower**i**

wedding ring de trouwring
tr**ow**ring

Wednesday woensdag v**oo**nsdak**h**

week de week vayk

a week (from) today
vandaag over een week
vand**ah**k**h oh**ver ayn

a week (from) tomorrow
morgen over een week m**o**rk**h**uh

weekend het weekend v**ee**kent

at the weekend in het weekend

weight het gewicht **kh**evi**kh**t

weird raar rahr

weirdo: he's a weirdo
hij is een raar figuur
hi is uhn rahr fik**h**00r

welcome: you're welcome
(don't mention it) graag gedaan
khrahk**h kh**ed**ah**n

well: I don't feel well ik voel
me niet l**e**kker vool muh neet

she's not well ze is niet erg lekker zuh is neet erkH

you speak English very well u spreekt erg goed Engels 00 spraykt erkH KHoot

well done! goed zo!

this one as well deze ook dayzuh ohk

well, well! (surprise) wel, wel! vel vel

how are you? (*pol*) hoe maakt u het? hoo mahkt 00 (*fam*) hoe gaat het ermee? KHaht uht ermay

very well, thanks, and you? uitstekend, en met u? 0wtstaykent en met 00

well-done (meat) goed doorbakken KHoot dohrbakkuh
Welsh Wels vels

I'm Welsh ik kom uit Wales 0wt
were: we/they were wij/ze waren vī/zuh vahruh

you were u was 00 vas
west het westen vestuh

in the west in het westen
western westelijk vestelik
West Indian Westindisch vestindees
wet nat
what? wat? vat

what's that? wat is dat?

what should I do? wat moet ik doen? moot ik doon

what a view! wat een uitzicht! ayn 0wtzikHt

what bus do I take? welke bus moet ik nemen? velkuh b00s moot ik naymuh

wheel het wiel veel
wheelchair de rolstoel rolstool
when? wanneer? vannayr

when we get back wanneer we terugkomen vuh ter00KH-kohmuh

when's the train/ferry? hoe laat gaat de trein/boot? hoo laht KHaht duh trīn/boht

where? waar? vahr

I don't know where it is ik weet niet waar het is vayt neet

where is the cathedral? waar is de kathedraal? kataydrahl

it's over there (die staat) daar (dee staht) dahr

could you show me where it is on the map? kunt u het me op de kaart aanwijzen? koont 00 uht muh op duh kahrt ahnvizuh

it's just here het is hier heer
see **way**

which: which bus? welke bus? velkuh b00s

which one? welke?
that one die dee
this one? deze? dayzuh
no, that one nee, die nay

while: while I'm here terwijl ik
hier ben tervil ik heer

whisky de whisky

white wit vit

white wine de witte wijn vittuh vīn

who? wie? vee

  who is it? wie is daar?
vee is dahr

  the man who... de man die...
dee

whole: the whole week
de hele week hayluh vayk

  the whole lot alles

whose: whose is this?
van wie is dit? vee

why? waarom? vahrom

  why not? waarom niet? neet

wide wijd vīt

wife: my wife mijn vrouw
muhn vrow

Wi-Fi de wifi wifee

will: will you do it for me?
wilt u dat voor mij doen?
vilt oo dat vohr muh doon

wind de wind vint

windmill de molen mohluh

window het raam rahm

  (of shop) de etalage aytalahJuh

  near the window bij het raam
bī uht

  in the window (of shop)
in de etalage duh

window seat de plaats bij het
raam plahts bī uht rahm

windscreen de voorruit vohr-rowt

windscreen wiper
de ruitenwisser rowtuhvisser

windsurfing windsurfen
vintsoorfuh

windy: it's so windy het is zo
winderig vinderikH

wine de wijn vīn

  **can we have some more
wine?** kunnen we nog wat
wijn krijgen? koonnuh vuh nokH
vat vīn krīkHuh

wine list de wijnkaart vīnkahrt

winter de winter vinter

  in the winter 's winters
svinters

winter holiday de
wintervakantie vintervakansee

wire het ijzerdraad īzerdraht

  (electric) het snoer snoor

wish: best wishes de beste
wensen bestuh vensuh

with met

  I'm staying with... ik logeer
bij... lohJayr bī

without zonder

witness de getuige кHetowкHuh

  **will you be a witness for
me?** wilt u mijn getuige zijn?
vilt oo mīn кHetowкHuh zīn

woman de vrouw vrow

wonderful geweldig кHeveldikH

  (weather) prachtig praкHtikH

won't: it won't start het wil niet
starten vil neet

wood (material) het hout howt

woods (forest) de bossen bossuh

wool de wol vol

word het woord vohrt

work het werk vairk

it's not working het werkt niet vairkt neet

I work in… ik werk in…

world de wereld vayrelt

worry: I'm worried ik maak me zorgen mahk muh zorkhuh

worse: it's worse het is erger airkher

worst het ergste airkhstuh

worth: is it worth a visit? is het de moeite waard om het te bezoeken? duh moo-ee-tuh vahrt om uht tuh bezookuh

would: would you give this to…? zou u dit aan… kunnen geven? zow oo dit ahn… koonnuh khayvuh

wrap: could you wrap it up? kunt u het inpakken? koont oo

wrapping paper het inpakpapier inpakpapeer

wrist de pols

write schrijven skhrivuh

could you write it down? kunt u het opschrijven? koont oo uht opskhrivuh

how do you write it? hoe schrijf je het? hoo skhrif yuh

writing paper het schrijfpapier skhrifpapeer

wrong: it's the wrong key het is niet de goede sleutel neet duh khooduh slurtel

this is the wrong train dit is de verkeerde trein duh verkayrduh trin

the bill's wrong de rekening klopt niet raykening klopt neet

sorry, wrong number sorry, ik ben verkeerd verbonden verkayrt verbonduh

sorry, wrong room sorry, verkeerde kamer verkayrduh kahmer

there's something wrong with… er is iets mis met… eets

what's wrong? wat is er? vat

X

X-ray de röntgenfoto roontkhuhfoto

Y

yacht het jacht yakht

yard de tuin town

year het jaar yahr

yellow geel khayl

yes ja ya

yesterday gisteren khisteruh

yesterday morning gistermorgen khistermorkhuh

the day before yesterday eergisteren ayrkhisteruh

yet nog nokh

(in questions) al

is it here yet? is het er al?

no, not yet nee, nog niet nay nokh neet

you'll have to wait a little longer yet u zult nog even moeten wachten oo zoolt nokh ayvuh mootuh vakhtuh

yoghurt de yoghurt yo**KH**hoort

you (*pol*) u oo

  (*sing, fam*) je yuh

  (*pl, fam*) jullie yoollee

  this is for you (*pol/fam*)
dit is voor u/jou vohr oo/yow

  with you (*pol/fam*) met u/jou

young jong yong

your (*pol*) uw oo

  (*sing, fam*) jouw yow

  (*pl, fam*) jullie yoollee

yours (*pol*) van u oo

  (*sing, fam*) van jou yow

  (*pl, fam*) van jullie yoollee

youth hostel de jeugdherberg
yur**KH**t-hairber**KH**

> **Travel tip** If you're on a tight
> budget, a hostel should be
> your accommodation of
> choice. They can be extremely
> good value, and offer clean
> and comfortable dorm beds
> as well as a choice of rooms
> at rock-bottom prices. Both
> city and country hostels
> can get very full between
> June and September, so you
> should book in advance.

Z

zero nul nool

zip de ritssluiting ritssl**o**wting

  **could you put a new zip
on?** kunt u er een nieuwe
ritssluiting inzetten? koont oo er
uh n**ew**-uh ritssl**o**wting

zip code de postcode
p**o**sstkohduh

zoo de dierentuin d**ee**ruht**o**wn

zucchini de courgette

DUTCH
→ ENGLISH

Colloquialisms

The following are words you might well hear. You shouldn't be tempted to use any of the stronger ones unless you are sure of your audience.

boeien! booyuh who cares?

donder op! bugger off!

effe dimme cool it

flex cool

fout fOWt uncool

gaaf KHahf cool

geintje! KHĪntjuh just joking

godverdomme! KHOtverdommuh bloody hell!, fucking hell!

hufter! arsehole!

je bent gek! KHek you're mad!

klootzak! stupid prick! (only to males)

klote wijf! klohtuh vīf mean bitch!

krijg de tyfus! teefOOs sod you!

kroeg (de) krooKH pub, bar

kut met peren! bullshit!

kutwijf kOOtvīf cunt (only to females)

lieve hemel! leevuh haymel good heavens!

lul! arsehole!, dickhead!

luldebehanger! stupid bugger! (only to males)

neem je me in de zeik? naym yuh muh in duh zīk are you having me on?

oprotten! get lost!

plee (de) play loo, john

rot op! get lost!

rotzak! bastard!

smeris smayris cop, pig

sodemieter op! sohduhmeeter fuck off!

tof great

trut! trOOt stupid bitch!

verdomme! ferdommuh damn!, shit!

verrek! damn!; sod you!

vet vayt cool

A

aan ahn to; on

aan zee by the sea

aan de kassa betalen pay at the cashdesk

aan/uit-schakelaar (de) ahn/owt-sкнahkelahr on/off switch

aanbellen to ring

aanbetaling (de) ahnbetaling deposit

aanbieding offer

aandoen ahndoon to turn on; to put on

aangebrand ahnкнebrant burnt

aangenaam ahnкнenahm enjoyable, pleasant; pleased to meet you

aangenaam kennis te maken tuh mahkuh pleased to meet you, how do you do?

aangenaam, hoe maakt u het? hoo mahkt oo how do you do?

aangetekende post (de) ahnкнetaykenduh posst registered mail

aanhangwagen (de) ahnhang-vahкнuh trailer (for carrying tent etc)

aankleden: zich aankleden ziкн ahnklayduh to get dressed

aankomen ahnkohmuh to arrive

aankomst (de) ahnkomst arrival

aankomsthal (de) arrivals hall

aankoop (de) purchase

aanlegsteiger (de) ahnleкнstiкнer jetty

aanmeldingspunt (het) check-in

aanpassen ahnpassuh to try on; to adapt

aanrijden ahnriduh to hit, to collide with

aanrijding (de) collision

aansluitende vlucht (de) ahnslowtenduh vlooкнt connecting flight

aansluiting (de) ahnslowting connection

aansprakelijkheidsverzekering (de) ahnspraнkelik-hïtsverzaykering personal liability insurance

aanstaande ahnstahnduh next

aansteker (de) ahnstayker cigarette lighter

aantal (het) ahntal number, amount

aantekenen: een brief laten aantekenen ahntaykenuh to register a letter

aantrekkelijk ahntrekkelik attractive

aanval (de) ahnval fit, attack

aanzetten ahnzettuh to switch on

aardewerk (het) ahrdevairk crockery; pottery; earthenware

aardig ahrdiкн nice

ik vind je aardig yuh ahrdiкн I like you

abdij (de) abdï abbey

abonnementen season tickets

accepteren aksept**ay**ruh
  to accept, to take

accu (de) akk**oo** battery (for car)

accukabels (de) akk**oo**kahbels
  jump leads

achter a**кн**ter behind; at the back

  achter mij mī behind me

achterkant (de) a**кн**terkant back
  (part)

  aan de achterkant
  at the back

achterlaten a**кн**terlahtuh to leave,
  to leave behind

achterlichten (de) a**кн**ter-li**кн**tuh
  rear lights

achternaam (de) a**кн**ternahm
  surname, family name

achteruitkijkspiegel (de)
  a**кн**ter**owt**kik-spee**кн**el rearview
  mirror

achteruitversnelling (de)
  a**кн**ter**owt**-versnelling
  reverse gear

adres (het) address

adresboek (het) adr**e**sboohk
  address book

advocaat/advocate (de)
  atvoh**kaht**/atvohka**h**tuh lawyer
  (*male/female*)

afdeling (de) a**f**dayling
  department; ward (in hospital)

afgelopen af**кн**elopuh to end

afgelopen vrijdag af**кн**elopuh
  last Friday

afgeprijsd reduced

afgesproken af**кн**esprohkuh
  agreed

afgezien van a**f**кн**e**zeen van
  apart from

afgezonderd af**кн**ezondert
  secluded

afhalen a**f**hahluh to pick up

aflopen a**f**lohpuh to finish

afrekenen a**f**raykenuh to pay

afschuwelijk afs**кн**oo-uhlik awful,
  dreadful

afslag (de) a**f**sla**кн** exit

afspraak (de) a**f**sprahk
  appointment; date

afspreken a**f**spraykuh to meet

afstand (de) a**f**stant distance

  afstand houden keep your
  distance

afval (het) a**f**-val rubbish, trash

afvalbak (de) bin

afvalzakken (de) bin liners

afvoerbuis (de) a**f**voorb**ow**s
  drain (in sink)

afvoerkanaal (het) a**f**voorkanahl
  drain (in road)

afwas: de afwas doen a**f**vas
  doon to do the washing-up

afwasmiddel (het) a**f**vasmiddel
  washing-up liquid

afzender (de) sender

afzonderlijk a**f**zonderlik
  separately

agenda (de) a**кн**enda diary

akelig ah**к**elik**кн** nasty

aktentas (de) a**к**tuhtas briefcase

al already; yet

algemeen al**кн**emayn general;
  generally

Algemene Nederlandse Wielrijders Bond Dutch motoring organization

alle alluh all

alle richtingen all directions

alleen allayn alone, by oneself; just, only

alleen op dokter's voorschrift only on prescription

alleen volgens voorschrift take only as prescribed

alleen voor uitwendig gebruik for external use only

allemaal allemahl all of them

allergisch allairкHees allergic

alles all of it; everything

   dat is alles that's all

alles inbegrepen everything included

allesreiniger all-purpose cleaner

als if

alsjeblieft als-yebleeft here you are

alstublieft alstoobleeft please; here you are

altijd altīt always

aluminiumfolie (het) aloomnium-**fohlee** tinfoil

amandelontsteking (de) ahmandel-ontstayking tonsillitis

ambassade (de) ambassahduh embassy

Amerikaans amayrikahns American

ander, andere anderuh different; other; others

   een ander another

andere richtingen other directions

anders different; otherwise

anjer (de) anyer carnation

annuleren annoolayruh to cancel

antiekwinkel (de) anteekvinkel, **antiquair** (de) antikair antique shop

antiseptisch antiseptees antiseptic

antivriesmiddel (het) antivreesmiddel antifreeze

ANWB Dutch motoring organization

apart distinctive; separate

apart wassen wash separately

aparte bedden separate beds

apenstaartje (het) ahpuh-stahrt-yuh @, at sign

apotheek (de) apotayk pharmacy, chemist's

arm (de) arm; poor

armband (de) armbant bracelet

artikelen goods

artikelen worden niet geruild zonder kassabon goods are not exchanged without a receipt

arts (de) doctor

a.s. next

as (de) axle

asbak (de) ashtray

aspirine (de) aspirinuh aspirin

atletiek atleteek athletics

attentie attention

a.u.b. please

augustus OWKHOOstOOs August

Australië owstrah**li**-uh Australia

Australisch owstrah**lis** Australian

auto (de) ow**to** car

autobanden car tyres

automaat (de) owto**maht** slot
machine; vending machine;
automatic (car)

automatiek fast-food counter

automatisch owto**mah**tees
automatic

automatische slagboom
automatic barrier

auto-onderdelen spare parts

autopech (de) ow**to**peкн
breakdown

autosnelweg (de) ow**tos**nelveкн
motorway, highway

autoveerboot (de) ow**to**vayrboht
car ferry

autoverhuur (de) ow**to**verhoor
car rental

autowasserette (de)
ow**to**vasserettuh carwash

avond (de) ah**vont** evening

's avonds sah**vonts** in the
evening

acht uur 's avonds 8pm

avondmaal (het) ah**vont**mahl
supper

avondmaaltijd (de) ah**vont**mahltīt
evening meal

B

baai (de) bī bay

baan (de) bahn job

baard (de) bahrt beard

babysit (de) baby-sitter

babyvoedsel baby**voot**sel
baby food

bad (het) bat bath

badhanddoek (de) bat**hand**ook
bath towel

badkamer (de) bat**kah**mer
bathroom

badkuip (de) bat**kow**p bathtub

badplaats (de) bat**plahts**
seaside resort

bagage (de) baкн**ah**Juh
luggage, baggage

bagage controle baggage check

bagage-afhaalpunt (het)
baкн**ah**Juh-afhahlp00nt, **bagage-
afhaalruimte** (de) baкн**ah**Juh-
afhahlr0wmtuh baggage claim

bagagedepot (het) baкн**ah**Juh-
depoh left luggage (office),
baggage checkroom

bagagekluis (de) baкн**ah**Juh-
kl0ws luggage locker

bagagekluizen luggage lockers

bagagewagentje (het)
baкн**ah**Juh-vaкнent-yuh
luggage trolley, cart

bakken to fry

bakkerij (de) bakker**ī** bakery

bal (de) ball

balkon (het) balcony; circle

balpen (de) ballpoint pen

band (de) bent band (musical);
tyre **bant**

banddruk (de) bant-dr00k
tyre pressure

bandje (het) bant-yuh strap

bank (de) bank; couch, sofa

> Travel tip Banks usually offer the best deals on changing money. Banking hours are Monday to Friday 9am to 4pm, with a few big-city banks also open on Thursday evenings until 9pm or on Saturday mornings.

bankbiljet (het) bankbil-yet banknote, (US) bill

banketbakkerij (de) banket-bakkerī cake shop

bankrekening (de) bank-raykening bank account

basiscrème (de) basiskrem foundation

basistarief (het) bahsis-tahreef basic tariff

batterij (de) batterī battery

beambte (de) be-amptuh official

bedankt thanks

beddegoed bedding

bediening service

bediening niet inbegrepen service not included

bedieningsgeld (het) bedeenings-KHelt service charge

bedoelen bedooluh to mean
  wat bedoelt u? vat bedoolt oo what do you mean?

bedrag (het) bedraKH amount (money)

bedrijf (het) bedrīf company, business

bedrijfsleider (de) bedrīfs-līder manager

bedroefd bedrooft sad

been (het) bayn leg

beet (de) bayt bite

beetje: een klein beetje uhn klīn bayt-yuh a little (bit)

begane grond (de) beKHahnuh KHront ground floor, (US) first floor

begijnhof homes for lay sisters

begin (het) beKHin start, beginning
  in het begin beKHin at the beginning

beginneling (de) beKHinneling beginner

beginnen beKHinnuh to begin

begraafplaats (de) beKHrahfplahts cemetery

begrafenis (de) beKHrahfenis funeral

begrijpen beKHrīpuh to understand
  ik begrijp het niet neet I don't understand

behalve behalvuh except

behandeling (de) behandeling treatment

behulpzaam behoolp-zahm helpful

beide bīduh both
  een van beide(n) ayn van either of them

geen van beiden KHayn van bīduh neither (one) of them

bejaarde (de) beyahrduh senior citizen

beker (de) bayker mug

bekeuring (de) bekuring fine

bel… ring …

ik bel je (wel)
I'll give you a ring

belachelijk belakHelik ridiculous

belangrijk belangrīk important

**belasting toegevoegde
waarde** value-added tax

belastingvrij belastingvrī
duty free

belastingvrije winkel
duty-free shop

beledigend belaydiKHent
offensive

beleefd belayft polite

België belkHee-uh Belgium

Belgisch belkHees Belgian

bellen to ring, to call

beloof: ik beloof het belohf uht
I promise

beloven belohvuh to promise

ben: ik ben I am

ben zo terug back in a minute

beneden benayduh downstairs;
at the bottom

bent: jij bent yī you are (*sing, fam*)

u bent ∞ you are (*pol*)

benzine (de) benzeenuh
petrol, gas

benzineblik (het) benzeenuh-blik
petrol can

benzinepomp (de) petrol pump,
gas pump

benzinestation (het) benzeenuh-
stashon petrol station, gas
station

beroemd beroomt famous

beroepsschool (de)
beroops-skHohl college

beschadigd beskHahdiKHt
damaged

beschadigen beskHahdiKHuh
to damage

beschermingsfactor (de)
beskHairmings-faktor
protection factor

beschikbaar available

beslissen to decide

beslissing (de) decision

beslist definitely

beslist niet neet definitely not

besmettelijk besmettelik
infectious

bespreken bespraykuh to book;
to discuss

best best

bestand (het) bestant file; stock

beste wensen (de) bestuh vensuh
best wishes

bestek (het) bestek cutlery

besteldienst (de) bestel-deenst
delivery service

bestelformulier (het)
bestel-formooleer order form

bestellen bestelluh to order

bestelling (de) delivery; order

bestelwagen (de) bestel-vahkHuh
delivery van

bestemming (de) destination

bestuurder (de) bestoorder driver

betaalpas (de) betahlpas cheque
card, check card

betalen beta**h**luh to pay

wie betaalt er? vee who's
paying?

beter ba**y**ter better

beurs (de) burs trade fair

bevatten beva**t**tuh to include;
to contain

bevelen beva**y**luh to recommend

bevestigen beve**s**tik**H**uh to confirm

bevroren bev**ro**hruh frozen

bewaakte fietsenstalling
supervised bicycle park/sheds

bewegen ba**v**ay**KH**uh to move

bewolkt bev**o**lkt cloudy

bewusteloos bev**oo**stelohs
unconscious

bezet engaged, occupied

is deze plaats bezet?
da**y**zuh is this seat taken?

bezichtigen bezi**KH**tik**H**uh
to see, to visit

bezienswaardigheden (de)
bezeens-va**h**rdik**H**-hayduh sights

bezoeken bez**oo**kuh to visit

bezorgen bez**o**rk**H**uh to deliver

b.g.g. if there is no answer

b.h. (de) bay-h**a** bra

bibliotheek (de) bibliota**y**k library

bij b**ī** at

bij Jan b**ī** at Jan's

bijbetaling (de) b**ī**betahling
supplement

bijna b**ī**na almost, nearly

bijvoorbeeld b**ī**v**oh**rbaylt
for example

binnen indoors, inside

binnen een uur weer
aanwezig back within an
hour

binnenbad (het) b**i**nnuhbat
indoor pool

binnenband (de) b**i**nnuhbant
inner tube

binnengaan to enter

binnenkomen to come in

binnenlands national, inland,
domestic

binnenlands tarief inland
postage rate

binnenlandse vlucht (de)
b**i**nnuhlantsuh vl**oo**K**H**t
domestic flight

bioscoop (de) biosk**oh**p cinema

bips (de) bottom (of person)

blaar (de) bla**h**r blister

blad (het) blat leaf

bladzijde (de) bla**t**ziduh page

blauw bl**ow** blue

blauwe plek (de) bl**ow**uh bruise

blauwe zone: parkeren alleen
met parkeerschijf blue zone:
parking only with parking disk

bleek blayk pale

bleekmiddel (het) bla**y**kmiddel
bleach

blij bl**ī** glad

blijven bl**ī**vuh to stay

blik (het) can, tin

blikje bier (het) bl**i**kyuh beer
can of beer

blikopener (de) can-opener,
tin-opener

bliksem (de) lightning

blindedarmontsteking (de) blinduh-darm-ontstayking appendicitis

bloed (het) bloot blood

bloem (de) bloom flower

bloembol (de) bloombol bulb (flower)

bloemist (de) bloomist florist

bloemwinkel (de) bloomvinkel flower shop

bloes (de) bloos blouse

blusapparaat (het) bloosapparaht fire extinguisher

bocht (de) boкнt bend, turning (in road)

boek (het) book book

boeken en tijdschriften books and magazines

boekwinkel (de) bookvinkel bookshop, bookstore

boerderij (de) boorderī farm

bof (de) mumps

bollenvelden (de) bolluhvelduh bulb fields

bont furs

boodschap (de) bohtsкнap message

boom (de) bohm tree

boord (het) bohrt collar (on shirt)

boos bohs angry

boot (de) boht boat

bootdienst ferry service

boottocht (de) bohttokнt boat trip

bootverhuur boat hire

bord (het) bort plate; sign

borgsom (de) borкнsom deposit

borrel (de) drink (alcoholic)

borst (de) breast; chest

borstbeeld (het) borstbaylt bust

borstel (de) brush

borstkas (de) borstkas chest

bos (het) forest

bossen (de) woods

bot (het) bone

botsing (de) crash

bougie (de) boo*Jee* spark plug

boulevard (de) boolev*art* seafront

boven boh*vuh* at the top; above;
    upstairs

bovenaan bohven*ahn* at the top

bovenop... bohven*op* on top of...

bovenste verdieping (de)
    bovenstuh verd*ee*ping top floor

brand (de) br*ant* fire

brandalarm (het) br*a*ntalarm
    fire alarm

brandblusapparaat (het)
    brantbl*oo*s-appahr*aht*
    fire extinguisher

brandgevaar fire risk

brandtrap (de) br*a*nt-trap
    fire escape

branduren... will burn for...

brandweer (de) br*a*ntvayr
    fire brigade

brandweerkazerne fire station

brandwond (de) br*a*ntvont burn

breken br*ay*kuh to break

brengen to bring; to take

breuk (de) br*u*rk fracture

brief (de) br*ee*f letter

briefje (het) br*ee*f-yuh note,
    (US) bill

briefkaart (de) br*ee*fkahrt
    postcard

bries (de) br*ee*s breeze

brievenbus (de) br*ee*vuhb*oo*s
    letterbox, mailbox

bril (de) glasses, eyeglasses

Brits British

broche (de) br*o*KHuh brooch

broek (de) br*oo*k trousers, pants

broer (de) br*oo*r brother

bromfiets (de) br*o*mfeets moped

brood en banket
    bread and pastries

brug (de) br*oo*KH bridge

bruin br*o*wn brown

bruine café (het) older style
    pub/café

bruine kleur (de) br*o*wnuh klur tan

bruingebrand br*o*wn-KHebrant
    suntanned

bruisend br*o*wsent fizzy

BTW VAT

buigtang (de) b*o*wKHtang pliers

buik (de) b*o*wk stomach

buiten b*o*wtuh outdoors, outside

buiten gebruik out of order

**buiten het bereik van kinderen
    houden/bewaren** keep out of
    the reach of children

buitenbad open-air swimming
    pool

buitenland (het) b*o*wtuhlant abroad
    in het buitenland abroad

buitenlander (de) b*o*wtuhlander
    foreigner

buitenlands b*o*wtuhlants foreign

buitenlands geld (het) KHelt
    foreign currency

buitenlucht: in de buitenlucht
    duh b*o*wtuhl*oo*KHt in the open air

buitensport (de) b*o*wtensport
    outdoor sports, field sports

buitentemperatuur (de)
bOWtuh-temperahtOOr
outside temperature

buitenwijk (de) bOWtuhvik suburb

bumper (de) bOOmper
bumper, fender

bureau voor gevonden
voorwerpen (het) bOOroh vohr
KHevOnduh vOhrvairpuh lost
property office, lost and found

bus (de) bOOs bus

bus naar het vliegveld (de)
airport bus

busdienst (de) bOOsdeenst
bus service

busdienst van NS bus service
run by Dutch Railways

bushalte (de) bOOs-haltuh bus stop

buskaart (de) bOOs-kahrt bus ticket

busstation (het) bOOs-stashon
bus station

bustocht (de) bOOstoKHt
coach trip

buurt (de) bOOrt neighbourhood
  in de buurt van in duh bOOrt
  van near

buurtcafe (het) bOOrtkafay
local pub/bar

BV Ltd, Inc

b.v. for example

C

cadeau (het) kahdOh gift

cadeauwinkel (de) kahdOh-vinkel
gift shop

café (het) kahfay café; pub

café-restaurant (het) restaurant,
café without a licence

cafetaria, cafeteria (het)
snack bar

camping (de) campsite

Canadees kanadays Canadian

caravan (de) caravan, trailer

cassettebandje (het)
kassettuh-bant-yuh cassette, tape

centraal sentrahl central

centrale verwarming (de)
sentrahluh vervarming
central heating

centrum (het) sentrOOm centre

check-in-balie (de)
check-in-balee check-in

chef (de) manager (restaurant)

chemisch reinigen dry-clean

chequeboek (het) shekbook
cheque book, check book

chic posh; upmarket

chips (de) ships crisps,
potato chips

chocola(de) (de) shokolah(duh)
chocolate

chocolaterie (de)
chocolate shop

chrysant (de) KHrisant
chrysanthemum

cijfer (het) sifer figure, number

coffeeshop (de) café (often selling
soft drugs)

collect gesprek (het) KHesprek
reverse charge call, collect call

conferentie (de) konferensee
conference

conferentiezaal conference room

conserveringsmiddel preservative

constipatie (de) konstip**ah**tsee constipation

consulaat (het) kons**oo**l**aht** consulate

contact opnemen kontakt **o**pnaymuh to contact

contactpunten (de) kontakt-p**oo**ntuh points (in car)

contant geld (het) к**н**elt cash

controle (de) kontr**o**luh check, inspection

controleren kontroh**lay**ruh to check

controleur (de) kontr**oh**l**u**r inspector

cosmetica (de) kosm**ay**tika cosmetics

couchette (de) bunk; sleeper

coupe (de) k**oo**p haircut

coupé (de) k**oo**p**ay** compartment

couvert cover charge

crème (de) krem cream, lotion

crèmespoeling (de) kr**e**m-sp**oo**ling conditioner

C.S. Central Station

CV Limited Partnership

c.v. central heating; co-op

D

daar dahr there; down there; over there

daar spreekt u mee speaking

daarboven dahrb**oh**vuh up there

daarginds dahrк**н**ins over there

dag (de) daк**н** day; hello

de dag ervoor erv**oh**r the day before

dagboek (het) daк**н**book diary

dagelijks dah**к**н**e**liks daily

dagexcursie (de) daк**н**-exk**oo**rsee day trip

dagkaart (de) daк**н**-kahrt ticket giving unrestricted bus, tram or metro travel within a zone for one day

dagretourtje (het) daк**н**-ret**oo**r-tyuh day-return ticket, round-trip ticket

dak (het) roof

dal (het) valley

dalurenkaart (de) dal**oo**ruhkahrt season ticket for off-peak travel

dame (de) dah**muh** lady

dames (de) dah**mes** ladies, ladies' restroom

damesconfektie (de) dah**mes-konfeksee ladies' wear

dameskapper (de) dah**meskapper ladies' hairdresser

dameskapsalon (de) dah**meskapsalon** ladies' hairdresser's

dameskleding (de) dah**mes-klayding ladies' wear

damesslipje (het) dah**muhs-slip-yuh panties

damestoilet (het) dah**mes-twa-let ladies' room

dan than; then

dankbaar dankbahr grateful

danken da*nk*uh to thank

dank je, dankjewel yuh vel
thank you

dank u, dank u wel ∞ thank you
  nee, dank u/je nay no, thanks

dans (de) dance

dansen to dance

dat that
  dat is... that's...
  is dat...? is that...?
  dat is zo that's true
  dat kan OK, no problem
  dat klopt that's right

datum (de) da*h*toom date

de duh the

de heer duh ha*y*r Mr

deel (het) da*y*l part

Deens da*y*ns Danish

defect duh*f*ekt faulty;
  out of order

dekbed (het) dekbet duvet

deken (de) da*y*kuh blanket

deksel (het) lid

dekstoel (de) dekstool deckchair

delen da*y*luh to share

deltavliegen (het) delta-vleeK*H*uh
  hang-gliding

Den Haag hah*KH* the Hague

Denemarken da*y*nemarkuh
  Denmark

denk aan uw lichten
  remember your lights

denken to think
  ik denk van niet neet
  I don't think so

ik denk van wel van vel
  I think so

deur (de) dur door

deur sluiten alstublieft please
  close the door

deuren sluiten doors close,
  last admission

deze da*y*zuh this; this one; these;
  these ones

Dhr duh ha*y*r Mr

dia (de) dee-a slide, transparency

diamant (de) diamond

diapositieven (de) dee-ah-
  posit*ee*vuh slides, transparencies

diarree (de) dee-arr*ay* diarrhoea

dicht shut

dichtbij diK*H*tb*ī* near; nearby

die dee that; those; that one

dieet (het) dia*y*t diet

dief (de) deef thief

dienblad (het) dee*n*blat tray

dienst inbegrepen
  service included

dienstdoend apotheker
  duty chemist

dienstdoend doktor
  doctor on call

diensten openbaar vervoer
  public transport services

dienstregeling (de) dee*n*strayK*H*eling timetable, schedule

diep deep deep

diepvries (de) deep-vrees freezer

diepvrieseten (het) deep-vrees-
  a*y*tuh frozen food

dier (het) deer animal

dierentuin (de) deeruh-town zoo

dij (de) dī thigh

dijk (de) dīk dyke

dik fat; thick

dimlichten dipped headlights, dimmed headlights

dim uw lichten dip your lights, dim your lights

diner (het) dinay dinner

dineren dinayruh to have dinner

ding (het) thing

dinsdag dinsdaKH Tuesday

directeur (de) deerektur director, president

dit this

  dit is... this is…

  is dit...? is this…?

  dit is voor u/jou vohr oo/yow this is for you

diverse smaken various flavours

dochter (de) doKHter daughter

doden dohduh to kill

doe-het-zelf-winkel (de) DIY shop

doek (de) dook cloth

doen doon to do

  wat is er te doen? tuh doon what's happening?, what's on?

dokter (de) doctor

dom thick, stupid

domkerk (de) cathedral

donderdag donderdaKH Thursday

donker dark

donkerblauw donkerblow dark blue

dood doht dead

doodlopende weg dead-end

doodop dohtop shattered, dead tired

doof dohf deaf

dooi (de) thaw

door dohr through; by

doorgaande trein through train

doorgang passage

doorsturen dohrstooruh to forward

doos (de) dohs box

dop (de) cap (of bottle)

dorp (het) village

dorst: ik heb dorst hep I'm thirsty

dosering voor kinderen dosage for children

dosering voor volwassenen dosage for adults

douane (de) duhwanuh Customs

douche (de) doosh shower

douchegel (de) doosh-Jel shower gel

downloaden download-uh to download

dozijn (het) dozīn dozen

draad (de) draht thread

draaien drah-yuh to dial

dragen drahKHuh to carry

drank (de) drink

  aan de drank zijn to be having a drink

drankje (het) drank-yuh drink (alcoholic); medicine

dringend dr**i**ngent urgent

drinken to drink

wil je iets drinken? vil yuh
can I get you a drink?

drinkglas (het) glass (for drinking)

drinkwater dr**i**nkvater
drinking water

drogisterij (de) droh-KH**i**ster**ī**
non-dispensing pharmacy

dronken drunk

dronken achter het stuur
a**KH**ter uht st**oo**r drunk driving

droog droh**KH** dry

droog föhnen f**oo**nuh to blow-dry

drooglijn (de) droh**KH**-l**ī**n
clothes line

droogtrommel (de) droh**KH**-
trommel spin-dryer

droom (de) drohm dream

druk dr**oo**k busy; crowded; lively

drukwerk dr**oo**kvairk
printed matter

D-trein (international) through
train with supplement

dubbel d**oo**bbel double

dubbeltje (het) d**oo**bbel-tyuh
10-cent coin

duidelijk d**o**wdelik clear, obvious

duikbril (de) d**o**wkbril goggles

duiken d**o**wkuh to dive; diving

duikplank (de) d**o**wk-plank
diving board

duim (de) d**o**wm inch; thumb

Duits d**o**wts German

Duitsland d**o**wtslant Germany

duizelig d**o**wzelik dizzy

dun d**oo**n thin

duur d**oo**r expensive

duwen d**oo**wuh to push

dwaas dvahs silly

d.w.z. i.e.

E

echt e**KH**t real, genuine; really

echtgenoot (de) e**KH**t-**KH**enoht
husband

echtpaar (het) e**KH**tpahr (married)
couple

echtwaar? e**KH**tvahr really?

een uhn a, an; ayn one

eenpersoonsbed (het)
aynpersohns-bet single bed

eenpersoonskamer (de)
aynpersohns-k**ah**mer
single room

eenrichtingverkeer
one-way traffic

eenvoudig aynv**o**wdi**KH**
plain; simple

eergisteren ayr**KH**isteruh
the day before yesterday

eerlijk **ay**rlik honest; fair

eerst ayrst first; at first

eerst kloppen alstubieft
please knock before entering

eerste hulp (bij ongelukken)
(de) **ay**rstuh h**oo**lp (b**ī**
on**KH**el**oo**kkuh) first aid

eerste hulpafdeling (de)
ayrstuh h**oo**lpafdayling
casualty department

eerste klas ayrstuh first-class

eerste straat links (de) straht first on the left

eerste straat rechts first on the right

eerste verdieping (de) ayrstuh verdeeping first floor, (US) second floor

eetcafé (het) aytkafay café-restaurant

eethuis (het) aythOws restaurant

Travel tip Restaurants tend to open in the evening only, usually from around 6pm, and the Dutch eat early, so you'll find many restaurant kitchens closed after 10pm. However, the majority of bars and cafés serve both lunch and evenings meals and are open until 1am during the week and 2am at weekends.

eetkamer (de) aytkahmer dining room

eet smakelijk! enjoy your meal!

eetzaal (de) aytzahl dining room

effen plain

EHBO first aid

eigenaar/eigenaresse (de) īKHenahr/īKHenaressuh owner (*male/female*)

eigen badkamer īKHuh batkahmer private bathroom

eind: aan het eind van... īnt at the bottom of... (**road**)

einde (het) īnduh end

einde autosnelweg end of motorway

einde bebouwde kom end of built-up area

einde parkeerverbod met verplicht gebruik van een parkeerschijf end of parking restriction and obligatory use of parking disk

eindje: een eindje uhn īnt-yuh a short distance

eindstation (het) īnt-stashon terminus

elastiekje (het) elasteek-yuh rubber band

elastisch aylastees elastic

elektricien (de) aylektrisyuh electrician

elektriciteit (de) aylektrisitīt electricity

elektriciteitsstoring (de) aylektrisitīts-stohring power cut

elektrisch aylektrees electric

elektrische apparaten (de) aylektrishuh electrical appliances

elektrische kachel (de) kaKHel electric fire

elk, elke elkuh each

elleboog (de) ellebohKH elbow

e-mailen email-uh to e-mail

emmer (de) bucket

en and

Engels English

in het Engels in English

enkel (de) ankle

enkele reis (de) enkeluh rïs single journey/ticket, one-way trip/ticket

enkeltje (het) enkel-tyuh single ticket, one-way ticket

entree entry

entreeprijs antrayprïs admission price

er: hij is er nog he is still here/there

er is... there is...

er is geen... meer mayr there's no... left

er zijn... zïn there are...

er kan nog een trein komen there may be a train after this one

erg airKH very

ergens airKHens somewhere

ergens anders airKHens somewhere else

erger: het is erger airKHer it's worse

ergste (het) airKHstuh worst

ernstig airnstiKH serious; nasty

ervaren airvahruh experienced

essentieel essenshayl essential

etage (de) aytahjuh floor

etalage (de) aytalahJuh shop window

eten (het) aytuh to eat; food

etenswaren (de) aytensvahruh food

etiket (het) label

EuroCity international fast train, may be boarded for local journeys

EuroNight night train with sleeping compartments

Europa urrohpa Europe

Europees urropays European

Europese kwaliteitsnachttrein European luxury night train

Europese kwaliteitstrein European luxury train

Evangelische Kerk Evangelical Church

even ayvuh just, for a moment

even weg gone for a minute

expres trein met toeslag express train with supplement

exprespost express mail

expresse expressuh express (mail)

per expresse sturen send by special delivery

expressepost van stukken tot en met 250gr. express mail for articles up to and including 250 gr.

F

fa firm

fabricage manufacture

fabriek (de) fabreek factory

fabrikaat make

familiekaarten family tickets

familielid (het) fameeleelit relative

fantastisch fantastees fantastic

favoriet fahvoreet favourite

feest (het) fayst party (celebration)

feestdag (de) fayst-daKH public holiday

fel bright

fiets (de) feets bicycle

fietsen (het) feetsuh cycling;
to cycle

fietsen en/of bagage
bicycles and/or luggage

fietsenmaker (de) feetsuh-mahker
bicycle repairer

fietsenreparatie bicycle repairs

fietsenstalling bicycle shed

**fietsenstalling, verkoop,
verhuur en reparatie**
bicycle storage, sale, rental
and repairs

fietsen te huur bicycles to rent

fietsverhuur bicycles to rent

fietsenwinkel bicycle shop

fietser (de) feetser cyclist

fietskluizen feetsklowzuh
bicycle lockers

Travel tip Bike stealing is
a big problem: in the larger
cities in particular, but really
anywhere around the coun-
try, you should never, ever,
leave your bike unlocked,
even for a few minutes.
Almost all train stations
have somewhere you can
store your bike safely for
less than a euro.

fietspad cycle path

fietspomp (de) feetspomp
bicycle pump

file (de) feeluh traffic jam,
tailback

filevorming (de) feeluh-vorming
traffic buildup, congestion

filiaal (het) fili-**ahl** branch

firma (de) firm

flat (de) flet flat, apartment

**flat met eigen
kookgelegenheid** īкниh
kohk-кнelayкнenhīt self-catering
apartment

flatgebouw (het) fletкнebow
apartment block

flauwvallen flowvalluh to faint

fles (de) bottle

flitser (de) flitser flash

föhnen furnuh to blow-dry

fontein (de) fontīn fountain

fooi (de) foy tip (to waiter etc)

fopspeen (de) fopspayn dummy,
pacifier

formeel formayl formal

formulier (het) formooleer form
(document)

fornuis (het) fornows cooker

fotoalbum (het) foto-alboom
photo album

foto-artikelen camera shop

fotograaf photographer

fototoestel (het) fototoostel
camera

fotowinkel (de) fotovinkel
camera shop

fourniturenzaak haberdashery

fout (de) fowt error, mistake

Frankrijk frankrīk France

Frans French

fris fresh

fruitmand (de) frowtmant
fruit basket

fruitschaal (de) fr**ow**tsKHahl
fruit bowl

fruitwinkel (de) fr**ow**tvinkel
fruitshop

G

gaan KHahn go

gaan liggen KHahn li̅KHuh
to lie down

gaan zitten to sit down

gaar KHahr cooked

gang (de) KHang corridor

garantie (de) KHar**a**ntsee
guarantee

garderobe (de) KHarder**o**buh
cloakroom, checkroom

gasfles (de) KH**a**sfles gas cylinder

gaspedaal (het) KH**a**s-ped**ah**l
accelerator, gas pedal

gast (de) KH**a**st guest

gastvrijheid (de) KHastvri̅hi̅t
hospitality

gat (het) KH**a**t hole

gauw KH**OW** soon

ga weg! KH**a** veKH go away!

ga zitten! KH**a** sit down!

geadresseerde addressee

geb. born

gebeuren KHeb**u**ruh to happen

wat is er gebeurd?
what's happened?

gebied (het) KHeb**ee**t area

geboortedatum date of birth

geboorteplaats place of birth

geboren KHeb**o**ruh born

gebouw (het) KHeb**OW** building

gebroken KHebr**oh**kuh broken

gebruik use

gebruik van wagentje/mandje
verplicht use of trolley/basket
obligatory

gebruikelijk KHebr**ow**kelik usual

gebruiken KHebr**ow**kuh to use

gebruiksaanwijzing
instructions for use

geeft: het geeft niet KH**ay**ft neet
it doesn't matter

geeft niks never mind

geel KH**ay**l yellow

geen KH**ay**n no, not any, none

ik heb geen... hep
I don't have any...

ik wil geen... vil
I don't want any...

geen een ayn none, not any

geen antwoord no answer

geen dank don't mention it

geen doorgaande weg
no through road

geen drinkwater
not drinking water

geen fietsen tegen het raam
plaatsen a.u.b. please do
not lean bicycles against the
window

geen honden no dogs

geen lawaai na 10 uur
alstublieft no noise after 10
o'clock please

geen lifters no hitchhikers

geen maximum snelheid
no speed limit

geen toegang no entry

geen uitgang no exit

geen zelfbediening
no self-service

gefabriceerd in... made in...

gefeliciteerd! KHefaylisitayrt
congratulations!

gegarandeerd KHeKHahrandayrt
guaranteed

gehandicapt KHehendikept
disabled

geheugenstick (de) KHehur-KHuh-
stik memory stick

geïnterresseerd KHeh-interresayrt
interested

gek KHek mad, crazy

geld (het) KHelt money

geld in sleuf werpen
put money in the slot

geld inwerpen insert coins

geld terug money back;
returned coins

geldautomaat (de)
KHeltowtomaht cash dispenser,
ATM

> Travel tip The Netherlands is
> a cash society: as a general
> rule, people prefer to pay for
> most things with notes and
> coins. However, debit cards
> are becoming increasingly
> popular, and most shops and
> restaurants accept these as
> well as credit cards.

geldig KHeldiKH valid

  geldig van... tot...
  valid from... to...

geleden: een uur geleden
KHelayduh an hour ago

  een week geleden a week ago

gelegen KHelayKHuh convenient

geleidelijk KHelidelik gradually

gelijk KHelik right

  je had gelijk yuh hat
  you were right

geloven KHelohvuh to believe

geluk (het) KHelook luck

gelukkig KHelookkikH happy;
fortunately

Gelukkig Nieuwjaar!
Happy New Year!

gemakkelijk KHemakkelik easy

gemarkeerde wandeling
signposted walk

gemeenschappelijke douches
communal showers

gemeente municipal

gemeentehuis town hall,
municipal buildings

gemiddeld KHemiddelt medium;
on average

genezen KHenayzuh to cure

genoeg KHenooKH enough

geopend KHuh-ohpent open

gepast geld the right change;
exact fare

gepensioneerd KHepenshonayrt
retired

gepensioneerde (de)
KHepenshonayrduh pensioner

Gereformeerde Kerk
Calvinist Church

gereserveerd KHeraysairvayrt
reserved

gescheiden KHesKH**ī**duh divorced;
separated

gesloten KHesl**oh**tuh closed

gesloten voor alle verkeer
closed to all traffic

**gesmaakt: heeft het
gesmaakt?** hayft uht KHesm**ah**kt
did you enjoy your meal?

gesprek (het) KHespr**e**k call;
conversation

  in gesprek engaged, busy

**gesprekken via de PTT
telefoniste** operator-
connected calls

gesprongen KHespr**o**nguh burst

gestoken KHest**oh**kuh stung

getij (het) KHet**ī** tide

getrouwd KHetr**ow**t married

geval: in geval van nood
in case of emergency

gevaar danger

gevaarlijk KHev**ah**rlik
dangerous

gevaarlijke bocht
dangerous bend

gevaarlijke stoffen
dangerous substances

gevaarlijke stroming
dangerous current

gevaarlijke wegkruising
dangerous junction

gevecht (het) KHev**e**KHt fight

geven KH**ay**vuh to give

gevonden KHev**o**nduh found

gevonden voorwerpen
KHev**o**nduh v**oh**rvairpuh lost
property, lost and found

geweldig KHev**e**ldiKH great,
excellent; exciting

gewicht (het) KHev**i**KHt weight

gewond KHev**o**nt injured

gewoon KHev**oh**n ordinary

gewoonte (de) KHev**oh**ntuh custom

gezagvoerder (de) KHez**a**KH-
voorder captain

gezellig cosy; warm, friendly

gezelschap (het) кнеz**e**lsкнap
party, group; company

gezicht (het) кнezi**к**нt face

gezien: heeft u… gezien? hayft
∞… кнezee**uh** have you seen…?

gezin (het) кнezin family

gezond кнezont healthy

gezondheid кнezont-hit health

  gezondheid! bless you!

gids (de) кнits tour guide

giftig кнiftiкн poisonous

girostortingen
girobank deposits

gisteravond кнister-**a**hvont
last night

gisteren кнist**e**ruh yesterday

gistermorgen кнister-morкнuh
yesterday morning

glad кнlat slippery

glimlachen кнlimlaкнuh to smile

gloeilamp (de) кнl**oo**-ee-lamp
light bulb

godsdienst (de) кн**o**ts-deenst
religion

goed кнoot good; all right, OK;
properly

  dat is goed all right

  zo is het goed keep the
  change

  goed meneer кнoot menayr
  yes sir

  goed zo! good!; well done!

  Goede Vrijdag кн**oo**duh vr**i**daкн
  Good Friday

  goedemiddag кн**oo**yuh-middaкн
  good afternoon

goedemorgen кн**oo**yuh-morкнuh
good morning

goedenacht кн**oo**yuh-naкнt
good night

goedenavond кн**oo**yuh-**a**hvont
good evening

goedendag кн**oo**yuh-daкн hello

goedkoop кн**oo**tkohp cheap,
inexpensive

goeie reis! кн**oo**yuh ris
have a good journey!

golf (de) кн**o**lf wave

golfbaan (de) кн**o**lfbahn golf course

golfen (het) кн**o**lfuh golf

gooien кн**oh**yuh to throw

gootsteen (de) кн**oh**tstayn sink

gordel (de) кн**o**rdel safety belt

gordijnen (de) кнordinuh curtains

goud (het) кн**ow**t gold

gouden gids (de) кн**ow**duh кнits
yellow pages

graag: ik wil graag… vil кнrahкн
I'd like…; I want…

  ik zou graag… zow I'd like…

graag gedaan кнrahкн кнed**a**hn
my pleasure, you're welcome

gracht (de) кнraкнt canal

grap (de) кнrap joke

grappig кнr**a**ppiкн funny, amusing

grasveld (het) кнr**a**svelt lawn

gratis кнr**a**htis free

grens (de) кнrens border

grenswisselkantoor (het)
кнrensvissel-kantohr
bureau de change

Griekenland кнr**ee**kuhlant Greece

Grieks KHreeks Greek

griep (de) KHreep flu

grijs KHrīs grey

groen KHroon green

groenten (de) KHroontuh vegetables

groentewinkel (de) KHroontuhvinkel greengrocer

groep (de) KHroop group

groepsreizen group travel

grond (de) KHront ground

  op de grond duh on the floor; on the ground

groot KHroht big, large

Groot-Brittannië KHroht-brittanni-uh Great Britain

grootmoeder (de) KHrohtmooder grandmother

grootvader (de) KHrohtvahder grandfather

grot (de) KHrot cave

grote KHrohtuh big, large

grote kerk cathedral

grote maat maht large size

grote weg (de) veg main road

GSM (de) KHay-ess-em mobile phone

gulzig KHoolzIKH greedy

gummetje (het) KHoommet-yuh rubber, eraser

H

haar (het) hahr hair; her

  dat is van haar van that's hers

haarborstel (de) hahrborstel hairbrush

haardroger (de) hahr-drohKHer hairdryer

haardvuur (het) hahrtvoor open fire

haargel (de) hahr-gel hair gel

haarlak (de) hahrlak hair spray

haarspelden (de) hahrspelduh hairgrips, barrettes

haarstudio hairdressing salon

haast nooit hahst noyt hardly ever

  ik heb haast hep I'm in a hurry

haasten: (zich) haasten (ziKH) hahstuh to hurry

hak (de) heel (of shoe)

hakkenbar (de) heelbar

halen hahluh to get, to fetch

halfpension half-penshon half board

hal (de) hall

halsketting (de) necklace

halte (de) stop

halve prijs (de) prīs half fare; half-price

hand (de) hant hand

hand- manual

handbagage (de) hant-baKHahJuh hand luggage

handdoek (de) handook towel

handrem (de) hantrem handbrake

handschoenen (de) hant-sKHoonuh gloves

handtas (de) hant-tas handbag, (US) purse

handtekening (de) hant-taykening signature

handvat (het) hantvat handle

handwerkartikelen handicrafts

handwerkwinkel (de) hantvairkvinkel handicraft shop

hangt: het hangt af van de... van duh it depends on the...

dat hangt ervan af airvan it depends

haring (de) hahring tent peg; herring

hartelijk gefeliciteerd! hartelik кнefaylisitayrt happy birthday!

haten hahtuh to hate

haven (de) hahvuh docks, harbour, port

hebben to have

heeft u...? hayft oo do you have...?

heel hayl very; quite

heerlijk hayrlik delicious, excellent

heet hayt hot

het is heet 'tis it's hot

hij/zij heet... hī/zī he/she is called...

hoe heet het? hoo what's it called?

ik heet... my name's...

heidevelden heathland

hek (het) gate

helaas haylahs unfortunately

helder clear

hele dag (de) hayluh all day

de hele week hayluh vayk the whole week

helemaal haylemahl altogether, completely

helemaal niet neet not in the least

helpen to help

hem him

dat is van hem van that's his

hemd (het) hemt vest

hemel (de) haymel sky

hen them

hengel (de) fishing rod

heren gentlemen; gents, men's room

herenconfectie (de) hayruh-konfeksee menswear

herenkapper (de) hayruh-kapper barber, gents' hairdresser

herenkapsalon barber's, gents' hairdresser's

herenkleding (de) hayruh-klayding menswear

herentoilet (het) hayruh-twalet gents' toilet, men's room

herfst (de) autumn, fall

herhalen hairhahluh to repeat

herinneren hairinneruh to remember

herkennen hairkennuh to recognize

hertenkamp (het) deer park

Hervormde Kerk (de) Reformed Church

het it; the

het is... it is...

is het...? is it...?

hete haytuh hot

heup (de) hurp hip

heuvel (de) hurvel hill

hiel (de) heel heel **(of foot)**

hier heer here; over here

hier is/zijn... zîn
here is/are...

hier beneden heer ben**ay**duh
down here

hier afscheuren tear off here

hier indrukken press here

hier lege wagentjes s.v.p.
leave your trolley here please

hier openmaken open here

hier spreken speak here

hij hî he

historisch gebouw
historic building

hitte (de) h**i**ttuh heat

hoe hoo how

hoe gaat het ermee?
кнaht uht air**may** how are you?

hoe gaat het met u? hoo
кнaht uht met oo how are you?

hoe heet het? hoo hayt
what's it called?

hoe laat is het? hoo laht
what's the time?

hoe maakt u het? hoo mahkt
oo how are you?

hoed (de) hoot hat

hoek: in de hoek duh hook
in the corner

op de hoek on the corner

hoest (de) hoost cough

hoestdrankje (het) h**oo**stdrank-
yuh cough medicine

hoestpastilles (de)
cough drops

hoeveel? hoov**ay**l how many?;

how much?

hoeveelheid (de) hoov**ay**lhît
amount

hoewel hoov**e**l although

hof (het) court **(royal household)**

hofje (het) h**o**fyuh courtyard;
almshouses **(in a courtyard)**

hoge kwaliteit high quality

homo (de) gay man

homocafé (het) gay bar

> **Travel tip** The country's big-
> gest gay and lesbian scene
> is in Amsterdam, where
> attitudes are tolerant, bars
> plentiful and support groups
> unequalled. Although not
> as extensive, Rotterdam,
> The Hague, Nijmegen and
> Groningen also have a
> vibrant gay nightlife, though
> the lesbian scene is smaller
> and more subdued.

homofiel homof**ee**l gay

hond (de) hont dog

hoofd (het) hohft head

hoofd- hohft- main

hoofddoek (de) h**o**hft-dook
headscarf

hoofdkussen (het) h**o**hft-k**oo**ssuh
pillow

hoofdpijn (de) h**o**hftpîn
headache

hoofdpostkantoor (het) h**o**hft-
posstkantohr main post office

hoofdweg (de) h**o**hft-veкн
main road

hoog hohкн tall; high

hoogte (de) hoh**KH**tuh
height, altitude

hooikoorts (de) hoy**koh**rts hayfever

hoop: ik hoop het hohp I hope so

hoorn (de) hohrn receiver, handset

hopelijk hoh**pe**lik hopefully

hopen hoh**puh** to hope

horentje (het) hoh**ruh**-tyuh
ice cream cone

horloge (het) horl**oh.**Juh
wristwatch

horlogebandje (het) horl**oh.**Juh-
bant-yuh watchstrap

hotelkamer (de) hotel-ka**hmer**
hotel room

houd je van...? how(t) yuh van
do you like...?

houd je kop! howt yuh kop shut up!

houd op! how stop it!

houden how**duh** to keep

houden van how**duh** van
to like; to love

  ik houd van jou how van yow
  I love you

hout (het) howt wood

huiduitslag (de) how**towt**slakH
rash

huilen how**luh** to cry

huis (het) hows house; home

huisarts (de) ho**ws**-arts GP,
family doctor

huishoudelijke artikelen
household goods

hulp (de) h**oo**lp help

hun h**oo**n their

huren h**oo**ruh to rent, to hire

hut (de) h**oo**t berth; cabin (on ship)

huur (de) h**oo**r rent

huurauto (de) h**oo**r**ow**to rented car

huwelijksreis (de) h**oo**liks**rī**s
honeymoon

I

I Inter-City

idee (het) ee**day** idea

idioot (de) eedi-y**oh**t idiot

ieder ee**der** every; each

  ieder van hen each of them

iedere ee**deruh** every; each

iedereen eede**rayn** everyone

iemand ee**mant** anybody;
somebody, someone

Iers eers Irish

iets eets anything; something

  nog iets? no**KH** anything else?

iets anders eets something else

ietsje meer eets-yuh mayr a little
bit more

ijs (het) īs ice

ijsbaan (de) ī**sbahn** ice rink

ijsje (het) ī**s**-yuh ice cream

ijskast (de) ī**skast** fridge

  in de ijskast bewaren
  keep refrigerated

ijslollie (de) ī**slollee** ice lolly,
popsicle

ijssalon (de) ice cream parlour

ijzel black ice

ijzerhandel (de) ī**zerhandel**
hardware store

ijzerwarenwinkel (de)
īzervaruhvinkel hardware store

ik I

ik ook ohk me too

in in; into; on

inbegrepen included

inbraak (de) inbrahk burglary

inchecken inchekuh to check in

Indiaas indiahs Indian

Indisch indees Indonesian

Indonesië indonaysi-uh Indonesia

Indonesisch indonaysees
Indonesian

indrukwekkend indr00k-vekkent
impressive

infectie (de) infeksee infection

informatie (de) informahtsee
information

informatiebalie (de)
informahtsee-bahlee
information desk

informeel informayl informal

ingang (de) entrance

ingang aan de achterkant
entry at rear

ingang aan de voorkant
entry at front

ingang vrijhouden
entrance – keep clear

inhalen inhahluh to overtake

inhalen verboden
overtaking prohibited

inhoud contents

inlegzool (de) inleKH-zohl insole

inlichtingen (de) inliKHtinguh
information; directory enquiries

inlichtingen binnenland
binnuhlant directory enquiries,
local and national numbers

inlichtingen buitenland
bowtuhlant directory enquiries,
international numbers

innemen in-naymuh
to take; to swallow

**innemen op de nuchtere
maag** to be taken on an empty
stomach

inpakken to wrap (up)

zal ik het inpakken?
shall I wrap it?

inpakpapier (het) inpak-papeer
wrapping paper

inruilen inrowluh to exchange

inschepen to embark

insekt (het) insect

insektenbeet (de) insektuh-bayt
insect bite

insektenwerend middel (het)
insektuh-vairent insect
repellent

insluiten inslowtuh to enclose

instapkaart (de) instapkahrt
boarding pass

instappen to get in; to get on,
to board

**Intercitytreinen stoppen
alleen op de met...
aangegeven stations**
Intercity trains stop only at
stations marked with...

interessant interesting

interlokaal gesprek (het)
interlokahl KHesprek
long-distance call

internationaal internashonahl
international

internationaal gesprek (het)
KHesprek international call

internationale lijndiensten
international scheduled services

internationale sneltrein (de)
international express train

invoegen get in lane

invullen invoolluh to fill in

inweekmiddel prewash powder

inwerpen invairpuh to insert

is is

is er...? is there...?

Italiaans eetal-yahns Italian

Italië itahli-uh Italy

J

ja ya yes

ja, graag KHrahKH yes, please

jaar (het) yahr year

jacht (het) yaKHt yacht

jacht (de) hunt; hunting

jachthaven (de) yaKHt-hahvuh
marina

jack (het) yek jacket

jammer: het is jammer yammer
it's a pity

wat jammer! vat
what a shame!

jas (de) yas coat

jasje (het) yas-yuh jacket

jazeker yazayker sure

je yuh you

jeugdherberg (de) yurKHt-
hairberkH youth hostel

jeugdherbergbeheerder
youth hostel warden

j.h. youth hostel

jong yung young

jongen (de) yonguh boy

Joods yohts Jewish

jouw yow your

juffrouw (de) yooffrow Miss

juffrouw! waitress!

juist yowst right, correct

juli yooli July

jullie yoollee you; your

juni yooni June

jurk (de) yoork dress

juwelen (de) yoo-ayluh
jewellery

juwelier (de) yoo-uhleer jeweller;
jeweller's

K

kaak (de) kahk jaw

kaal kahl bald

kaars (de) kahrs candle

kaart (de) kahrt card; map

**kaarten met/zonder
enveloppe** cards with/without
envelope

kaartje (het) kahrt-yuh ticket

kaartjes tickets

kaartjesautomaat
ticket-machine

kaarttelefoon (de) kahrt-telefohn
cardphone

kaasschaaf (de) kahs-sкнahf
cheese slicer

kaaswinkel (de) kahs-vinkel
cheese shop

kachel (de) kaкнel heater

kade: op de kade duh kaduh
on the quayside

kadowinkel gift shop

kakkerlak (de) cockroach

kam (de) comb

kamer (de) kahmer room

kamer met bad en w.c.
room with bath and toilet

kamer met bad zonder w.c.
room with bath and no toilet

**kamer met twee
eenpersoonsbedden** (de) tvay
aynpersohns-bedduh twin room

kamerjas (de) kahmer-yas
dressing gown

kamermeisje (het) kahmer-
mīshuh maid

kamers (de) kahmers rooms;
accommodation

kamerservice (de) kahmer-
service room service

kamers vrij vacancies, rooms free

kampeerterrein (het) kampayr-
terrīn campsite

kamperen kampayruh to camp

kamperen verboden no
camping

kan (de) jug

kan ik...? can I...?

ik kan niet... neet I can't...

kanaal (het) kanahl canal (shipping)

kano (de) canoe

kanoën kahno-uhn to canoe

kant (de) side

kantoor (het) kantohr office

kantoorartikelen office supplies

kantoorboekhandel office
stationery shop

kapot kahpot broken

kapot gaan кнahn to break
down; to fall to pieces

kapper (de) hairdresser

kapsalon hairdressing salon

kapsel (het) hairdo; haircut

kapster hairdresser

karretje (het) karruh-tyuh
trolley, cart

kassa (de) cash desk, checkout

kassabon (de) receipt

kast (de) cupboard

kasteel (het) kastayl castle

kater (de) kahter hangover

katoen (het) kahtoon cotton

kauwgum (het) kowкнoom
chewing gum

keel (de) kayl throat

keelpastilles (de) kaylpastee-uhs
throat pastilles

keer kayr time

een keer once

een andere keer some other
time, another time

kelderverdieping (de)
kelder-verdeeping basement

kelner (de) waiter

kennen to know

kentekenbewijs (het) vehicle
registration certificate

kentekennummer (het) kentaykuh-noommer registration number

kerk (de) church

kermis (de) fair, funfair

kerstboom (de) kairst-bohm Christmas tree

kerstmis Christmas

kerstnacht kairstnaKHt Christmas Eve

keuken (de) kurkuh kitchen

keukenrol (de) kurkuhrol kitchen roll, paper towel

kiespijn (de) keespin toothache

kiestoon (de) dialling tone

kiezen keezuh to choose

kijk uit! kik owt look out!

kijken kikuh to see; to look

kijken naar nahr to look at

kin (de) chin

kind (het) kint child

kinderbad (het) kinderbat children's pool

kinderbedje (het) kinderbet-yuh cot

kinderen (de) children

Travel tip If you're travelling with children, you'll find that extra beds are usually easy to arrange in hotel rooms, many restaurants have kids' menus and discounts are the rule – from public transport to museums. Baby-changing facilities are commonplace and pharmacists sell nappies (diapers), baby food and other supplies.

kinderen beneden… jaar worden niet toegelaten children under… not admitted

kinderen niet toegelaten children not admitted

kinderkleding (de) kinderklayding children's clothes

kinderkleren (de) kinder-klayruh children's clothes

kinderoppas (de) child minder

kinderportie (de) kinder-porsee children's portion

kinderspeelbad (het) kinderspaylbat paddling pool

kinderstoel (de) kinderstool highchair

klaar klahr ready

ben je klaar? yuh are you ready?

klaar terwijl u wacht ready while you wait

klaar zijn klahr zin to be ready; to have finished

klacht (de) klaKHt complaint

klachten complaints

klagen klahKHuh to complain

klant (de) customer

klantenservice (de) customer service

klederdracht (de) traditional costume

kleding (de) klayding clothing

kleedkamer (de) klayt-kahmer changing room

kleerhanger (de) klayr-hanger coathanger

kleermaker (de) klayr-mahker
tailor

klein klīn little, small; short

kleiner dan klīner smaller than

kleindochter (de) klīn-doкНter
granddaughter

kleine: de kleine maat klīnuh
maht small size

kleingeld (het) klīn-кНelt change,
small change

kleinzoon (de) klīnzohn grandson

klem stuck

kleren (de) klayruh clothes

kleur (de) klur colour

kleurenfilm (de) klurruhfilm
colour film

kliniek (de) klineek clinic

klompen (de) clogs

klooster (het) klohster monastery;
convent

kloppen to knock; to tally;
to make sense

**kloppen alvorens binnen te
komen** knock before entering

klopt: dat klopt that's right

het klopt it's right

KNAC Royal Dutch Motoring
Club

knap k-nap clever; pretty

knie (de) k-nee knee

knippen k-nippuh to cut

knoop (de) k-nohp button

KNT children not admitted

koe (de) koo cow

koekenpan (de) kookuhpan
frying pan

koel kool cool

koel bewaren
keep in a cool place

koel serveren serve cooled

koelkast (de) koolkast fridge

koerier (de) kooreer courier

koers (de) koors exchange rate

koffer (de) suitcase

kofferbak (de) boot, trunk

koffiehuis (het) koffeehows
coffee shop

koffieshop café selling soft drugs

koken to cook

kom binnen come in!

komen kohmuh to come

kon: ik kon niet... neet
I couldn't...

koning (de) king

koninklijk royal

**Koninklijke Nederlandse
Automobiel Club** Royal
Dutch Motoring Club

kooi (de) koy bunk; cage

kookgerei (het) kohk-KHeri cooking utensils

koopavond late shopping

koortsachtig kohrts-aKHtiKH feverish

kop (de) cup

kopen to buy

koplampen headlights

koppeling (de) clutch

kort short, brief

korte broek (de) kortuh brook shorts

korte invoegstrook! short slip road!

korte verhalen verhahluh short stories

kortere weg (de) korteruh veKH shortcut

korting (de) discount

kost: wat kost het? vat how much is it?

koud kowt cold

kousen (de) kowsuh stockings

kraag (de) krahKH collar

kraan (de) krahn tap, faucet

krant (de) newspaper

> **Travel tip** British newspapers are on sale in every major city on the day of publication for around €4; newsagents at train stations almost always have copies. Current issues of UK and US magazines are widely available too, as is the *International Herald Tribune*.

krantenkiosk (de) newspaper kiosk

kredietcrisis (de) kredeet-kreesis credit crunch

krijgen krīKHuh to get

krik (de) jack (for car)

kroon (de) krohn crown (on tooth)

kruidenier(swinkel) (de) krowdeneer(svinkel) grocer

kruising (de) krowsing junction

kruispunt (het) krows-poont crossroads, intersection

krullend kroollent curly

kun: kun je...? koon yuh can you...?

kunnen we...? koonnuh vuh can we...?

zou u kunnen...? zow oo could you...?

kunst (de) koonst art

kunst- koonst- imitation

kunstbont (het) koonstbont artificial fur

kunstenaar/kunstenares (de) koonstenahr/koonstenares artist

kunstgalerij (de) koonst-KHahlerī art gallery

kunstgebit (het) koonst-KHebit dentures

kunstnijverheid (de) kunst-nīverhīt handicrafts

kunstnijverheidswinkel (de) koonst-nīverhīts-vinkel craft shop

kunt u...? koont oo can you...?

kurk (de) koork cork

kurkentrekker (de) koorkentrekker corkscrew

kus (de) kOOs kiss

kussen (het) kOOssuh cushion

kussen kOOssuh to kiss

kussensloop (het) kOOssuh-slohp
pillow case

kust (de) kOOst coast

  aan de kust ahn on the coast

kwaliteit (de) kvahlitīt quality

kwart (het) kvart quarter

kwartje (het) kvart-yuh 25-cent coin

kwekerij (de) kwaykerī nursery
(for plants)

kwitantie (de) kvitansee receipt

L

laag lahKH low

laan (de) lahn avenue

laars (de) lahrs boot

laat laht late

laatst lahtst last

laatste lahtstuh last; latest

lachen laKHuh to laugh

lade (de) lahduh drawer

laden en lossen
loading and unloading

laken (het) lahkuh sheet

lampenwinkel lighting shop

land (het) lant country

landschap (het) lantsKHap scenery

landweg country road

lang long; tall

lange-afstandsgesprek (het)
languh-afstants-KHesprek
long-distance call

langzaam langzahm slow; slowly

langzaam rijden drive slowly

laten lahtuh to let, to allow

laten we... let's...

lawaai (het) lavī noise

lawaaierig lavah-yuhriKH noisy

laxeermiddel (het) laxayr-middel
laxative

lederwaren leather goods

leeftijd (de) layftīt age

leeg laykH empty

leer (het) leather

legitimatiebewijs (het) laykHiti-
mahti-bewīs proof of identity

leiden līduh to lead

leiding (de) līding pipe

lekkage (de) lekkahJuh leak

lekke band (de) lekkuh bant
puncture, flat tyre

lekken to leak

lekker nice

  ik vind het lekker fint
I like it

  ik voel me niet lekker neet
I'm not feeling well

lelie (de) laylee lily

lelijk laylik ugly

lenen laynuh to borrow; to lend

lengte (de) lengtuh height

lensvloeistof (de) lens-vloo-ee-
stof soaking solution

lente (de) lentuh spring

lepel (de) laypel spoon

leraar (de) layrahr secondary-
school teacher (*male*)

lerares (de) layrahres secondary-school teacher (*female*)

leren layruh to learn; to teach

les (de) lesson

lesbisch lesbees lesbian

let op 'Niet Parkeren' borden please observe the 'No Parking' signs

let op stap mind the step

let op! deuren sluiten automatisch caution, doors close automatically

leuk lurk nice

   ik vind het leuk I like it

leven (het) layvuh life; to live

levendig layvendiKH lively

levensmiddelen (de) layvens-middeluh food; groceries

levensmiddelenwinkel (de) – vinkel grocer's, food store

lever (de) layver liver

lezen layzuh to read

lichaam (het) liKHahm body

licht (het) liKHt light

licht light (not heavy)

licht verteerbaar easily digestible

lichten aan lights on

lichten uit lights off

lied (het) leet song

liefde (de) leefduh love

liegen leeKHuh to lie, to tell a lie

liever: ik heb liever… hep leever I'd rather…, I prefer…

liever niet roken op vol balkon no smoking please when this area is crowded

lift (de) lift, elevator

liften to hitchhike

ligstoel (de) liKHstool sun lounger

lijm (de) lïm glue

lijn (de) lïn line

lijnvlucht (de) lïn-vlooKHt scheduled flight

linkerkant: aan de linkerkant ahn duh on the left, to the left

links left

links aanhouden ahnhowduh keep left

lip (de) lip

lippenstift (de) lipstick

lippenzalf (de) lip salve

lits jumeaux (het) lee joomoh twin beds

logeert: waar logeert u? vahr loJayrt oo where are you staying?

logies en ontbijt lohJees en ontbït bed and breakfast

lokaal local

lokale gesprek(het) lokahluh KHesprek local call

loket (het) lohket box office; ticket office; counter

loket voor pakketafgifte parcels counter

longen (de) lungs

loodgieter (de) loht-KHeeter plumber

loodvrije benzine (de) lohtvrï-uh benzeenuh unleaded petrol

lopen to walk

los loose

lounge (de) lobby; lounge

lucht (de) lOOKHt air

luchtdruk air pressure

luchthaven (de) lOOKHt-hahvuh airport

luchtpost lOOKHt-posst airmail

   per luchtpost by airmail

luchtpost-enveloppe (de) – anvelop airmail envelope

lucifers (de) lOOsifers matches

lui lOw lazy

luid lOwt loud

luier (de) lOw-yer nappy, diaper

luik (het) lOwk shutter (on window)

luisteren lOwster-uh to listen

Lutheraanse Kerk (de) Lutheran Church

luxe lOOxuh luxury

luxueus lOOx-yurs luxurious

M

ma mum

maag (de) mahKH stomach

maagpijn (de) mahKHpin stomach ache

maal mahl meal; time

   drie maal three times

maaltijd (de) mahltit meal

maan (de) mahn moon

maand (de) mahnt month

maandag mahndaKH Monday

maandkaart (de) mahntkahrt monthly ticket

maandverband (het) mahnt-verbant sanitary towel(s), sanitary napkin(s)

maar mahr but; only

maart mahrt March

maat (de) maht size

maatschappij company

machtig maKHtiKH rich; powerful

mag ik...? maKH ik may I...?

   mag ik... hebben? maKH ik may I have...?

mager mahKHer thin, skinny; low fat

magnetron (de) maKHnaytron microwave

mama mum

maken mahkuh to make; to mend, to repair

mand (de) mant basket

mandje (het) mant-yuh basket

mandje gebruiken a.u.b. please use a shopping basket

man (de) man

mannenklooster (het) mannuh-klohster monastery

marihuana (de) marOOwahna marijuana

marineblauw mareenuh-blOw navy blue

markering ontbreekt no road markings

markt (de) market; town square

maximum snelheid (de) maximOOm speed limit

mazelen (de) mahzeluh measles

me muh me

mededelingenbord notice board bulletin board

medicijn (het) medis**ī**n medicine

dit medicijn kan uw rijvaardigheid beïnvloeden this medicine may influence your driving ability

meebrengen m**a**ybrenguh to bring

meemaken m**a**ymahkuh to experience; to go through

meenemen m**a**ynaymuh to take; to bring

meer (het) lake

meer mayr more

wilt u nog wat meer? vilt ∞ noКН vat mayr would you like some more?

meermanskaarten tickets for small groups

meestal m**a**ystal most of the time

meeste m**a**ys-tuh most

mei mī May

meisje (het) m**ī**shuh girl

meisjesnaam (de) m**ī**shuhs-nahm maiden name

melden: zich melden zĭКН to check in (at hotel)

melk milk

melkchocolade (de) melk-shokol**ah**duh milk chocolate

meneer muhn**a**yr Mr; sir

menigte (de) m**a**yniКНtuh crowd

mensen people

mentholsnoepjes (de) m**e**ntol-snoop-yuhs mints

merk (het) make, brand

merkwaardig merkv**ah**rdiКН peculiar

mes (het) knife

met with

met de auto by car

met Jan it's Jan, Jan speaking

met aansluiting op… connecting with…

met conserveringsmiddel contains preservatives

met mij is het goed mī is uht КН**oo**t I'm fine

met wie spreek ik? who's calling?

meteen met**a**yn at once, immediately

metro (de) m**a**ytro underground, subway

meubel (het) m**u**rbel piece of furniture

meubilair (het) murbil**a**yr furniture

mevrouw mevr**ow** Mrs; Miss; Ms; madam

middag (de) m**ĭ**ddakН afternoon

's middags sm**ĭ**ddakНs in the afternoon

twee uur 's middags ∞r sm**ĭ**ddakНs 2pm

om twaalf uur 's middags tvahlf ∞r sm**ĭ**ddakНs at noon

middelgroot m**ĭ**ddel-КНroht medium-sized

midden: in het midden in the middle

middenin de nacht duh naКНt in the middle of the night

middernacht middernaKHt
midnight

mij mī me (emphatic)

het is van mij van it's mine

mij. company

mijn mīn my

mijn eigen… mīn īKHuh
my own…

mijnheer muhnayr Mr; sir

minder less

**minderjarigen worden niet
toegelaten** no admittance to
minors

minister-president (de) minister-
presid**ent** prime minister

minuut (de) min**oo**t minute

misbruik misuse; abuse

misbruik wordt gestraft
penalty for misuse

misschien missKH**euh** maybe;
perhaps

misselijkheid (de) misseliKHīt
nausea

mist (de) fog; mist

mistig mistikH foggy

misverstand (het) misverstant
misunderstanding

mobiele telefoon (de) mob**ee**luh
telef**oh**n mobile phone

mobiele winkel mobile shop

modder (de) mud

mode (de) m**oh**duh fashion

in de mode in fashion

modieus modi**u**rs fashionable

moe moo tired

moeder (de) m**oo**der mother

moeilijk m**oo**-ee-lik difficult, hard

moeilijkheid (de) m**oo**-ee-lik-hīt
difficulty; trouble

moet: ik moet moot I have to,
I must

je moet yuh you have to,
you must

moeten: wij moeten vī m**oo**tuh
we have to, we must

mogelijk mohKHelik possible

zo… mogelijk
as… as possible

Mohammedaans
mohammed**ah**ns Muslim

molen (de) m**oh**luh windmill

mond (de) mouth

mondzweer (de) montzvayr
mouth ulcer

monteur (de) mont**u**r mechanic

mooi moy beautiful; pretty; fine;
nice

ik vind het mooi I like it

morgen (de) morKHuh
morning; tomorrow

's morgens smorKHens
in the morning

's morgens om zeven uur
oor at 7am

's morgens vroeg smorKHens
early in the morning

morgen over een week
morKHuh a week (from)
tomorrow

morgenmiddag morKHuh-
m**i**ddakH tomorrow afternoon

morgenochtend morKHuh-
oKHtent tomorrow morning

moskee (de) mos**kay** mosque

motor (de) engine

motor afzetten alstublieft
please switch off engine

motorfiets (de) m**o**torfeets
motorbike

motorkap (de) bonnet, hood

mouw (de) m**o**w sleeve

mp-drie-formaat (het) em-pay-
dree-form**ah**t MP3 format

mug (de) m**oo**KH mosquito

muis (de) m**o**ws mouse

munt (de) m**oo**nt coin

munten coins

munttelefoon (de) m**oo**nt-telefohn
payphone

museum (het) m**oo**s**ay**uhm
museum; art gallery

museumjaarkaart (de)
m**oo**s**ay**uhm-**yah**r-kahrt museum
year card

Travel tip If you're planning
to visit even a handful of
museums, you'll save money
with a Museumkaart (muse-
um card), which gives free
entry to over 400 museums
and galleries nationwide. It
costs €40 for a year (less if
you're 24 or under) and can
be purchased at any partici-
pating museum.

musicienne (de) m**oo**sish**e**nnuh
musician (*female*)

musicus (de) m**oo**sik**oo**s musician

muur (de) m**oo**r wall

muziek (de) m**oo**z**ee**k music

N

'n a, an

na after

na opening beperkt houdbaar
will keep for limited period
only after opening

naaien n**ah**-yuh to sew

naald (de) n**ah**lt needle

naam (de) n**ah**m name

wat is uw naam? vat is **oo**
n**ah**m what's your name?

naar nahr for; to

naar binnen gaan to go in(side)

naar boven gaan b**oh**vuh KH**ah**n
to go up(stairs)

naast n**ah**st next to

naast de... beside the...

nacht (de) naKHt night

's nachts snaKHts at night;
overnight

om twaalf uur 's nachts
tvahlf **oo**r at midnight

nachtclub (de) naKHtkl**oo**p
nightclub

nachtjapon (de) naKHt-yapon
nightdress

nachtportier (de) naKHtporteer
night porter

nachttrein (de) naKHt-trin
night train

nadere bijzonderheden
further details

naderhand nahderhant
afterwards

nagel (de) n**ah**KHel fingernail

nagellak (de) nahKHellak
nail varnish

nagesynchroniseerd dubbed
(in Dutch)

nakijken nahkikuh to check

narcis (de) narsis daffodil;
narcissus

nat wet

nationaal nashonahl national

nationaal gesprek (het) KHesprek
inland call

**Nationale Maatschappij der
Belgische Spoorwegen**
Belgian Railways

nationaliteit (de) nashonalitit
nationality

natte verf wet paint

natuurgebied (het)
national park

natuurlijk natoorlik natural;
of course

natuurlijk niet neet
of course not

natuurresservaat (het)
nature reserve

nauw now narrow

nauwelijks noweliks hardly

Nederland nayderlant
the Netherlands

Nederlander (de) nayderlander
Dutchman

Nederlanders (de) the Dutch

Nederlands nayderlants Dutch

Nederlands Hervormde Kerk
(de) Dutch Reformed Church

Nederlandse (de) nayderlantsuh
Dutchwoman

Nederlandse Spoorwegen
Dutch Railways

nee nay no

nee, bedankt no, thanks

neef (de) nayf cousin (*male*);
nephew

neem me niet kwalijk naym
muh neet kvahlik I'm sorry

neer nayr down

nemen naymuh to take

netnummer (het) netnoommer
area code, dialling code

netto gewicht net weight

neus (de) nurs nose

N.H. North Holland

nicht (de) nikHt cousin (*female*);
niece

niemand neemant nobody

nieren (de) neeruh kidneys

niet neet not

niet-alcoholisch neet-
alkohohlees non-alcoholic

niet aankomen do not touch

niet buiten koelkast bewaren
keep refrigerated

niet centrifugeren
do not spin-dry

niet chemisch reinigen
do not dry-clean

niet geschikt voor... not
suitable for...

niet goed, geld terug money
back if not satisfied

niet inrijden no entry

**niet op de onderste trede
staan** do not stand on the
bottom step

niet op het ijs komen
  keep off the ice

niet openen voordat de trein stilstaat do not open until the train has stopped

niet op zaterdag not on Saturdays

niet op zaterdag, zon- en feestdagen not on Saturdays, Sundays and public holidays

niet parkeren no parking

niet roken no smoking

niet-roken coupé (de) neet-rohkuh koopay non-smoking compartment

niet-rokers non-smokers

niets neets none; nothing

  ik wil niets vil
  I don't want anything

  niets anders nothing else

niets te danken tuh don't mention it, you're welcome

niet storen a.u.b.
  please do not disturb

niet strijken do not iron

niet toegestaan not allowed

niet voor inwendig gebruik
  not to be taken internally

nieuw new new

nieuwe oogst newly harvested

Nieuwjaar new-yahr New Year

niezen neezuh to sneeze

NMBS Belgian Railways

noch... noch... noKH
  neither... nor...

nodig nohdiKH necessary

noemen noomuh to mention

nog noKH yet

  nog een uhn another one

  nog iets (anders)? anything else?

  nog meer more

  nog niet neet not yet

noodgeval (het) nohtKHeval emergency

noodknop deurbediening
  emergency button to operate door

noodrem emergency brake

nooduitgang (de) noht-owtKHang emergency exit

noodzakelijk nohtzahkelik necessary

nooit noyt never

noordelijk nohrdelik northern

noorden (het) nohrduh north

  ten noorden van Amsterdam van
  north of Amsterdam

  naar het noorden nahr
  to the north

noordoosten (het) nohrt-ohstuh northeast

noordwesten (het) nohrt-vestuh northwest

Noordzee (de) nohrt-zay
  North Sea

Noors nohrs Norwegian

Noorwegen nohrvayKHuh Norway

normaal normahl normal

notitieboekje (het) nohteetsee-book-yuh notebook

NP, n.p. no parking

NS Dutch Railways

nu noo now

nu even niet ayvuh neet
not just now

nuchter nookHter sober

nul nool zero

nummer (het) noommer number

nummerplaat (de) noommer-plaht
number plate

nuttig noottikH useful

NV Ltd, Inc

O

o nee (toch)! nay (tokH) oh no!

ober! waiter!

oefenen oofenuh to practise

oever (de) oover shore

of or

of... of... either... or...

**ogenblik: een ogenblik,
alstublieft!** uhn ohкHenblik
alstoobleeft just a minute!

ogenblikje: een ogenblikje
uhn ohкHenblik-yuh just a second

oké! okay OK!, right!

olie (de) ohlee oil

oliepeil (het) ohlee-pil oil level

om mee te nemen may tuh
naymuh to take away, (US) to go

omdat because

omgeving (de) omкHayving
surroundings

in de omgeving van near

omgooien omкHohyuh to knock
over

omheining (de) omhining fence

omhoog omhohкH up

omkeren omkayruh to turn

omkleden: zich omkleden ziкH
omklayduh to get changed

omleiding diversion

onbeleefd onbelayft rude

onbeperkt aantal kilometers
(het) ahntal kilomayters
unlimited mileage

onbevoegd unauthorized

onder under, below; among

onderbroek (de) onderbrook
underpants

onderjurk (de) onder-yoork slip
(garment)

ondersteboven onderstebohvuh
upside down

ondertiteling (de) subtitles

onderwijzer/onderwijzeres
(de) ondervizer/ondervizeres
teacher (*male/female: junior*)

ondiep ondeep shallow

oneffen wegdek uneven road
surface

ongelegen onкHelaykHuh
inconvenient

ongelofelijk onкHelohfelik
unbelievable

ongeluk (het) onкHelook accident

ongeveer onкHevayr about,
roughly

ongewoon onкHevohn unusual

onlangs recently

onmiddelijk onmiddelik
immediately

onmogelijk onmohкHelik
impossible

ons our; us

onschuldig onsKHOoldiKH
innocent

ontbijt (het) ontbi̅t breakfast

ontbrekend ontbraykent missing

onthoudt u van refrain from

ontmoetingsplaats (de)
ontmootings-plahts meeting place

ontsmettingsmiddel (het)
disinfectant

ontsteek uw lichten
switch on your lights

ontsteking (de) ontstayking
ignition; inflammation

ontvangstbewijs (het)
ontvangst-bevi̅s receipt

ontwikkelen (het) ontvikkeluh
film processing; to develop

onverharde weg unpaved road

onweersbui (de) onvayrs-bow
thunderstorm

onze onzuh our

onzin! (de) rubbish!

oog (het) ohKH eye

oogarts (de) ohKH-arts
opthalmologist

oogdruppels (de) ohKH-drooppels
eye drops

oogschaduw (de) ohKH-sKHahdoo
eye shadow

ooit oyt ever

ook ohk also, too

  ik ook niet neet do I, nor have
  I, nor am I

  heeft u ook...? hayft oo have
  you got any...?

  ik ook me too

oom (de) ohm uncle

oor (het) ohr ear

oorknopjes (de) ohrknop-yuhs
ear-studs

oorringen (de) ohrringuh earrings

oostelijk ohstelik eastern

oosten (het) ohstuh east

  in het oosten in the east

op on; at

op slot doen doon to lock

**op zon- en feestdagen,
echter niet op...** on Sundays
and public holidays but not
on...

open doen doon to open;
to answer the door

open haard (de) hahrt fireplace

openbaar vervoer (het)
public transport

openbare bibliotheek
public library

openbare toiletten (de)
openbahruh tva-lettuh
public toilets

openen to open

openingstijden (de) ohpenings-
tiduh opening times

openlucht zwembad
outdoor swimming pool

openmaken opuh-mahkuh
to open; to unlock

operatie (de) operahtsee operation

opgezet opкнezet swollen;
stuffed (animal)

ophaalbrug drawbridge

ophalen to collect; to pick up

opklaren opklahruh to
brighten up

opname (de) withdrawal;
recording

opnemen opnaymuh
to withdraw; to record;
to answer the phone

opnieuw opnew again

oponthoud (het) opont-howt delay

opruiming clearance

opschrijven op-skHrivuh
to write down

opspattend grind! loose
chippings

opstaan opstahn to get up (in the
morning)

opstapplaats touringcars
boarding point for long-
distance buses

opticien (de) optee-shuh optician

opwindend opvindent exciting

opzettelijk opzettelik deliberately

opzij on/at the side; aside

oranje ohran-yuh orange (colour)

orde: bent u in orde? oo in
orduh are you OK?

orkest (het) orchestra

oud owt old; stale

oude stadsdeel (het) owduh
stats-dayl old town

Oudejaarsavond owduh-
yahrsahvont New Year's Eve

ouders (de) owders parents

ouderwets owdervets
old-fashioned

oven (de) ohvuh oven

over ohver about, concerning

over twee dagen tvay daкнuh
in two days' time

over vijf minuten
in five minutes

er is er geen een over кнayn
ayn there's none left

overal ohveral everywhere

overdekt zwembad indoor
swimming pool

overgeven ohver-кнayvuh
to vomit

overgewicht (het) ohver-кнeviкнt
excess weight

overhemd (het) ohverhemt shirt

overige bestemmingen
other destinations

overjas (de) ohver-yas overcoat

**overkant: aan de overkant
van de straat** ahn duh

** oh**verkant van duh straht
across the road

overmorgen **oh**vermorⱩHuh
the day after tomorrow

overnachting (de) ohverna**ⱩH**ting
night

overstappen **oh**verstappuh
to change

u moet in… overstappen
you have to change at…

overstapverbinding
connection, change

oversteekplaats (de) pedestrian
crossing

oversteekplaats voor fietsers
crossing for cyclists

overstroming (de) ohverstro**h**ming
flood

overtocht (de) **oh**vertoⱩHt crossing
(on ship)

overtreding offence

P

paar (het) pahr couple; pair

een paar dagen da**ⱩH**uh
a few days

paard (het) pahrt horse

paardrijden (het) pa**h**rt-riduh
horse riding; to ride

pad (het) pat path

pak (het) carton; pack; suit

pakhuis (het) warehouse

Pakistaans pakista**h**ns Pakistani

pakje (het) small package, parcel;
packet

pakken to pack; to fetch

paleis (het) pal**i**s palace

pannenkoekenhuis (het)
pannuh-kookuhhows pancake
restaurant

panty (de) pen**t**i tights, pantyhose

papier (het) pap**ee**r paper

papieren zakdoekjes (de)
pap**ee**ruh zakdook-yuhs
paper tissues

paraplu (de) paraploo umbrella

pardon excuse me

pardon, wat zei u? vat zi oo
pardon (me)?, sorry?

parfum (het) parfoom perfume

parkeergelegenheid (de)
park**a**yr-ⱩHelayⱩHenhit parking

parkeerplaats (de) park**a**yr-plahts
car park, parking space

parkeerschijf (de) park**a**yr-sⱩHif
parking disk

parkeerterrein (het) park**a**yr-terrin
car park, parking lot

parkeerverbod op even dagen
no parking on even days

**parkeerverbod op oneven
dagen** no parking on odd days

parkeren park**a**yruh to park

**parkeren alleen voor
hotelgasten** parking for hotel
guests only

parterre ground floor,
(US) first floor

particulier partikooleer private

partij (de) par**t**i game, match

pas step; pass; passport; the
other day; just; as late as

Pasen Easter

paskamer (de) fitting room

passagier (de) passaJeer
passenger

passen to try on

pauze (de) pOWzuh interval

pct. per cent

p.d. per day

penseel (het) pensayl brush
(artist's)

pension (het) penshon guesthouse

pepermunt (de) paypermOOnt
peppermint

per pair by

per aangetekende post
ahnкккetaykenduh posst
by registered mail

per dag per day

per nacht naкнt per night

per persoon per dag
per person per day

per spoor spohr by rail

per stuk each

per uur OOr per hour

per vliegtuig vleeкнtOWKH by air

perron (het) platform, track

persen pairsuh to press

personenwagen private car

persoon (de) persohn person

pet (de) cap

petit pacquet small packet,
airmail parcels up to 1kg

pijn (de) pīn ache, pain

pijn doen doon to hurt

pijnlijk pīnlik painful

pijnstillers (de) pīnstillers
painkillers

pijp (de) pīp pipe

pinda's (de) pindas peanuts

pittig pittiкн hot, spicy

plaat (de) plaht record (music)

plaats (de) plahts place

  in plaats daarvan dahrvan
  instead

  in plaats van... instead of...

  deze plaats is bezet
  this seat is taken

plaats bij het raam (de) bī uht
rahm window seat

plaatsbespreking (de) plahts-
bespreking seat reservation

plaatsbewijs (het) plahtsbevis
ticket

plaatselijk spoornet
local railway system

plaatselijke tijd local time

plafond (het) plahfon ceiling

plak (de) slice

plakband (het) plakbant
adhesive tape

plank (de) shelf

plastic (het) plestik plastic

plastic tas (de) plastic bag

plat flat

platteland (het) plattelant
countryside

plein (het) plīn square (in town);
courtyard

pleister (de) plīster plaster, Bandaid

plezier hebben plezeer
to enjoy oneself

ploeg (de) plooкн team

plotseling suddenly

poelier poulterer

polder(land) land reclaimed from the sea

polikliniek outpatient clinic

politie (de) pol**ee**tsee police

politieagent (de) pol**ee**tsee-ahKH**ent** policeman

politieagente (de) pol**ee**tsee-ahKH**ent**uh policewoman

politiebureau (het) pol**ee**tsee-b**oo**roh police station

pols (de) wrist

pond (het) pont pound

pony (de) p**o**nnee pony

poosje: een poosje p**o**hs-yuh a while

pop (de) doll

popzanger/popzangeres (de) pop singer *(male/female)*

poreuze lenzen (de) por**u**rzuh gas-permeable lenses

porselein (het) porsel**i**n china, porcelain

port betaald postage paid

portefeuille (de) portuh-f**u**r-yuh wallet

portemonnee (de) portuh-monn**ay** wallet; purse

portier (de) port**ee**r doorman; porter

portokosten postage, postal charges

porto luchtpostbrieven tariff for airmail letters

post (de) p**o**sst mail, post

posten p**o**sstuh to mail, to post

postkantoor (het) p**o**sstkantohr post office

postpakket (het) parcel, package

posttarieven voor binnen- en buitenland postage rates for home and abroad

postwissel (de) p**o**sstvissel money order

postzegel (de) p**o**sst-zayKHel stamp

postzegelautomaat stamp vending machine

postzegelboekje (de) p**o**sst-zayKHel-b**oo**kyuh book of stamps

pot (de) jar

potlood (het) p**o**tloht pencil

p.p.p.d per person per day

p.r. public relations; poste restante, **(US)** general delivery

praatpaal emergency roadside phone

prachtig praKH-tiKH lovely, wonderful

praten pr**ah**tuh to talk

precies pres**ee**s accurate

precies! exactly!

prettige dag! pr**e**ttiKHuh have a nice day!

priester (de) pr**ee**ster priest

prijs (de) pr**i**s price; charge; fare

prijslijst price list

prijzen vanaf… prices from…

prikbord notice board, bulletin board

prima! excellent!

privéadres home address

privéterrein private grounds

proberen probayruh to try

procent per cent

proeflokaal (het) proof-lohkahl old-fashioned bar that serves only spirits and closes at around 8pm

proeven proovuh to taste

proost! prohst cheers!

p.st. each

P.T.T. Post Office

p.u. per hour

pure chocolade (de) pooruh shokolahduh plain chocolate

puur poor straight (whisky etc)

p.w. per week

R

R.K. Roman Catholic

raadhuis town hall

raam (het) rahm window

raar rahr weird

radio- en televisiewinkel radio and television shop

ramp (de) disaster

recept (het) resept prescription; recipe

receptie (de) resepsee reception; reception desk

receptioniste (de) resepshonistuh receptionist

rechtdoor reKHtdohr straight ahead, straight on

rechterkant: aan de rechterkant ahn duh reKHterkant on the right hand side

rechtuit gaan reKHtowt KHahn keep straight ahead

rechts reKHts right; on the right, to the right

rechts aanhouden ahnhowduh keep right

rechtstreeks reKHt-strayks direct; directly

rechtstreeks bellen direct dialling

rechtstreekse vlucht (de) direct flight

reclame special offer

recreatiegebied, recreatieterrein recreation area

reddingsgordel (de) reddings-KHordel lifebelt

reddingsvest (het) reddings-vest life jacket

redelijk raydelik reasonable

reep: een reep chocolade uhn rayp shokolahduh a bar of chocolate

reformhuis (het) reeform-hows, **reformwinkel** (de) reeform-vinkel health food shop

regel (de) rayKHel line

regelen rayKHeluh to arrange, to order

regen (de) rayKHuh rain

in de regen in the rain

het regent rayKHent it's raining

regenbui (de) rayKHuhbow shower

regenjas (de) rayKHuh-yas raincoat

regering (de) reKHayring
government

reinigingsmelk (de) rīnikKHings-
melk cleansing lotion

reis (de) rīs journey, trip

reisbureau (het) rīsbooroh
travel agency

reischeque (de) rīs-chek
traveller's cheque

reisgids (de) rīsKHits
guidebook

reisinformatie
travel information

reiskaart (de) rīskahrt
season ticket

reisonderbreking (de) rīsonder-
brayking stopover

reisorganisatie (de) rīs-
orKHanisahtsee tour operator

reiswieg (de) rīsveeKH
carry-cot

reiswinkel (de) rīsvinkel
travel agency

reizen rīzuh to travel

rekenen raykenuh to charge

rekening (de) raykening
bill, check; account

rem (de) brake

rennen to run

repareren reparayruh
to repair

reserveband (de) resairvuh-bant
spare tyre

reserveonderdeel (het) reservuh-
onderdayl spare part

reserveren raysairvayruh
to reserve, to book

reserveren aanbevolen
reservation recommended

reserveren verplicht
reservation compulsory

> Travel tip Rooms are in
> high demand in Amsterdam
> at all times of the year, so
> advance booking is always
> required. Hotel prices are
> also about thirty percent
> higher than in the rest of
> the country.

reservering (de) reservayring
reservation

restauratiewagen (de)
restOwrahtsee-vahKHuh
buffet car, restaurant car

retour(tje) (het) retoor(t-yuh)
return ticket, round-trip ticket

reusachtig rursaKHtiKH enormous

richting (de) riKHting direction

  in de richting van van towards

richtingaanwijzer (de) riKHting-
ahnvīzer indicator

riem (de) reem belt; strap

rij (de) rī queue, line

rijbewijs (het) rībevīs driving
licence

rijden rīduh to drive

**rijdt niet op zon- en
feestdagen** does not run on
Sundays and public holidays

rijk rīk rich

rijksmuseum (het) rīks-
musayuhm national museum

rijksweg (de) rīksveKH motorway,
freeway

rijp rip ripe

rijrichting direction of traffic

rijstrook (de) rīstrohk lane (on motorway)

rijtuig (het) rītOWKH carriage, coach

riskant risky

ritsen over 100m please get in lane over the next 100 metres

ritssluiting (de) rits-slOWting zip

rivier (de) riveer river

rodehond (de) rohde-hont German measles

roeien (het) roo-yuh to row; rowing

rok (de) skirt

rokers smokers

rolgordijnen (de) rol-KHordīnuh blinds

rolstoel (de) rolstool wheelchair

roltrap escalator

roman (de) rohmahn novel

rondje (het) ront-yuh round

rondleiding (de) ront-līding guided tour

rondreis (de) ront-rīs tour

rondvaart (de) rontvahrt pleasure cruise, boat trip

rondvaart door de haven boat trip round the harbour

rondvaartboot (de) rontvahrt-boht sightseeing boat

rondweg by-pass

rood roht red

rook (de) rohk smoke

   ik rook niet neet I don't smoke

   rookt u? ᴏᴏ do you smoke?

roomkleurig rohm-klurriKH cream (colour)

Rooms Katholiek Roman Catholic

roos (de) rohs rose

rotonde (de) rotonduh roundabout, traffic circle

rots (de) rock

rotzooi (de) rotzoy mess

roze rozuh pink

rug (de) rooKH back

rugpijn rooKHpīn backache

ruilen rowluh to change, to exchange

ruïne (de) roo-eenuh ruins

ruitenwisser (de) rowtuhvisser windscreen wiper

ruiterpad bridle path

rustig roostiKH quiet

S

saai sī boring

saldo (het) bank balance

samen sahmuh together

sandalen (de) sandahluh sandals

sanitaire voorzieningen washing and toilet facilities

schaakspel (het) sKHahk-spel chess

schaal (de) scale; dish

schapenwol wool

schaar (de) sKHahr scissors

schaatsen (de) sKHahtsuh ice skates

schaatsen (het) sĸᴴahdoo ice skating;
to ice skate

schaduw (de) sĸᴴahdoo shade;
shadow

schakelaar (de) sĸᴴahkelahr
switch

scheerapparaat (het) sĸᴴayr-
apparaht razor

scheermesjes (de) sĸᴴayr-
meshus razor blades

scheerschuim (het) sĸᴴayr-
sĸᴴowm shaving foam

scheerwol (de) wool

scheerzeep (de) sĸᴴayrzayp
shaving foam

scheren sĸᴴayruh to shave

scherp sĸᴴairp sharp

scheutje (het) sĸᴴurt-yuh drop

schiet op! sĸᴴeet hurry up!

schilderij (het) sĸᴴilderī painting

schip (het) sĸᴴip ship

schoen (de) sĸᴴoon shoe

schoenenzaak (de) sĸᴴoonuh-
zahk shoe shop

schoenmaker (de) sĸᴴoon-
mahker shoe repairer

schoensmeer (de) sĸᴴoon-smayr
shoe polish

schoenveters (de) sĸᴴoon-vayters
shoelaces

schokbreker (de) sĸᴴok-brayker
shock-absorber

schokkend sĸᴴokkent shocking

schoon sĸᴴohn clean

schoondochter (de) sĸᴴohn-
doĸᴴter daughter-in-law

schoonheidsartikelen
cosmetics

schoonheidssalon (de)
sĸᴴohnhīts-salon beauty salon

schoonmaakartikelen
cleaning articles

schoonmaken sĸᴴohn-mahkuh
to clean

schoonmoeder (de) sĸᴴohn-
mooder mother-in-law

schoonouders (de) sĸᴴohn-
owders parents-in-law

schoonvader (de) sĸᴴohn-vahder
father-in-law

schoonzoon (de) sĸᴴohn-zohn
son-in-law

schoonzus (de) sĸᴴohn-zoos
sister-in-law

schoteltje (het) sĸᴴotelt-yuh
saucer

Schots sĸᴴots Scottish

schouder (de) sĸᴴowder shoulder

schouwburg (de) sĸᴴow-boorĸᴴ
theatre

schram (de) sĸᴴram scratch

schreeuwen sĸᴴray-wuh to shout

schrijfpapier (het) sĸᴴrīf-papeer
writing paper

schrijven sĸᴴrīvuh to write

schudden voor gebruik
shake before use

schuifdak (het) sĸᴴowfdak
sunroof

seconde (de) sekonduh second

septisch septis septic

serveerster (de) servayrster
waitress

servet (het) sairv**e**t serviette, napkin

sigarenwinkel tobacconist, tobacco store

sinds since

sinterklaas sinterkl**ah**s Saint Nicholas

sinterklaasavond sinterkl**ah**s-**ah**vont St. Nicholas Eve (December 5th)

> Travel tip If you're visiting in December and have Dutch friends, it's worth knowing that they exchange presents on December 5 – St. Nicholas Eve or 'present evening' (*Pakjesavond*) – rather than Christmas Day. It's traditional to give a present plus an amusing poem you have written caricaturing the recipient.

sjaal (de) sh**ah**l scarf

slaan sl**ah**n to hit

slaapcoupé (de) sl**ah**p-koopay couchette

slaapkamer (de) sl**ah**p-kahmer bedroom

slaapwagen (de) sl**ah**p-vahkHuh sleeping car

slaapzaal (de) dormitory

slaapzak (de) sl**ah**pzak sleeping bag

slager (de) sl**ah**kHer butcher's

slagerij (de) slahkHer**ī**, **slagerswinkel** (de) sl**ah**kHers-vinkel butcher's shop

slapen sl**ah**puh to sleep

slecht slekHt bad; poor; badly

niet slecht neet not bad

slecht wegdek poor road surface

sleutel (de) sl**uR**tel key

sleutelring (de) sl**uR**telring keyring

slijterij (de) sl**ī**ter**ī** off-licence, liquor store

slim clever

slipgevaar danger of skidding

slipje (het) slip-yuh panties

slot (het) lock; fortified castle

sluis (de) sl**ow**s lock (on canal)

sluiten sl**ow**tuh to close, to shut

sluitingstijden closing times

smaak (de) sm**ah**k flavour; taste

smaakstoffen flavourings

smerig sm**ay**rikH filthy

sms'je es-em-**e**s-yuh text (message)

snee (de) snay slice

sneeuw (de) sn**ay**-oo snow

sneeuwstorm blizzard

sneeuwval snowfall

snel fast, quick; quickly

snelbuffet (het) snackbar

snelheid (de) sn**e**lh**ī**t speed

snelheidsmeter (de) sn**e**lh**ī**ts-mayter speedometer

snelkassa (de) quick checkout (in supermarket, 7 items or less)

sneltrein (de) sn**e**ltr**ī**n express (train)

snelweg (de) sn**e**lvekH motorway, highway

snijden sn**ī**duh to cut

snijwond (de) sn**ī**vont cut

snoepgoed (het) sn**oo**p-κ**H**oot sweets, candy

snoepjeswinkel (de) sn**oo**p-yuhs-vinkel sweet shop, candy store

snor (de) moustache

soms sometimes

soort (het) s**oh**rt sort, type

wat voor soort…? vohr what sort of…?

welke soort wilt u? v**e**lkuh which sort do you want?

soortgelijk s**oh**rtκ**H**elk similar

souterrain (het) s**oo**terr**ay**n basement

spaak (de) spahk spoke

Spaans spahns Spanish

spaarbank savings bank

Spanje span-yuh Spain

spannend sp**a**nnent exciting

speciale aanbieding special offer

speelgoed toys

speelgoedwinkel (de) sp**ay**l-κ**H**oot-vinkel toy shop

speelplaats (de) sp**ay**lplahts playground

speld (de) spelt pin

spelen sp**ay**luh to play

spelletje (het) sp**e**llet-yuh game

spiegel (de) sp**ee**κ**H**el mirror

spijkerbroek (de) sp**ī**kerbrook jeans

spijt: (het) spijt me sp**ī**t muh I'm sorry

het spijt me echt sp**ī**t muh I'm really sorry

spin (de) spider

spirituosa spirits

spitsuur (het) sp**i**ts**oo**r rush hour

spoedgeval (het) sp**oo**tκ**H**eval emergency

spoedzendingen express post

spoor platform, track

spoorboek(je) train timetable

het nieuwe spoorboekje is weer verkrijgbaar the new train timetable is available now

spoorkaart van Nederland rail map of Holland

spoorkaartjes train tickets

spoorlijn track

spoorvorming! ruts on road!

spoorweg (de) sp**oh**rveκ**H** railway

spoorwegovergang level crossing, grade crossing

spoorwegpolitie railway police

sportartikelen sports goods

sportkleding sports wear

sportvelden sports fields

sportwinkel sports goods shop

spreek: ik spreek geen…
sprayk KHayn I don't speak…

spreekt u… spraykt ∞
do you speak…?

spreekuur office hours;
surgery hours

spreken spraykuh to speak

springen to jump

staan stahn: **het staat me niet**
staht muh neet it doesn't suit me

staanplaatsen standing room

we hebben staanplaatsen
standing room only

staat (de) staht state

stad (de) stat city; town

stadhuis (het) stathOWs town hall

stadsbussen town buses

stadscentrum (het) stats-sentrOOm
city centre; town centre

stadslichten (de) stats-liKHtuh
side lights

stadsplattegrond street map

stalletjes stalls

standbeeld (het) stantbaylt statue

stapvoets rijden drive at
walking pace

stedelijk municipal

steelpan (de) staylpan saucepan

steen (de) stayn stone, rock

steil stīl steep

steile helling steep gradient

stekend staykent sharp

stekker (de) plug

stelen stayluh to steal

stem (de) voice

stempelautomaat
ticket-stamping machine

ster (de) star

sterk strong

sterke drank spirits

sterven stairvuh to die

stilte (de) stiltuh silence

stoel (de) stool chair

stoel bij het middenpad (de)
bī uht midduhpat aisle seat

stoel bij het raam (de) bī uht
rahm window seat

stoep (de) stoop pavement,
sidewalk

stof (de) cloth, material, fabric

stof (het) dust

stofdoeken dusters

stoffeerderij upholsterer

stoffen materials, fabrics;
substances

stoffig stoffiKH dusty

stofzuiger (de) stofzOWKHer
vacuum cleaner

stom stupid

stomerij (de) stomerī dry-cleaner

stommeling stommeling idiot

stop (de) plug (in sink); fuse

stopcontact (het) power point,
socket

**stopcontact voor
scheerapparaten** (het)
shaving point

stoppen to stop

stopt niet in…
does not stop in…

stoptrein slow train stopping at most stations

storen to disturb

storingsdienst faults service

stortingen deposits

straat (de) straht street

strafbaar punishable

strak tight

strand (het) strant beach

op het strand on the beach

strandwacht (de) strantvaкHt lifeguard

stratenplan (het) strahtuhplan streetmap

streek (de) strayk region

streekpost local mail

streekvervoer regional transport

strijken striːkuh to iron

strijkijzer (het) striːkizer iron

strippenkaart (de) strippuhkahrt ticket strip for bus, tram and metro

stroom (de) strohm current; stream

stroomafwaarts strohmafvahrts downstream

stroomopwaarts strohmopvahrts upstream

stropdas (de) tie, necktie

stuk (het) stook piece; article

stukje (het) stook-yuh bit

een stukje… a bit of…

een stukje verderop
a little further down

stukje bij beetje bit by bit

sturen stooruh to send

stuurinrichting (de) stoor-inrikHting steering

suikergehalte sugar content

suikergoed confectionery

suikerpatient (de) sowker-pahshent diabetic

super four-star petrol, premium gas

supermarkt (de) soopermarkt supermarket

surfplank (de) soorfplank sailboard

T

taal (de) tahl language

taalcursus (de) tahl-koorsoos language course

tabak (de) tobacco

tabakswaren tobacconist

tafel (de) tahfel table

tafellaken (het) tablecloth

tafeltennis (het) table tennis

taille (de) tah-yuh waist

talkpoeder (de) talkpooder talcum powder

tamelijk tahmelik quite, fairly, rather

tand (de) tant tooth

tandarts (de) tant-arts dentist

tandenborstel (de) toothbrush

tandpasta (de) toothpaste

tandvlees (het) tant-vlays gum

tandzijde (de) tant-zīduh dental
   floss

tante (de) tantuh aunt

tapijt (het) tapīt carpet

tapvergunning licence to sell
   alcoholic drinks

tarief charges; price list

tarieven buitenland overseas
   postage rates

tas (de) bag

tas aan de haak hang your bag
   on the hook

tax-free-winkel (de) tax-free-
   vinkel duty-free shop

taxi-standplaats (de)
   taxi-stantplahts taxi rank

te tuh too

te hard kost teveel!
   speed kills!; speeding fines

te huur hoor for hire, to rent

te koop kohp for sale

te veel vayl too much

te voet voot on foot

tearoom café selling drinks,
   cakes and snacks, and
   sometimes alcoholic drinks

TEE Trans European Express

teen (de) tayn toe

**tegemoetkomend verkeer
   heeft voorrang** oncoming
   traffic has right of way

tegen tayKHuh against

tegen de halve prijs half-price

tegenover tayKHenohver opposite

tegenovergestelde
   tayKHenohver-KHestelduh
   opposite

tekening (de) taykening
   picture, drawing

tekst (mededeling) (de)
   mayduhdayling text (message)

telefoneren telefonayruh
   to phone

telefonist/telefoniste (de)
   telefonist/telefonistuh operator

telefoon (de) telefohn phone

telefoonboek (het) telefohn-book
   phone book

telefooncel (de) telefohn-sel
   phone box

telefoongesprek (het)
   telefohn-KHesprek phone call

telefoongids (de) telefohn-KHits
   phone book

telefoonkaart (de) telefohn-kahrt
   phonecard

telefoonnummer (het) telefohn-
   noommer phone number

telefoonoplader (de) telefohn-
   oplahder phone charger

teleurgesteld telurKHestelt
   disappointed

teleurstellend telurstellent
   disappointing

televisie (de) televeesee television

ten minste minstuh at least

tenminste houdbaar tot…
   can be kept until…

tennisbaan (de) tennisbahn
   tennis court

tent (de) tent; dive

tentharing (de) tent peg

tentoonstelling (de) tentohnstelling exhibition

tentstok (de) tent pole

terug terooKH back

ik ben zo terug
I'll be right back

terugbellen terooKH-belluh
to ring back, to call back

teruggaan terooKH-KHahn
to go back, to return

teruggeven terooKH-KHayvuh
to give back

terugkomen terooKH-kohmuh
to come back, to get back

terwijl tervil while

thee (de) tay tea

theedoek (de) taydook tea towel

theelepel (de) taylaypel teaspoon

thermosfles (de) tairmosfles
Thermos flask

thuis tows at home

bij hem thuis at his place

ticket (de) ticket

tiener (de) teener teenager

tijd (de) tit time

tijdens tidens during

tijdschrift (het) tidsKHrift magazine

tijdschriftenwinkel (de)
tidsKHriftuh-vinkel newsagent's

tijdslot (het) titslot time lock

tik unit

t/m up to and including

tocht met de rondvaartboot
(de) canal trip

tochtig toKHtiKH draughty

toegang (de) too-KHang
admission; access

toegang alleen voor

kaartenhouders
ticket-holders only

toegang verboden
no admittance

toegangsbewijs (het) tooKHangs-
bewis ticket

toegangsprijs (de) tooKHangs-pris
admission charge

toegelaten tooKHelahtun allowed

toegestaan too-KHestahn allowed

toekomst (de) tookomst future

toen toon then

toerist (de) toorist tourist

toeristenbureau (het)
tooristuh-booroh tourist
information office

toeristische rondrit (de)
tooristeesuh rontrit sightseeing
tour (by bus)

toeristische rondvaart (de)
ront-vahrt sightseeing tour
(by boat)

toeslag (de) tooslaKH supplement

u moet toeslag betalen
you must pay a supplement

toestel (het) toostel extension;
apparatus

toestelnummer (het) toostel-
noommer extension number

toeter (de) tooter horn

**toezichthouder/toezicht-
houdster** (de) toozikHt-howder/
toozikHt-howtster caretaker

toilet (het) twa-let toilet, rest room

toiletartikelen toiletries

toiletpapier (het) twalet-papeer
toilet paper

toiletten toilets, rest rooms

tol toll

tolk (de) interpreter

tolken to interpret

toneel (het) stage; drama

toneelstuk (het) tonaylstook play

tonen to show

tot until

tot en met up to and including

tot straks see you later

tot ziens zeens goodbye, see you, cheerio

touringcar (de) tooringkar coach, bus

touw (het) tow rope; string

traject (het) trahjekt route; section of rail track

tramhalte (de) tramhaltuh tram stop

transportkaart (de) transportkahrt network map

trap (de) stairs; steps

trefpunt meeting point

trein (de) trīn train

   de trein naar... staat gereed op spoor... the train for... is waiting at platform...

   de trein staat gereed op... the train is about to depart from...

trein met toeslag train with supplement payable

treinkaart train ticket

treinstel section of the train

treintaxi station taxi

trek: heeft u trek? hayft oo are you hungry?

trekken to pull

trouwdag (de) trowdakH wedding day; wedding anniversary

trouwerij (de) trowerī wedding

trouwring (de) trowring wedding ring

trui (de) trow jersey, jumper

tuin (de) town garden; yard

tulp (de) toolp tulip

tussen toossuh between

   tussen de middag duh at midday

   tussen de middag gesloten closed at lunchtime

tussenlanding (de) stopover

twee eenpersoonsbedden tvay aynpersohns-bedduh twin beds

twee keer tvay kayr twice

twee keer zoveel zovayl twice as much

twee weken tvay vaykuh fortnight

tweede tvayduh second

tweede klas second-class

tweede straat links second on the left

tweedehands tvayduh-hants second-hand

tweepersoonsbed (het) tvaypersohns-bet double bed

tweepersoonskamer (de) tvaypersohns-kahmer double room

tweerichtingsverkeer two-way traffic

tweesprong (de) tvaysprong fork (in road)

typisch tipees typical

U

u oo you

u bent hier, u bevindt zich hier you are here

uit Owt out; exit

ik kom uit… I come from…

uitbetaling (de) Owtbetahling payment

uitdoen Owtdoon to turn off

uiteindelijk Owtindelik eventually

uiterst Owterst extremely

uiterste verkoopdatum sell-by date

uitgaan OwtKHahn to go out

uitgang (de) OwtKHang exit, way out; gate

uitgeput OwtKHepoot exhausted

uitgesteld postponed

uitgeven OwtKHayvuh to spend

uitgezonderd op… …days excepted

uitlaat (de) Owtlaht exhaust (pipe)

uitleggen OwtleKHuh to explain

uitlekgewicht dry weight

uitnodigen OwtnohdiKHuh to invite

uitnodiging (de) OwtnohdiKHing invitation

uitpakken Owtpakkuh to unpack

uitrit vrijlaten please keep exit clear

uitrusten Owtroostuh to rest

uitrusting (de) Owtroosting equipment

uitschakelen OwtsKHahkeluh to switch off

uitstappen Owtstappuh to get off, to get out

uitstekend Owtstaykent fine; excellent

uitverkocht sold out

uitverkoop (de) Owtverkohp sale

uitverkoopartikelen worden niet geruild we do not exchange sales goods

uitvoering (de) Owtvooring performance

uitzicht (het) OwtziKHt view

uitzoeken Owtzookuh to find out

universiteit (de) OOnivairsitit university

uur (het) OOr hour; o'clock

uw oo your

uw lichten! remember your lights

V

vaag vahKH vague; dull

vaak vahk frequent; often

niet vaak neet not often

vaart minderen reduce speed

vaatdoek (de) vahtdook dishcloth

vader (de) vahder father

vakantie (de) vakansee holiday, vacation

op vakantie on holiday/vacation

vakantie-reizen holiday travel

valhelm (de) valhelm helmet

vallen va**l**luh to fall

vallend gesteente
falling rocks

valuta foreign currency

van van from; of

  van wie is dit? vee
  whose is this?

  van nu af aan n∞ af ahn
  from now on, in future

van hen theirs

van jou y**OW** yours

van jullie y**OO**llee yours

van ons ours

van u ∞ yours

vanaf vanaf from

vanavond vana**h**vont tonight;
this evening

vandaag vanda**h**KH today

  vandaag over een week
  ohver uhn a week (from) today

vangen va**n**guh to catch

vanmiddag vanmi**dd**akH
this afternoon

vanmorgen vanmo**rk**Huh
this morning

vanochtend vano**k**Htent
this morning

vanuit fan**OW**t from

vanwege… vanvay**k**Huh
because of…

vast: het zit vast vast
it's jammed

vasthouden vast-h**OW**duh to hold

vatbaar voor wijzigingen
subject to change

veel vayl a lot, lots; many; much

niet veel neet not a lot; not
many; not much

niet zo veel not so much, not
so many

veel succes! s∞kses good luck!

veerboot (de) va**y**rboht ferry

vegetariër (de) vaykHeta**h**ri-er
vegetarian

> Travel tip Vegetarians don't
> have to worry about finding
> something decent to eat in
> the Netherlands. Most *eet-
> cafés* and restaurants have at
> least one meat-free item on
> the menu, and you'll find a
> few veggie restaurants in the
> larger towns, offering reason-
> ably priced two- and three-
> course set meals.

vegetarisch vaykHeta**h**rees
arian

veilig v**i**likH safe

veiligheidsgordel (de)
v**i**likHhits-kHordel seat belt

veiligheidsgordels omdoen
fasten seat belts

veiligheidsspeld (de)
v**i**likHhits-spelt safety pin

veld (het) velt field

ventilator (de) ventila**h**tor fan

ventilatorriem (de)
ventila**h**tor-reem fan belt

ver vair far

verband (het) verba**n**t bandage;
dressing

verbanddoos (de) verba**n**t-dohs
first-aid kit

verbazingwekkend verbahzing-vekkent amazing, astonishing

verbergen verbairKHuh to hide

verbeteren verbayteruh to improve

verbind: ik verbind u door I'll put you through

verbinding (de) verbinding connection

verbindingstoon ringing tone

verblijfsvergunning (de) verblijfs-vergOOnning residence permit

verboden prohibited

verboden de dieren te voederen do not feed the animals

verboden in te halen no overtaking

verboden inrij behalve voor plaatselijk verkeer no access except local traffic

verboden te roken no smoking

verboden te vissen no fishing

verboden te zwemmen no swimming

verboden toegang behalve voor plaatselijk verkeer no access except local traffic

verboden toegang voor onbevoegden no access for unauthorized persons

verbranden verbranduh to burn

verder vairder further

verder dan beyond

verderop verderop further down; further up

verdieping (de) verdeeping floor, storey

verdwaald verdvahlt lost

verdwijnen verdvinuh to disappear

Verenigde Staten (de) veraynikHduh stahtuh United States

Vereniging voor Vreemdelingenverkeer tourist information

verf (de) vairf paint

vergadering (de) verkHahdering meeting

vergeet het maar! verkHayt uht mahr no way!

vergeten verkHaytuh to forget

vergif verkHif poison

vergissing (de) verkHissing mix-up

vergoeding (de) verkHooding refund

vergroting (de) verkHrohting enlargement

vergunning (de) verkHOOnning licence, permit; permission

verharde berm hard shoulder

verhoging (de) verhohKHing temperature, fever

verhuren to rent

verhuur rental

verhuurtarief hire charge

verjaardag (de) ver-yahrdakH birthday

verkeer (het) verkayr traffic

verkeer van rechts heeft voorrang give way to traffic from the right

verkeerd verkayrt wrong

verkeerd nummer noommer wrong nummer

verkeerd verbonden verbonduh wrong number

verkeersbord (het) verkayrsbort roadsign

verkeerslichten (de) verkayrs-liKHtuh traffic lights

verkeersomleiding diversion

verkeersopstopping (de) verkayrs-opstopping traffic jam

verkeersplein roundabout

verkeerstekens traffic signs

verkoop strippenkaart sale of bus/tram/metro tickets

verkopen verkohpuh to sell

verkouden: ik ben verkouden verkowduh I have a cold

verkrachting (de) verkraKHting rape

verlaat uw kamer alstublieft om... please vacate the room by...

verleden: in het verleden verlayduh in the past

verlegen verlayKHuh shy

verlengsnoer (het) verlengsnoor extension lead

verliezen verleesuh to lose

verloofd verlohft engaged

verloofde (de) verlohfduh fiancé; fiancée

verloren voorwerpen lost property, lost and found

verontreinigd verontrinikHt polluted

verontschuldiging (de) veront-sKHooldikHing apology

verpleger/verpleegster (de) verplayKHer/verplayKHster nurse

verplicht rondgaand verkeer compulsory to follow roundabout before taking chosen exit

vers vairs fresh

verscheidene versKHīdenuh several

verschil (het) versKHil difference

verschillend versKHillent different

verschilt: het verschilt versKHilt it varies

verschrikkelijk versKHrikkelik terrible

vershoudfolie (de) vershowt-folee cling film

versnellen to accelerate

versnellingen (de) versnellinguh gears

versnellingsbak (de) versnellings-bak gearbox

versnellingspook (de) versnellings-pohk gear lever

versperd verspairt blocked

verstaan verstahn to hear

 ik versta u niet I can't hear you

verstopt verstopt blocked

versturen verstooruh to send

vertalen vertahluh to translate

vertaling (de) vertahling translation

verte: in de verte duh vairtuh in the distance

vertellen vertelluh to tell

vertraging (de) vertrahKHing delay

vertrek (het) vertrek departure

vertrekhal (de) vertrekHal departure lounge

vertrekken vertrekkuh to leave

vervaldatum (de) verval-datoom expiry date

vervalsing (de) vervalsing fake

verveel: ik verveel me vervayl muh I'm bored

vervelend vervaylent annoying

verven vairvuh to paint, to dye

vervoerprijs (de) vervoorpris fare

verwachten vervaKHtuh to expect

verwarmd openluchtbad heated outdoor swimming pool

verwarming (de) vervarming heater; heating

verzekering (de) verzaykering insurance

verzilveren verzilveruh to cash

vest (het) vest cardigan; waistcoat

vet (het) vet fat

vijver (de) vīver pond

vind: ik vind het niet erg vint uht neet airKH I don't mind

vinden vinduh to find

vindt u dat goed? vint oo dat KHoot is that OK with you?

vinger (de) vinger finger

vis (de) vis fish

visboer (de) visboor fishmonger

visitekaartje (het) viseetuh-kahrt-yuh business card

visrestaurant (het) visrestowrant seafood restaurant

visum (het) veesoom visa

viswinkel (de) vísvinkel fishmonger's

Vlaams vlahms Flemish

vlag (de) vlakH flag

vlakbij vlakbī near; just off

vlees (het) vlays meat

vleugelboot (de) vlURKHelboht hydrofoil

vlieg (de) vleeKH fly

vliegen vleeKHuh to fly

vliegtuig (het) vleeKHtowKH aeroplane, airplane

per vliegtuig by air

vliegveld (het) vleeKHvelt airport

vlo (de) vlo flea

vloeibare zeep liquid soap

vloer (de) vloor floor

vlooienmarkt flea market

vlucht (de) vlooKHt flight

vluchtduur (de) vlooKHt-dōor flight time

vluchtheuvel traffic island

vluchtnummer (het) vlooKHt-nōommer flight number

vluchtstrook hard shoulder

vochtig voKHtikH damp; humid

vochtinbrengende crème (de) voKHt-inbrengenduh krem moisturizer

voedsel (het) vōotsel food

voedselvergiftiging (de) vōotselver-KHiftiKHing food poisoning

voelen vōoluh to feel

voet (de) vōot foot

voetbal (het) vōotbal football

voetbalstadion (het) football stadium

voetbalwedstrijd (de) vōotbal-vetstrīt football match

voeten vegen alstublieft please wipe your feet

voetgangers pedestrians

voetgangersgebied, voetgangerszone pedestrian precinct

voetgangersoversteekplaats pedestrian crossing

voetzool (de) vōotzohl sole

vogel (de) voKHel bird

vol vol full; no vacancies

volgeboekt fully booked; no vacancies

volgen volKHuh to follow

volgend volKHent next

de volgende bocht/straat links the next turning/street on the left

volgende lichting next collection

volgorde van de rijtuigen order of cars

volksdansen (het) volksdansuh folk dancing

volkenkunde folklore

volksmuziek (de) volks-mōozeek folk music

volledig verzorgde vakantie (de) vollaydikH verzorKHduh vakansee package holiday

volop... volop plenty of...

volpension vol-penshohn full board

voluit volOWt in full

volwassene (de) volvassenuh
adult

voor vohr for; before

  voor donderdag by Thursday

  voor het hotel in front of the
  hotel

  voor hoe laat? hoo laht
  for what time?

vooraan vohrahn in front

vooral vohral especially; mostly

voorbeeld (het) vohrbaylt
example

**voorbehoedsmiddel
(het)** vohrbehoots-middel
contraceptive

voorbij vohrbI over, finished

voorhoofd (het) vohr-hohft
forehead

voorkant (de) vohrkant front

aan de voorkant at the front

voornaam (de) vohrnahm
Christian name, first name

voorrang vohr-rang priority;
right of way

voorrangsweg main road

voorruit (de) vohr-rowt
windscreen, windshield

voorschrijven to prescribe

voorsorteren get in lane

voorstellen vohrstelluh
to introduce

  **mag ik… aan u
  voorstellen?** maKH – ahn oo
  may I introduce…?

voorstelling (de) vohrstelling
show, performance

vooruit vohrOWt in advance

voorzichtig vohrziKHtiKH careful

  voorzichtig! look out!

**voorzichtig, deze bus zwaait
uit** caution! this bus swings out

voorzichtig, kinderen
caution! children

voorzichtig rijden
drive carefully

voorzichtig, stoepje
mind the step

voorzichtig! breekbaar
handle with care! fragile

voorzichtig! trambaan
caution! tramway

**voorzieningen voor
gehandicapten** facilities for
the handicapped

vorig vohriKH last

vork (de) vork fork

vorst (de) vorst frost

vraag (de) vrahKH question

vrachtwagen (de) vraKHt-vahKHuh
lorry, truck

vragen vrahKHuh to ask

vredig vraydiKH peaceful

vreemd vraymt odd, strange

vreemdeling (de) vraymdeling
stranger

vreemdelingenpolitie
immigration police

vriend (de) vreent
friend; boyfriend

vriendelijk vreendelik
friendly; kind

vriendin (de) vreendin
friend; girlfriend

vriesvak freezer

vrij vrī vacant; free; quite

vrij duur d0or quite expensive

vrij toegankelijk admission free

vrijdag (de) vrīdakH Friday

vrije entree admission free

vroeg vrooKH early

vrolijk kerstfeest! vrohlik
kairstfayst merry Christmas!

vrouw (de) vrOw woman; wife

vrouwen women

vrouwenklooster convent

V.S. (de) vay-ess USA

VTB Flemish tourist organization

vuil (het) vOwl dirt; dirty

vuilnisbak (de) vOwlnisbak
dustbin, trashcan

vullen vOOlluh to fill up

vulling (de) vOOlling filling

vuur (het) vOOr fire

vuurtje: heeft u een vuurtje?
hayvt 00 uhn vOOrt-yuh do you
have a light?

VVV(-kantoor) tourist
information (office)

W

waakhond guard dog

waar vahr true

waar? where?

waar komt u vandaan? komt
00 vandahn where are you from?

waarborgsom (de) vahrborKHsom
deposit

waarde (de) vahrduh value

waardevol vahrdevol valuable

waarom? vahrom why?

waarom niet? neet why not?

waarschijnlijk vahr-sKHīnlik
probably

waarschuwing (de) warning

wachten vaKHtuh to wait

wacht op mij vaKHt op mī
wait for me

wachtkamer waiting room

wachtwoord (het) vaKHt-vohrt
password

wagentje (het) vahgent-yuh
supermarket trolley, cart

wagon (de) vahKHon carriage

walgelijk valKHelik revolting

wandelen (het) vandeluh
to walk; walking

wandelgebied hiking area

wandeling (de) vandeling walk

wandelwagen (de) vandelvahKHuh pushchair, buggy

wang (de) vang cheek

wanneer? vannayr when?

waren: wij/ze waren vī/zuh
vahruh we/they were

warenhuis (het) vahruh-hOws
department store

warm varm warm; hot

warme en koude dranken
hot and cold drinks

was (de) vas washing, laundry

was: ik was vas I was

hij/zij/het was hī/zī
he/she/it was

u was oo vas you were

wasautomatiek launderette, laundromat

wasbak (de) vasbak washhand basin, sink

wasgoed (het) vasкнoot washing, laundry

washandje (het) vashant-yuh flannel

wasknijper (de) vask-nīper clothes peg

wasmachine (de) vasmasheenuh washing machine

waspoeder (het) vaspooder washing powder, soap powder

wassen vassuh to wash

wassen en watergolven vassuh en vahterкнolvuh shampoo and set

wasserette (de) vasserettuh launderette, laundromat

wasserij (de) vasserī laundry

wastafel (de) vastahvel washbasin

wat? vat? what?

wat is er (aan de hand)? (ahn duh hant) what's wrong?

wat wil je? vil yuh what do you want?

wat wil je hebben? what would you like?

water (het) vahter water

in water oplossen dissolve in water

waterdicht vahterdikнt waterproof

waterfiets (de) vahterfeets pedalboat

waterpokken (de) vahterpokkuh chickenpox

waterskiën (het) vahterski-uhn waterskiing

watten (de) vattuh cotton wool, absorbent cotton

WC, w.c. (de) vay-say toilet, rest room

we vuh we

wedstrijd (de) vetstrīt match

weekkaart (de) vayk-kahrt weekly ticket

weer (het) vayr weather

wees voorzichtig! vays vohrzikнtiкн be careful!

weet: ik weet het niet vayt uht neet I don't know

ik weet het nog noкн I remember

weet jij het nog? yī do you remember?

weg (de) veкн road

is het ver weg? vair is it far away?

ze is weg zuh she's gone

wegafsluiting, weg afgesloten road closed

wegenkaart (de) vayкнuhkahrt road map

wegenwacht (de) vayкнuh-vaкнt breakdown service

weggaan veкн-кнahn go away

weggetje (het) veкннet-yuh lane

weggooien veкн-кнohyuh to throw away

wegkruising junction

wegomlegging, wegomleiding diversion

wegongeluk (het) veKHonKHelook road accident

wegrestaurant roadside restaurant

wegvernauwing road narrows

wegwerpluiers (de) veKHverplOW-yers disposable nappies/diapers

wegwijzer (de) veKHvizer signpost

weigering (de) vīKHering refusal

bij weigering knop indrukken press button in event of fault

wekken vekkuh to wake

wekker (de) vekker alarm clock

welke? velkuh which?; which one?; which ones?

welkom in... welcome to...

Wels vels Welsh

wenkbrauwpotlood (het) venkbrOW-potloht eyebrow pencil

wereld (de) vayrelt world

werk (het) vairk work

werk in uitvoering roadworks

werkdagen workdays

werkeloos vairkelohs unemployed

wesp (de) vesp wasp

westelijk vestelik western

westen (het) vestuh west

in het westen in the west

wet (de) vet law

weten vaytuh to know

wie? vee who?

wie is daar? dahr who is it?

wiel (het) veel wheel

wij vī we (emphatic)

wijd vīt wide

wijkplattegrond district map

wijn (de) vīn wine

wil: ik wil... I want...

hij wil... hī he wants...

ik wil niet... neet I don't want...

wildpark nature reserve

wilt u...? would you like...?

wilt u alstublieft vooruit betalen please pay in advance

wind (de) vint wind

windsurfplank (de) vint-soorfplank sailboard

winderig vinderiKH windy

windmolen (de) vintmohluh windmill

windsurfen (het) vintsoorfuh sailboarding, windsurfing

winkel (de) vinkel shop

winkelcentrum (het) vinkel-sentroom shopping centre

winkelen: gaan winkelen KHahn vinkeluh to go shopping

Travel tip When it comes to shopping, all the big cities are home to scores of specialist shops. There are certain obvious Dutch specialities – tulips, clogs and porcelain windmills to name the big three – but it's the Dutch flair for design that is the most striking feature, whether it's reflected in stylish furniture or clothes.

winkelwagen (de) vinkel-vahKHuh, **winkelwagentje** (het) vinkel-vahKHent-yuh trolley, cart

winteruitverkoop winter sale

wisselautomaat money-changing machine

wisselen visseluh to change (money)

wisselgeld (het) vissel-KHelt change, small change

wisselkantoor (het) visselkantohr bureau de change

wisselkoers (de) visselkoors exchange rate

wist: dat wist ik niet vist I didn't know that

wit vit white

woensdag voonsdaKH Wednesday

wol (de) vol wool

wolk (de) volk cloud

woon: waar woon je? vahr vohn yuh where do you live?

ik woon in... I live in…

woonboot (de) vohnboht barge, houseboat

woonerf residential area with ramps to slow down traffic

woonplaats domicile

woord (het) vohrt word

Z

zacht zaKHt soft; mild

zachte berm soft verge

zachte lenzen (de) zaKHtuh soft lenses

zadel (het) zahdel saddle

zak (de) pocket

zakdoek (de) zakdook handkerchief

zaken business

zakkenroller (de) pickpocket

zaklantaarn (de) zaklantahrn torch, flashlight

zakmes (het) penknife

zalf (de) ointment

zand (het) zant sand

zanger/zangeres (de) singer (*male/female*)

zaterdag zahterdaKH Saturday

zaterdags en op zon- en feestdagen on Saturdays, Sundays and public holidays

ze zuh she; they; her

dat is ze that's her

zee zay sea

aan zee ahn by the sea(side)

zeep (de) zayp soap

zeer zayr sore

het doet zeer doot it's sore

zeggen zeKHuh to say

zeil zil sail

zeilen (het) to sail; sailing

zeker zayker sure; certainly

zeldzaam zeltzahm rare, uncommon

zelfbediening (de) zelfbedeening self-service

zelfde: het zelfde zelfduh the same

zelfs even

zelfs als... even if…

zet uw motor af switch off your engine

zetmeel starch

zetten to put

zie bodem/deksel see bottom/cap

ziek zeek ill, sick

ziekenhuis (het) zeekuh-hows hospital

ziekenwagen (de) zeekuh-vahkʜuh ambulance

ziekte (de) zeektuh disease

zien zeuh to see

zij zī she; they (emphatic)

zijde (de) zīduh silk

zijkant side

zijn zīn to be; are; his

zijn er…? are there…?

zijstraat (de) zīstraht side street

zilver (het) zilver silver

zin (de) sentence; meaning; liking

het heeft geen zin hayft kʜayn there's no point

heb je zin in een ijsje? would you like an ice cream?

zingen to sing

zitplaats (de) zitplahts seat

zitten to sit

zn. son

z.o. south-east

zo so

zo… mogelijk as… as possible

zo groot als as big as

zo meteen metayn in a minute

zoeken zookuh to look for, to search

zoet zoot sweet

zolen en hakken heelbar, shoe repairs

zomer (de) sohmer summer

's zomers in the summer

zomeruitverkoop summer sale

zon (de) sun

zondag zondakʜ Sunday

zonder without

zonder badkamer batkahmer without bathroom

zonder bon wordt niet geruild no goods exchanged without a receipt

zonder douche without shower

zonder pension no meals

zonder toevoeging van conserveringsmiddelen contains no preservatives

zonnebrand (de) zonnebrant sunburn

zonnebrandcrème (de) zonnebrant-krem suntan lotion

zonnebrandolie (de) zonnebrant-ohlee suntan oil

zonnebril (de) zonnebril sunglasses

zonnen to sunbathe

zonneschijn (de) zonneskʜīn sunshine

zonnesteek (de) zonnestayk sunstroke

zonnig zonnikʜ sunny

zonsondergang (de) zonsonderkHang sunset

zonsopgang (de) zonsopKHang dawn

zool (de) zohl sole

zoon (de) zohn son

zorgen (de) zorkHuh worries

ik maak me zorgen mahk muh I'm worried

zorgen voor zorkHuh vohr to look after

zou u… kunnen? zow ∞… k∞nnuh could you…?

z.o.z. please turn over

zo-zo average, so-so

z.s.m. as soon as possible

zuidelijk zowdelik southern

zuiden (het) zowduh south

in het zuiden in the south

zuidenwind (de) southerly wind

zuiderling (de) zowderling southerner

Zuid-Holland South Holland

zuidoosten (het) zowt-ohstuh southeast

zuidwesten (het) zowt-vestuh southwest

zuipen zowpuh to booze

zuivelproduct (het) zow-vel-prohd∞kt dairy product

zuivere scheerwol pure wool

zus (de) z∞s sister

zuur z∞r sour

zwaar zvahr badly; heavy

zwager (de) zvahkHer brother-in-law

zwak zvak weak

zwanger zvanger pregnant

zwart zvart black

Zweden zvayduh Sweden

Zweeds zvayts Swedish

zwembad (het) zvembat swimming pool

zwembroek (de) zvembrook swimming trunks

zwemmen zvemmuh to swim

zwemmen verboden no swimming

zwempak (het) zvempak swimming costume

zwemvest (het) zvemvest life jacket

Zwitsers zvitsers Swiss

MENU READER

Food

Essential terms

bread het brood broht
butter de boter
cup de kop
dessert het nagerecht
  nah-KHereKHt
fish de vis
fork de vork
glass het (drink)glas
knife het mes
main course het hoofdgerecht
  hohft-KHereKHt
meat het vlees vlays
menu het menu menoo,
  de kaart kahrt
pepper de peper payper

plate het bord
salad de salade salahduh
salt het zout zowt
set menu het vaste menu
  vastuh menoo
soup de soep soop
spoon de lepel laypel
starter het voorgerecht
  vohrKHereKHt
table de tafel tahfel

another…, please nog een…,
  alstublieft noKH uhn – alstoobleeft
excuse me! (to call waiter/
  waitress) pardon!
could I have the bill, please?
  kan ik afrekenen, alstublieft?

A–Z

aalbessen ahlbessuh (black, red or white) currants

aardappelen ahrdappeluh potatoes

aardappelpuree ahrdappelpooray mashed potatoes

aardbeien ahrdbī- uh strawberries

abrikoos abrikohs apricot

abrikozencompote abrikohzuh-kompot apricot compote

abrikozenjam abrikohzuh-jam apricot jam

abrikozenvlaai abrikohzuh-vlī apricot flan

ajam ahyam chicken (Indonesian)

ajuin ahyown onion

amandelen ahmandeluh almonds

amandelkoekjes ahmandelkook-yuhs crispy biscuits/cookies with almonds or soft almond-paste filling

amerikaanse biefstuk amayrikahnsuh beefstook hamburger with a fried egg

ananas pineapple

andijvie andīvee endive

andijvie a la crème krem cooked endives in cream sauce

anijs anīs aniseed

ansjovis anshohvis anchovies

appel apple

appelcompote apple compote, stewed apples

appelflap apple turnover

appelgebak appel-kнebak apple and cinnamon tart or cake

> **Travel tip** Dutch cakes and biscuits are always good, and best eaten in a *ban-ketbakkerij* (patisserie) with a small serving area. Top of the list is the ubiquitous Dutch speciality *appelge-bak* – chunky, memorably fragrant apple and cinnamon pie, served hot in huge wedges, and often topped with whipped cream.

appelgelei appelJeleī apple jelly

appelmoes appelmoos apple sauce; puréed apples

appelpannenkoek appel-pannuhkook apple pancake

appelstroop appelstrohp kind of treacle made with apples, used as a sandwich spread

appelstrudel appel-stroodel apple strudel

appeltaart (met slagroom) appeltahrt (met slaкнrohm) apple cake (with whipped cream)

Ardennerham Ardennes ham (smoked)

artisjok artishok artichoke

asperges asperJes asparagus

atjar tampoer at-yar tampoor mixed pickles (Indonesian)

au jus ow yoos in gravy

augurken OW-KHOOrkuh gherkins

azijn ahzīn vinegar

baars bahrs bass

babi bahbi pork (Indonesian)

bak- en braadvet brahtvet
cooking fat

baklappen frying steak

balkenbrij balkuhbrī
white pudding

bami noodle dish with meat and
vegetables (Indonesian)

bamivlees bahmivlays
diced pork, served with
Indonesian bami dish

banaan banahn banana

banketbakkersroom banket-
bakkers-rohm confectioner's
custard

banketletter banketletter puff
pastry with almond paste filling

basilicum basilikoom basil

bearnaise saus bayarnaysuh
sows hollandaise sauce with
tarragon vinegar, chopped
tarragon or chervil

belegen kaas belayKHuh kahs
mature cheese

berliner berleener doughnut filled
with custard

beschuit besKHOWt crispbread

**bevat…% meervoudig (on)
verzadigde vetzuren**
contains… % poly(un)saturates

bevat geen kleurstof
no artificial colouring

biefstuk (hollandse) beefstook
(hollandsuh) steak

biefstuk van de haas duh hahs
fillet steak

biefstuk van de lende lenduh
sirloin steak, rump steak

bieslook beeslohk chives

bieten beetuh, **bietjes** beet-yuhs
beetroot

bijgerecht bī-KHereKHt side dish

bitterballen bitterballuh
hot, savoury forcemeat for
cocktail snacks

bitterkoekjespudding bitter-
kookyuhs-poodding milk pudding
containing almond macaroons

blauwgekookte forel blow-
KHekohktuh poached trout

bleekselderij blayk-selderī
celery

blinde vinken blinduh finkuh
rolled slice of veal stuffed with
minced meat

bloedworst blootvorst black
pudding, blood sausage

bloemkool bloomkohl cauliflower

boerenmeisjes booruh-mīshuhs
apricots in brandy

boerenham booruhham
smoked ham

boerenkaas booruhkahs
farmhouse cheese

boerenkool booruhkohl kale

boerenleverworst
booruhlayvervorst coarse liver
sausage

boerenmetworst booruhmetvorst
coarse sausage

boerenomelet boorenommelet
omelette with potatoes and
bacon

boheemse saus bohhaymsuh
sows béchamel sauce with
mayonnaise

bokking smoked herring

bonen bohnuh beans

bonensla bohnuhsla bean salad

borrelnootjes borrelnoht-yuhs
cocktail nuts

borst breast

bosbessen bilberries

bot flounder

boter bohter butter

boterham bohterham slice
of bread and butter; open
sandwich

boterham met... ... sandwich

boterham met kaas kahs
cheese sandwich

boterhamworst bohterhamvorst
sliced sausage used on
sandwiches

boterletter puff pastry with
almond paste filling

bouillon stock, consommé

braadlappen brahtlappuh
frying steak

braadworst brahtvorst sausage
for frying

bramen brahmuh blackberries,
brambles

brasem bream

brood broht bread

broodje broht-yuh roll; sandwich

bruinbrood brownbroht
brown bread

bruine bonen brownuh bohnuh
brown beans resembling
kidney beans

bruine bonensoep brownuh
bohnuhsoop brown bean soup

bruine suiker sowker
brown sugar

caramelpudding karamel-
poodding caramel custard

casselerrib kasseler-rip
salted, boiled ribs of pork

champignons shampin-yons
mushrooms

champignonsoep shampin-
yonsoop mushroom soup

chantillysaus shantihyee-sows
mayonnaise and whipped
cream sauce

Chinese fondue shinaysuh fondoo
Chinese fondue – individual
portions of vegetables or meat
dipped in boiling stock

Chinese kool kohl Chinese leaf

chips ships crisps, potato chips

chocolade hagelslag
shokolahduh hahкнelslaкн
chocolate vermicelli

chocolade vlokken flokkuh
chocolate flakes

chocoladepasta shokolahduh-
pasta chocolate spread

chocoladevla shokolahduh-vla
kind of chocolate custard

citroen sitroon lemon

citroenvla sitroonvla kind of
lemon custard

compote kompot compote,
stewed fruit

contrefilet kontrefilay rump steak

courgette courgette, zucchini

croquet krohket croquette

croquetje krohket-yuh small
croquette

dadels dahdels dates

daging dahging beef (Indonesian)

dagschotel daKH-sKHohtel
dish of the day

dame blanche dahm blansh
ice cream with chocolate sauce

doperwten dop-airtuh garden peas

dragon drahKHon tarragon

drie in de pan dree in duh pan
small pancakes with currants
and raisins

droogkokende rijst drohKH-
kohkenduh rist instant rice

drop Dutch liquorice

druiven drowvuh grapes

duitse biefstuk dowtsuh
beefstook minced beef and
onion hamburgers

Edammer (kaas) kahs Edam
(cheese)

eend aynt duck

eendenei aynduh-ī duck egg

ei, eieren ī, ī-uhruh egg, eggs

eierkoeken ī-uhrkookun flat,
round sponge cakes

eisbein īsbīn pickled upper leg
of pork

erwt(en) airt(uh) pea(s)

erwtensoep airtuhsoop
thick pea soup

erwtensoep met spek
thick pea soup with bacon

erwtensoep met worst vorst
thick pea soup with sausage

fazant fahzant pheasant

fijngehakt fīnKHehakt
finely minced

filet americain filay amayrikan
tartar steak

filosoof filosohf stew with meat
and potatoes

forel fohrel trout

frambozen frambohzuh
raspberries

fricandeau frikandoh
lean pork or veal

friet(en) freet(uh)
chips, French fries

frietsaus freetsOWs mayonnaise
to put on French fries

frikadel freekahdel deep-fried
sausage made from minced
meat

frites freet chips, French fries

gado gado vegetables in peanut
sauce (Indonesian)

ganzenlever KHanzuhlayver goose liver

garnalen KHarnahluh prawns; shrimps

garnalencocktail KHarnahluh-koktayl prawn cocktail

garnalensaus KHarnahluh-sows shrimp sauce

gebak KHebak fancy pastries or cakes

gebakjes KHebak-yuhs small, fancy pastries or cakes

gebakken KHebakkuh fried

gebakken aardappelen ahrtappeluh fried potatoes

gebakken ei met spek ī fried egg with bacon

gebakken mosselen fried mussels

gebakken paling pahling fried eel

gebakken uitjes owt-yuhs fried onions

gebonden KHebonduh thickened

gebraden KHebrahduh roast

gebraden eend aynt roast duck

gebraden gehakt KHehakt roast meatloaf

gedroogd KHedrohKHt dried

gefileerd KHefilayrt filleted

geglaceerde kastanjes KHeKHlasayrduh kastan-yuhs glazed chestnuts

gegrild KHeKHrilt grilled

gehakt KHehakt minced meat

gehaktbal KHehaktbal meatball

gekookt KHekohkt boiled

gekruid KHekrowt seasoned with herbs or spices

gele erwten KHayluh airtuh yellow split peas

gelei Jelī jelly

gemarineerd KHemarinayrt marinated

gemarineerd rundvlees roontvlays marinated beef

gemarineerde runderlappen KHemarinayrduh roonderlappuh marinated braising steak

gember KHember ginger

gemberkoek KHemberkook gingerbread

gemberpoeder KHember-pooder ground ginger

gemengde noten KHemeng-duh mixed nuts

gepocheerd KHeposhayrt poached

gepocheerde eieren
KHeposh**ay**rduh **ī**-uhruh
poached eggs

gepocheerde vis poached fish

gepofte kastanjes KHep**o**ftuh
kastan-yuhs roast chestnuts

geraspt KHer**a**spt grated

gerecht KHer**e**KHt dish

gerookt KHer**oh**kt smoked

gerookte bokking KHer**oh**ktuh
smoked herring

gerookte paling p**a**hling
smoked eel

gerookte zalm smoked salmon

geroosterd KHer**oh**stert grilled

geroosterd brood broht toast

gerst KH**ai**rst barley

gesmoord KHesm**oh**rt braised

gestampte muisjes KHest**a**mptuh
m**ow**shuhs powdered aniseed
eaten on bread

gestoofd KHest**oh**ft stewed

gestoofde andijvie KHest**oh**fduh
and**ī**vee steamed endive

gevulde kalfsborst KHev**oo**lduh
k**a**lfsborst stuffed breast of veal

gevulde koek kook pastry with
almond paste filling

**gevulde omelet met groene
kruiden** KHr**oo**nuh kr**ow**duh
stuffed omelette with green
herbs

goreng fried (Indonesian)

Goudse kaas KH**ow**tsuh kahs
Gouda cheese

goulash goulash

griet KHreet brill

groene haring KHr**oo**nuh lightly
salted young herring

groene saus s**ow**s mayonnaise
with fresh herbs

groenten KHr**oo**ntuh vegetables

groentesoep KHr**oo**ntesoop
vegetable soup

grof gesneden bladspinazie
KHr**o**f KHesn**ay**duh bl**a**tspinahzee
coarsely chopped leaf spinach

gula djawa Javanese brown
sugar (Indonesian)

haas hahs hare

haasbiefstuk h**a**hsbeefst**oo**k
fillet steak

hachée hahsh**ay** stew of diced
meat, onions, vinegar and cloves

halfvolle melk half-v**o**lluh
skimmed milk

halfvolle yoghurt yoKHh**oo**rt
skimmed milk yoghurt

halvarine halvar**ee**nuh half butter,
half margarine

hamlappen pork steak from the
fat part of the pig's heel

handappelen eating apples

handperen h**a**ntpayruh
dessert pears

hangop hang**o**p buttermilk dessert

hardgekookt ei hardKHek**oh**kt **ī**
hard-boiled egg

haring herring

haring met uitjes **ow**t-yuhs
herring with chopped onions

haringsalade hahringsaladuh
herring salad

havermout hahvermowt,
havermoutse pap
hahvermowtsuh porridge made
with milk

hazelnoten hahzelnotuh hazelnuts

hazenpastei hahzuhpasti hare pâté

hazenpeper hahzuhpayper
jugged hare

hazenrug hahzuhrooKH
saddle of hare

heilbot hilbot halibut

hertenvlees hairtuhvlays venison

hete bliksem haytuh potatoes
and apples mashed together

hollandse biefstuk hollandsuh
beefstook thick slice of frying
steak

hollandse saus sows
hollandaise sauce

hom soft roe

honing hohning honey

honingkoek hohningkook type of
gingerbread made with honey

hoofdgerecht(en)
hohfdKHereKHt(uh)
main course(s)

hopjesvla hopyesvla kind of
caramel custard

houtsnip howtsnip woodcock

hutspot hootspot hotpot with
potatoes, onions and carrots

huzarensalade hoozahruhsaladuh,
huzarensla hoozahruhslah
potato salad with beetroot,

gherkins, meat, mayonnaise
and hard-boiled eggs

ijs is ice cream

ikan fish (Indonesian)

ikan terie tayree very small dried
fish (Indonesian)

in het zuur zoor pickled

jachtschotel yaKHt-sKHohtel
oven dish with meat, potatoes,
apples and onions

janhagel yanhahKHel crumbly
biscuit/cookie sprinkled with
tiny bits of sugar

jeneverbessen yenayver-bessuh
juniper berries

jong yong young

jonge kaas yonguh kahs
immature cheese

kaas kahs cheese

kaas 20+ low-fat cheese

kaas 40+ full fat cheese

> **Travel tip** Most Dutch chees-
> es vary little from the familiar
> pale yellow, semi-soft Gouda,
> though the various levels
> of maturity impart different
> flavours: *jong* cheese has a
> mild taste, *belegen* is much
> stronger, while *oud* can be
> pungent and strong, with a
> grainy, flaky texture. The best
> way to eat it is as the Dutch
> do, in thin slices rather than
> large chunks.

kaascroissant kahskrwassan
cheese croissant

kaaskoekje kahskook-yuh
cheese biscuit

kaassaus kahs-sows
cheese sauce

kaassoesje kahs-sooshuh
cheese puff

kabeljauw kabel-yow cod

kadetje kahdet-yuh soft roll

kalfsfricassee kalfs-frikassay
veal fricassee

kalfsbiefstuk kalfs-beefstook
fillet of veal

kalfsgehakt kalfs-KHehakt
minced veal

kalfslappen veal slices

kalfslever kalfs-layver calf's liver

kalfsleverworst kalfs-layvervorst
veal liver sausage

kalfsniertjes kalfs-neert-yuhs
calf's kidneys

kalfsoester kalfs-ooster
escalope of veal

kalfsschnitzel kalfs-shnitzel
veal schnitzel

kalfstong calf's tongue

kalfsvlees kalfsvlays veal

kalkoen kalkoon turkey

kandijsuiker kandī-sowker
crystallized sugar (used in coffee)

kaneel kanayl cinnamon

kapucijners kapoosīners
marrowfat peas

karbonade karbonahduh chop;
small piece of meat from the

back, shoulder, rib or loin of a
calf, lamb, sheep or pig

karnemelk karnemelk
buttermilk

karnemelkse pap karnemelksuh
pap buttermilk porridge

karper carp

kastanjepuree kastanye-pooray
puréed chestnuts

kastanjepudding kastanye-
poodding chestnut pudding

kastanjes kastanyes chestnuts

katjang kat-yang pulses; peanuts
(Indonesian)

katjang idjoe it-yoo small green
peas (Indonesian)

kerrie kerree curry

kerriesaus kerreesows
curry sauce

kerriesoep kerreesoop
curry soup

kersen cherries

kersenvlaai kersuhvlī
cherry pie

kervel kervel chervil

kervelsoep kervelsoop
chervil soup

ketjap asin ket-yap salty soy
sauce (Indonesian)

ketjap manis ket-yap sweet soy sauce
(Indonesian)

ketoembar kaytoombar
coriander seeds (Indonesian)

keukenstroop kurkuhstrohp
golden syrup

kievitsei keeveets-ī plover's egg

kikkerbillen kikkerbilluh,
kikkerbilletjes kikkerbillet-yuhs
frogs' legs

kinderijsje kinder-īshuh
small ice cream

kinderportie kinderporsee
children's portion

kindersurprise kinder-
sOOrpreesuh children's dessert

kip chicken

kip aan het spit ahn
spit-roasted chicken

kippenlever kippuhlayver
chicken-liver

kippensoep kippuhsoop
chicken soup

klapper coconut

klapstuk klapstOOk piece of beef
from the rib

klaverhoning klahverhoning
clover honey

knäckebrood k-nekkebroht
crispbread

knakworst k-nakvorst
Frankfurter

knoflook k-noflohk garlic

knolselderij k-nolselderī
celeriac

koekjes kook-yuhs biscuits,
cookies

koenjit koon-yit spice (Indonesian)

koffietafel koffeetafel cold buffet
lunch, sometimes including
soup

kogelbiefstuk kohkHel-beefstOOk
thick end of rump

kokosnoot kohkosnoht coconut

komijnekaas kohmīnekahs
cheese with cumin seeds

komkommer cucumber

konijn kohnīn rabbit

koninginnesoep kohning**i**nnesoop
cream of chicken soup

kool koh**l** cabbage

koolraap koh**l**rahp swede

koolvis koh**l**vis coalfish

korst crust

kotelet chop, cutlet

koud ko**w**t cold

krabbetjes kra**b**bet-yuhs
spare ribs

kreeft krayft lobster

kreeftensoep kra**y**ftuhsoop
lobster soup

krenten currants

krentenbrood kr**e**ntuhbroht
currant loaf

kroepoek kr**oo**pook prawn
crackers

kroket(ten) croquette(s) of spiced
minced meat covered with
breadcrumbs and deep-fried

krop sla krop sla**h** (head of)
lettuce

kropsla kropsla**h** cabbage lettuce

kroten kroh**t**uh, **krootjes**
kro**h**tyuhs beetroot

kruiden kr**ow**duh spices; herbs

kruidenboter kr**ow**duhbohter
herb butter

kruidenkaas kr**ow**duhkahs
herb cheese

kruidnagel kr**ow**t-nah**K**Hel clove

kruisbessen kr**ow**sbessuh
gooseberries

kuikenvleugels k**ow**kuh-vl**ur**KHels
chicken wings

kuikenbouten k**ow**kuhbo**w**tuh
chicken legs

kuit ko**w**t hard roe

kwark kvark quark, low-fat soft
white cheese

kwarktaart kvarktahrt cheesecake

kwartel kva**r**tel quail

lamsborst breast of lamb

lamsbout lamsbo**w**t leg of lamb

lamskotelet lamb chop

lamslapje lamslap-yuh
escalope of lamb

lamslappen lamb slices

lamsragout lams-rah**K**Hoo diced
lamb in a thick white sauce

lamsschouder lams-s**K**Ho**w**der
shoulder of lamb

lamstong lamb's tongue

lamsvlees lamsvlays lamb

laurierblad lo**w**re**e**rblat bayleaf

Leerdammer layrda**m**mer
nutty-tasting cheese with holes

Leidse kaas l**i**dsuh kahs Gouda
cheese with cumin seeds

lekkerbekjes le**k**kerbek-yuhs deep-
fried whiting fillets in batter

lever la**y**ver liver

leverworst la**y**vervorst
liver sausage

Limburgse vlaai limb**oo**r**K**Hsuh vl**i**
fruit flan from Limburg

linzen lentils

loempia l**oo**mpia spring roll
(Indonesian)

lombok hot red peppers
(Indonesian)

maaltijd mahltīt meal

maaltijdsoep mahltīdsoop thick
meat and vegetable soup,
served as a meal in itself

Maasdammer mahsdammer
strong, creamy cheese with
holes

Maaslander mahslander
type of cheese

maatjesharing maht-yuhshahring
young herring

maderasaus mahdayra-sows
brown sauce with madeira

mager mahkHer low fat; lean

magere melk mahkHeruh
skimmed milk

maiskolf mīskolf corn on the cob

maiskorrels mīskorrels sweet corn

makreel mahkrayl mackerel

marsepein marsepīn marzipan

meloen meloon melon

menu van de dag menoo van duh
dakH today's menu

mergpijpjes merkHpīp-yuhs
marrowbone

metworst metvorst pork sausage

mie mee thin Chinese noodles

mierik meerik horseradish

mihoen mihoon very fine Chinese
rice noodles

moerbeien moorbī-uh mulberries

moes moos puréed fruit

moesappelen moosappeluh
cooking apples

mosselen mussels

mosselensoep mosseluhsoop
mussel soup

mosterd mostert mustard

mousseline saus mousseleenuh
sows hollandaise sauce with
whipped cream and lemon juice

munt moont mint

nagerecht(en) nahkHerekHt(uh)
dessert(s)

nasi nassee rice (Indonesian)

nasi goreng gohreng fried rice
dish with meat and vegetables
(Indonesian)

Travel tip The Dutch
are particularly partial to
Indonesian food: *nasi goreng*
and *bami goreng* are good
basic dishes, though there
are usually more exciting
items on the menu. You
could ask for a *rijsttafel* – a
sampler meal, comprising
boiled rice and/or noodles
plus a selection of small and
often spicy meat, fish and
vegetable dishes, with hot
sambal sauce on the side.

---

nasi rames various spicy dishes
served with rice (Indonesian)

nasivlees nasseevlays diced pork

natrium-arme kaas nahtri-oom-
armuh kahs low-salt cheese

nekkarbonaden neck-end chops

nieren neeruh kidneys

nieuwe haring new-uh herring
caught early in the season

noedels noodels noodles

nootmuskaat nohtmooskaht
nutmeg

oesters oosters oysters

olie ohlee oil

oliebol ohleebol deep-fried,
ball-shaped cake containing
currants or raisins, sprinkled
with icing sugar

olijfolie ohlīf-ohlee olive oil

olijven ohlīvuh olives

ongepelde rijst ongepelduh rīst
brown rice

ongezoet ongezoot unsweetened

ontbijt ontbīt breakfast

ontbijtkoek ontbītkook
type of gingerbread

ontbijtspek ontbītspek
streaky bacon

opzij opzī on the side; as a side
dish

ossestaart ossestahrt oxtail

ossestaartsoep ossestahrtsoop
oxtail soup

ossetong ossetong ox tongue

oud owt old, mature

oude kaas owduh kahs
well-matured cheese

paardenrookvlees
pahrduhrohkvlays
smoked horsemeat

paling eel

paling in het groen KHroon
eel in sorrel sauce and herbs

palingworst pahlingvorst
type of sausage

paneermeel pahnayrmayl
breadcrumbs

panggang grilled (Indonesian)

pannenkoek pannuhkook pancake

pannenkoek met stroop strohp
pancake with syrup

paprika (rode/groene/gele)
rohduh/KHroonuh/KHayluh
pepper (red/green/yellow)

parijzer worst parīzer vorst
type of sausage

pastei pastī vol-au-vent; pie

pasteitje pastīt-yuh
small vol-au-vent

pastinaak pastinahk parsnip

patat (friet) freet
chips, French fries

patates frites patat freet
chips, French fries

patrijs patrīs partridge

pedis paydis hot and spicy
(Indonesian)

peer payr pear

peper payper pepper

peperkorrels peppercorns

pepermunt paypermoont
peppermint

pepersaus payper-sows
creamy white sauce with
crushed peppercorns

perencompote payruhkompot
pear compote

perenmoes payruhmoos
puréed pears

perenstroop payruhstrohp kind
of treacle made from pears,
used as sandwich spread

perziken perzikkuh peaches

peterselie paytersaylee parsley

pinda's pindahs peanuts

pindakaas pindahkahs
peanut butter

pisang banana (Indonesian)

plakje plak-yuh slice

plantaardig vet plant-ahrdiKHt
vegetable fat

plantaardige olie plantahrdiKHuh
ohlee vegetable oil

poffertjes poffert-yuhs small
pancakes served with lots of
butter and icing sugar

pommes frites pom freet
French fries

pompelmoes pompelmoos
grapefruit

pompoen pompoon pumpkin

poon pohn gurnard

postelein postelin purslane

prei prī leek

preisoep prī-soop leek soup

pruimedant prowmedant
type of prune

pruimen prowmuh plums; prunes

pruimenjam prowmuh-jam
plum jam

rabarber rhubarb

radijs rahdīs radish

rauw row raw

rauwkost rowkost raw vegetables

ravigote saus rahvigotuh sows
vinaigrette made with shallots,
capers and herbs

ree(bok) ray(bok) roe(buck)

reebout raybowt haunch of
venison

reerug rayrooKH saddle of venison

regenboogforel rayKHuhbohKH-
fohrel rainbow trout

remoulade saus remowlahduh
sows mayonnaise with
anchovies

riblappen rib steak

rietsuikerstroop
reetsowkerstrohp treacle

rijst rīst rice

rijsttafel rīsttafel rice and/or
noodles served with a variety
of spicy side dishes and hot
sambal sauce (Dutch Indonesian)

rijstebrij rīstebrī rice pudding

rijstevlaai rīstevlī creamed rice
flan

rivierkreeft riveerkrayft crayfish

riviervis riveervis freshwater fish

rode bessen rohduh
red currants

rode bessengelei bessuhgelī
red currant jelly

rode bieten beetuh beetroot

rode kool kohl red cabbage

roerei roorī scrambled eggs

rog roKH ray (fish)

roggebrood roKHKHebroht
ryebread

rolmops rolmops, pickled herring

rookvlees rohkvlays thinly sliced smoked beef

rookworst rohkvorst smoked sausage

room rohm cream

roomboter rohmboter butter

roomijs rohmīs ice cream

roomijstaart rohm-īstahrt ice cream gateau

roomsoes rohmsoos éclair

rosbief rosbeef roast beef

roti flat pancake-like bread (Indonesian, Surinamese, Indian)

rozemarijn rohzemarīn rosemary

rozijn(en) rohzīn(uh) raisin(s)

rug van de haas rooKH van duh hahs saddle of hare

rundergehakt roonderKHehakt minced beef

runderlap roonderlap braising steak

runderlever roonder-layver ox liver

rundvlees roondvlays beef

Russische salade rooseesuh salahduh Russian salad

sajoer sah-yoor vegetable soup (Indonesian)

salami (met knoflook) k-noflohk salami (with garlic)

sambal very hot chilli sauce (Indonesian)

sardientjes sardeent-yuhs sardines

saté satay Indonesian kebab, usually spicy chicken or beef, served with peanut sauce

satésaus sataysows peanut sauce served to accompany meat broiled (grilled) on skewers

saucijs sowsīs unsmoked sausage

saucijzenbroodje sowsīzuh-broht-yuh sausage roll

saus sows sauce

savooiekool savoh-uhkohl Savoy cabbage

schaaldieren sKHahldeeruh shellfish

schapenvlees sKHahpuhvlays mutton

schar sKHar dab (fish)

scharreleieren sKHarrel-ī-uhruh free-range eggs

schartong sKHartong lemon sole

schelvis sKHelvis haddock

schenkel sKHenkel shin of beef

schildpadsoep sKHildpatsoop turtle soup

schnitzel shnitzel veal cutlet rolled in breadcrumbs

schol sKHol plaice

schorseneren sKHorsenayruh salsify (root vegetable)

schouderham sKHOWderham shoulder of ham

schouderlappen sKHOWderlappuh shoulder steak

schuimomelet sKHOWmomelet omelette with stiffly beaten egg white

schuimgebak sKHOWmKHebak
meringue

schuimpjes sKHOWmp-yuhs
sweets made of stiffly beaten
egg and sugar

selderij selderī celery

sereh seray lemon grass
(Indonesian)

seroendeng seroendeng
shredded coconut and peanuts
fried with spices (Indonesian)

shoarma kebab

sinaasappel sinahsappel orange

sinaasappelsaus
sinahsappelsows orange sauce

sjis kebab shis kebap shish kebab

sla lettuce; salad

slaatje slaht-yuh small salad with
mayonnaise

slagroom slaKHrohm
whipped cream

slagroomtaart slaKHrohm-tahrt
whipped cream cake

slagroomwafels slaKHrohm-
vafels waffles with whipped
cream

slakken snails

slaolie slah-ohlee salad oil

slasaus slahsows salad dressing

slavinken slahvinkuh minced
pork or beef rolled in bacon

smeerkaas smayrkahs
cheese spread

sneetje snayt-yuh slice

snelkookrijst snelkohkrīst
quick-cook rice

snert thick pea soup

snijbonen snībohnuh string beans

snoekbaars snookbahrs perch
(fish)

soep soop soup

soep Lady Curzon turtle soup
finished with cream and a
pinch of curry powder

soep van de dag duh daKH
soup of the day

soepvlees soopvlays meat for
soup

spaanse omelet spahnsuh
Spanish omelette, omelette
with vegetables

specerijen spayserī-uh spices

speculaas spaykoolahs
cinnamon-flavoured biscuit/
cookie

spek streaky bacon

spekpannenkoek
spekpannuhkook pancake with
bacon

sperziebonen spairzeebohnuh
French beans

spiegelei speeKHelī fried egg

spiering speering smelt (fish)

spijskaart spīskahrt menu

spinazie spinahzee spinach

spliterwten splitertuh split peas

spruiten sprowtuh, **spruitjes**
sprowt-yuhs Brussels sprouts

stamppot stamppot mashed
potatoes mixed with vegetables

stokbrood stokbroht French bread

stokvis stockfish

stoofperen stohfpayruh cooking pears

stoofvlees stohfvlays stewing meat

stroopwafel strohpvafel wafer-type biscuit/cookie with syrup filling

studentenhaver stoodentuhhahver mixed nuts and raisins

sucadelappen sookahdelappuh stewing steak

suiker sowker sugar

sukade sookahduh candied peel

taart tahrt cake

tahoe tahoo, **tofoe** tohfoo tofu, bean curd

tarbot turbot (fish)

tartaar tartahr raw minced steak, steak tartare

tarwebloem tarvebloom wheatflour

tarwebrood tarvebroht wheat bread

taugé towgay bean sprouts

tempé tempay tempeh (kind of tofu)

tijm tim thyme

toeristenmenu tooristuhmenoo tourist menu

tomaat tomaht tomato

tomatensaus tomahtuhsows tomato sauce

tomatensoep (met gehaktballetjes) tomahtuhsoop (met KHehaktballet-yuhs) tomato soup (with meat balls)

tompoes tompoos vanilla slice

tong sole

tong in bakdeeg bakdayKH sole in batter

tongeworst tongevorst tongue sausage

tongrolletjes tongrollet-yuhs rolled fillets of sole

tonijn tonin tuna

tosti toasted sandwich

trassi trassi condiment made with dried fish and shrimps (Indonesian)

tuinbonen townbohnuh broad beans

tuinkruiden townkrowduh garden herbs

ui(en) OW(uh) onion(s)

uiensoep OWuhnsoop onion soup

uiringen OWringuh onion rings

uitgebreide koffietafel OWtkHebrīduh koffeetafel full buffet lunch, i.e. with soup and a dessert

uitsmijter OWtsmiter one, two or three fried eggs on buttered bread, topped with either ham, cheese or roast beef

vanillevla vanilluhvla kind of vanilla custard

varkensbiefstuk varkens-beefstɤk fillet of pork

varkensfilet varkens-filay fillet of pork

varkenshaas varkens-hahs fillet of pork

varkenskrabbetjes varkens-krabbet-yuhs spare ribs

varkenslap varkens-lap pork chop; pork steak

varkenslever varkens-layver pig's liver

varkensnieren varkens-neeruh pig's kidneys

varkensnierstuk varkens-neerstɤk boned, rolled pork with kidney

varkensoester varkens-ooster pork escalope

varkenspoot varkens-poht leg of pork

varkenspootjes varkens-poht-yuhs pig's trotters

varkensrib varkens-rip pickled, smoked rib of pork

varkensrollade varkens-rollahduh rolled pork

varkensschnitzel varkens-shnitzel pork schnitzel

varkenstong varkens-tong pig's tongue

varkensvlees varkens-vlays pork

venkel venkel fennel

vermicellisoep vermisellisoop chicken noodle soup

vers(e) vairs(uh) fresh

verse worst vorst sausage

vet fat

vijgen vīkHuh figs

vis fish

viscroquetten viskrokettuh fish croquettes

vissoep vissoop fish soup

vla kind of custard, usually eaten cold

vlaai vlī fruit flan/pie

Vlaamse frites vlahmsuh freet chips; French fries

vlees vlays meat

vleet vlayt skate

vlierbessen vleerbessuh elderberries

volkorenbrood volkohruhbroht wholemeal bread

voorgerecht(en) vohrkHerekHt(uh) starter(s), appetizer(s)

voorn vohrn roach (fish)

vruchten vrooKHtuh fruit

vruchtensla vrooKHtuhsla fruit salad

wafel vahfel waffle; wafer

warm varm hot

waterkers vahterkairs watercress

Weens bakkippetje vayns bakkippet-yuh chicken coated in flour, egg yolk and bread crumbs and fried

wijting viting whiting

witte bonen vittuh bohnuh haricot beans

witte suiker vittuh sowker white sugar

wittebrood vittebroht white bread

wittekool vittekohl white cabbage

worst vorst sausage

wortel vortel carrot

zachtgekookt eitje zaKHt-KHekohkt it-yuh soft-boiled egg

zalm salmon

zalmslaatje zalmslaht-yuh salmon salad

zandgebak zantKHebak shortcrust pastry

zandkoekje zantkook-yuh shortbread

zandtaart zant-tahrt shortcrust pastry

zeebanket zaybanket seafood

zeekreeft zaykrayft lobster

zeelt zaylt tench (fish)

zeepaling zaypahling eel

zeekraal zaykrahl glasswort, seaweed

zeetong zaytong Dover sole

zeevis zayvis salt-water fish

zeewolf zayvolf wolf fish

zigeunerschnitzel zikhurner-shnitzel schnitzel with garlic and paprika

zilveruitjes zilverowt-yuhs pickled onions

zoet zoot sweet

zoet-zuur zoot-zoor sweet-and-sour

zout zowt salt; salted

zoute haring zowtuh salted herring

zoutjes zowt-yuhs salty cocktail biscuits/cookies/nuts

zoutwatervis zowt-vahtervis salt-water fish

zuivere bijenhoning zowveruh bi-uhnhoning pure honey

zult zoolt brawn, head cheese (a kind of meat terrine)

zure haring zooruh pickled herring

zuurkool zoorkohl sauerkraut

zuurkool met spek/worst vorst sauerkraut with bacon/sausage

zwarte bessen zvartuh blackcurrants

zwarte kersenjam kersuh-jam black cherry jam

zwarte peper payper black pepper

zwezerik zvayzerik sweetbread

Drink

Essential terms

beer het bier beer

bottle de fles

brandy de cognac

coffee de koffie koffee

cup de kop

    a cup of..., please een kop..., alstublieft alstOObleeft

fruit juice het vruchtensap vrOOKHtuhsap

gin de gin

    Dutch gin de jenever yenayver

    a gin and tonic een gin en tonic uhn

glass het (drink)glas

    a glass of... een glas...

milk de melk

mineral water het spawater spah-vahter

orange juice het sinaasappelsap seenahs-appelsap

port de port

red wine de rode wijn rohduh vin

rosé rosé rosay

soda (water) het sodawater sohda-vahter

soft drink het glas fris KHlas

sugar de suiker sowker

tea de thee tay

tonic (water) de tonic

vodka de wodka vodka

water het water vahter

whisky de whisky

white wine de witte wijn vittuh

wine de wijn vin

wine list de wijnkaart vinkahrt

another..., please nog een..., alstublieft noKH uhn - alstOObleeft

A–Z

advocaat advokaht advocaat, eggnog

alcoholvrij alkoholvrī non-alcoholic

anijslikeur anīslikur anisette

anijsmelk anīsmelk aniseed-flavoured warm milk

appelsap apple juice

bessenjenever bessuh-yenayver blackcurrant-flavoured gin

bessensap redcurrant juice/blackcurrant juice

bier beer beer

> **Travel tip** You can find the most common Dutch beer brands (Heineken, Amstel, Grolsch) nationwide, but expect them to be stronger and more distinctive than the watery approximations brewed abroad. Alternatively, try some local or seasonal brews: Bavaria beer in Noord-Brabant, Brand bitter from the country's oldest brewer in Limburg or rich, fruity *bokbier* in autumn.

bier van het vat draught beer

bittertje bittert-yuh gin with angostura

boerenjongens booruh-yongens brandy with raisins

borreltje borrelt-yuh straight gin

brandewijn brandevīn brandy

cassis kassis blackcurrant fizzy soft drink

chocolademelk shokolahdemelk chocolate milk

chocomel shohkomel chocolate milk

citroenjenever sitroon-yenayver lemon-flavoured gin

citroensap sitroonsap lemon juice

citroenthee sitroontay lemon tea

cognac French brandy

donkerbier donkerbeer dark beer

dranken drinks (non-alcoholic)

drinkyoghurt drinking yoghurt

droog drohKH dry

elske elskuh strong spirit made from the leaves, berries and bark of alder bushes

frappé frappay yoghurt shake

frisdranken soft drinks

fruitsap frowtsap fruit juice

gedistilleerde dranken KHedistillayrduh spirits

gemalen koffie KHemahluh koffee ground coffee

halfdroog half-drohKH medium-dry

halfvolle melk half-volluh melk semi-skimmed milk

huiswijn howsvīn house wine

jenever yenayver Dutch gin
jonge jenever yonguh
young Dutch gin
jonge klare yonguh klahruh
young Dutch gin

kamillethee kamilluhtay
camomile tea
karnemelk karnuhmelk buttermilk
koffie koffee coffee
de koffie is klaar freshly
made coffee (literally: coffee's
ready)
koffiemelk koffeemelk
evaporated milk for coffee
koffieroom koffeerohm
creamy milk for coffee
koffie verkeerd verkayrt
coffee with warm milk
kopstoot kopstoht beer with a
gin chaser
korenwijn kohrenvin high-quality,
well-aged, mature Dutch gin
kriek kreek dark beer fermented
with black cherries
kruidenthee krowdentay
herbal tea
kwast kvast lemon squash

landwijn landvin
local/regional wine
licht bier liKHt beer light beer
limonade limonahduh lemonade

magere melk mahKHeruh
skimmed milk

melk milk
mousserend moosayrent
fizzy, sparkling
mousserende dranken
moosayrenduh fizzy drinks

oploskoffie oploskoffee
instant coffee
oude klare owduh klahruh
mature Dutch gin
pisang ambon banana liqueur

rode bessensap rohduh red
currant juice
rode port red/ruby port wine
rode wijn vin red wine

santen coconut milk
sap juice

sec sweet white wine made from
dried grapes

sinaasappelsap sinahs-appelsap
orange juice

sinas fizzy orange drink

spawater spahvahter
mineral water

spiritualiën spiritooahli-uhn spirits

sterke drank stairkuh spirits

tafelwijn tahfelvīn table wine

thee tay tea

thee met citroen sitroon
lemon tea

thee met melk en suiker
sowker tea with milk and sugar

tomatensap tomato juice

trappistenbier trappistenbeer
strong, dark beer

vers citroen/sinaasappelsap
vairs sitroon/sinahsappel-sap
fresh lemon juice/orange juice

vieux vyur Dutch brandy

volle melk volluh
pasteurised milk

vruchtensap vrookHtensap
fruit juice

warme chocolademelk varmuh
shokolahdemelk hot chocolate

wijn vīn wine

wijnkaart vīnkahrt wine list

witte wijn vittuh vīn white wine

zeer oud zayr owt very old

zoet zoot sweet

zwarte bessensap zvartuh
blackcurrant juice

Picture credits

GET LOST

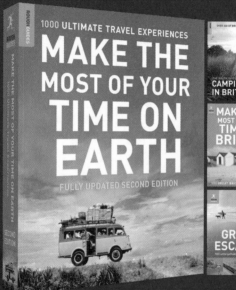

ESCAPE THE EVERYDAY
WITH OVER 700 **BOOKS**, **EBOOKS**, **MAPS** AND
APPS YOU'RE SURE TO BE INSPIRED

Start your journey at **roughguides.com**
MAKE THE MOST OF YOUR TIME ON EARTH™